A CENTURY OF DISHONOR

ʜᴀʀᴘᴇʀ ⚜ ᴛᴏʀᴄʜʙᴏᴏᴋs

A reference-list of Harper Torchbooks, classified by subjects, is printed at the end of this volume.

AMERICAN PERSPECTIVES

EDITED BY BERNARD WISHY AND

WILLIAM E. LEUCHTENBURG

Ray Stannard Baker: FOLLOWING THE COLOR LINE: *American Negro Citizenship in the Progressive Era*, edited by Dewey W. Grantham, Jr. TB/3053

George Bancroft: *THE ORIGIN OF THE AMERICAN REVOLUTION, from "The History of the United States," edited by Edmund S. Morgan.

Hyman Berman (ed.): *THE RISE OF AMERICAN LABOR: *A Reader*.

Randolph S. Bourne: WAR AND THE INTELLECTUALS: *Collected Essays, 1915-1919*, edited by Carl Resek. TB/3043

Louis D. Brandeis: *OTHER PEOPLE'S MONEY, edited by Richard M. Abrams.

Edmund Burke: *EDMUND BURKE AND THE AMERICAN REVOLUTION, edited by Elliott Robert Barkan.

Dixon Ryan Fox: THE DECLINE OF ARISTOCRACY IN THE POLITICS OF NEW YORK, edited by Robert V. Remini. TB/3064

Charlotte Perkins Gilman: *WOMEN AND ECONOMICS: *A Study of the Economic Relation Between Men and Women as a Factor in Social Evolution*, edited by Carl N. Degler.

Alexander Hamilton: THE REPORTS OF ALEXANDER HAMILTON, edited by Jacob E. Cooke. TB/3060

Daniel R. Hundley: SOCIAL RELATIONS IN OUR SOUTHERN STATES, edited by William R. Taylor. TB/3058

Robert Hunter: *POVERTY, edited by Peter d'A. Jones

Helen Hunt Jackson: A CENTURY OF DISHONOR: *The Early Crusade for Indian Reform*, edited by Andrew F. Rolle. TB/3063

Thomas Jefferson: NOTES ON THE STATE OF VIRGINIA, edited by Thomas P. Abernethy. TB/3052

O. G. Libby: *THE GEOGRAPHICAL DISTRIBUTION OF THE VOTE OF THE THIRTEEN STATES ON THE FEDERAL CONSTITUTION: 1787-1788, edited by Lee Benson.

Abraham Lincoln *and* Stephen A. Douglas: *THE LINCOLN-DOUGLAS DEBATES, edited by William H. Freehling.

William G. McLoughlin (ed.): *THE AMERICAN EVANGELICALS: *A Reader*.

Alfred T. Mahan: *AMERICA'S ROLE IN WORLD AFFAIRS: *Collected Essays*, edited by Ernest R. May.

S. Walter Poulshock *and* Robert A. Skotheim, (eds.): *THE BUSINESSMAN AND MODERN AMERICA: *A Reader*.

Walter Rauschenbusch: CHRISTIANITY AND THE SOCIAL CRISIS, edited by Robert D. Cross. TB/3059

Whitelaw Reid: *AFTER THE WAR, edited by C. Vann Woodward.

James Ford Rhodes: *THE COMING OF THE CIVIL WAR (Vol. I); THE CIVIL WAR (Vol. II): an abridgment of "The History of the United States from the Compromise of 1850," edited by Grady McWhiney.

Jacob Riis: *THE MAKING OF AN AMERICAN, edited by Roy Lubove.

Charles Howard Shinn: MINING CAMPS: *A Study in American Frontier Government*, edited by Rodman Paul. TB/3062

Ida M. Tarbell: *THE HISTORY OF THE STANDARD OIL COMPANY: *Selections*, edited by David M. Chalmers.

George B. Tindall (ed.): *A POPULIST READER.

Walter E. Weyl: THE NEW DEMOCRACY: *An Essay on Certain Political and Economic Tendencies in the United States*, edited by Charles B. Forcey. TB/3042

* *in preparation*

HELEN HUNT JACKSON

A CENTURY OF DISHONOR

THE EARLY CRUSADE FOR INDIAN REFORM

EDITED BY
Andrew F. Rolle

HARPER TORCHBOOKS
THE UNIVERSITY LIBRARY
HARPER & ROW, PUBLISHERS
NEW YORK, EVANSTON AND LONDON

A CENTURY OF DISHONOR

CONTENTS.

CHAPTER VIII.

CHAPTER IX.

CHAPTER X.

Introduction to the Torchbook edition

By Andrew F. Rolle

"President after president has appointed commission after commission to inquire into and report upon Indian affairs," the indignant Helen Hunt Jackson wrote in her *A Century of Dishonor*. Her impassioned book, published in 1881, further declaimed that federal Indian reports were "filled with eloquent statements of wrongs done to the Indians, of perfidies on the part of the Government." And, she lamented, these testimonials were buried in Government archives, "bound up with the Government's Annual Reports, and that is the end of them."[1]

Mrs. Jackson had vowed to stir up national indignation on behalf of Indian rights. In her *A Century of Dishonor* and subsequent *Ramona* she found a momentous issue to which she gladly gave the last years of her life. By the 1880's the United States approached the end of its thirty-seven Indian wars. A time for healing the wounds inflicted on the Indian by the nation had arrived.

In a period of four years before her death in 1885, Mrs. Jackson aroused the country to the Indian's plight. No longer could congressional leaders turn their backs on the Indian. No longer could his cause be

---

[1] *A Century of Dishonor* (New York, 1881), 338.

shrouded from presidential eyes. As if in anticipation
of solid reform, she wrote President Grover Cleveland
four days before her death:

> From my deathbed I send you a message of heartfelt
> thanks for what you have already done for the Indians. I
> ask you to read my *Century of Dishonor*. I am dying hap-
> pier for the belief I have that it is your hand that is des-
> tined to strike the first steady blow toward lifting this
> burden of infamy from our country and righting the wrongs
> of the Indian race.[2]

Most of Helen Hunt Jackson's life had been spent in
other pursuits than the championing of Indian rights.
Born Helen Maria Fiske in 1830 at Amherst, Massachusetts, she was the childhood friend of Emily Dickinson.
In that lovely New England village, they played under
the shade of the cherry trees and her youth passed
placidly and quietly. Her professor father gave her a
superior education in New England private schools and
at Amherst College. By the age of twenty-two she had
married an army officer, Edward B. Hunt. There followed eleven years of wandering military life during
which she was a homemaker.

Then came a series of tragedies. Her first child, Mur-
ray, died as an infant. During the Civil War, Major
Hunt suffocated while testing a submerged naval vessel
he had designed.[3] Only two years later another disaster,

---

[2] Ruth Odell, *Helen Hunt Jackson* (New York, 1939), 219
quotes this letter of August 8, 1885.

[3] Several writers have averred that Major Hunt was in love
with Emily Dickinson, but this legend rests upon slender foundations. See Josephine Pollitt, *Emily Dickinson: The Human
Background of Her Poetry* (New York, 1930), 119, *passim*, and
the play *Brittle Heaven* (New York, 1934) by Vincent York and
Frederick J. Pohl. The relationship with Emily Dickinson is

the loss from diphtheria of her idolized nine-year-old son, Rennie, again plunged the thirty-five-year-old widow into bereavement.

In the company of the sculptors, Horatio Greenough and William Wetmore Story, and the authors, Nathaniel Hawthorne and Horace Greeley, Mrs. Jackson dabbled with spiritualism and clairvoyance. Finally, she turned to writing in order to earn a livelihood, claiming that her best plots came from dreams.

It was while she was closeted for a time with Emily Dickinson after her husband's death that she had resolved to embark on a writing career. She was also inspired by the publicist and literary critic, Thomas Wentworth Higginson, whom she met at Newport and who also stimulated Miss Dickinson. His fondness for Mrs. Hunt led to a correspondence so delicate that he found it necessary to burn her frankest letters. About the fascinating widow, with whom he frequently was seen, Higginson once wrote that she was "brilliant, impetuous, and thoroughly individual . . . a personality so unique and . . . so fascinating that few could comprehend the curious thread of firm New England texture that ran through her whole being, tempering waywardness, keeping impulse from making shipwreck itself."[4]

Spurred on by Higginson, she began in 1865 to turn out travel sketches, children's stories, poems and essays. Under the pseudonyms "H.H." and "Saxe Holm," she

---

sketched in Thomas H. Johnson, *Emily Dickinson, An Interpretive Biography* (Cambridge, 1955), 155–180, and in Martha Dickinson Bianchi, *The Life and Letters of Emily Dickinson* (Boston, 1924), 74ff.

[4] Quoted in Anna Mary Wells, *Dear Preceptor, The Life and Times of Thomas Wentworth Higginson* (Boston, 1963), 269.

wrote more than thirty books and hundreds of articles.
The modest use of these initials and name, in fact, kept
her from becoming even more famous. The conventional
role of women writers still called for them to cloak their
authorship with at least partial anonymity. Only years
later, after she began to write *A Century of Dishonor*,
and her later *Ramona*, did she openly affix her full
name to her writings. By then she had become perhaps
the most prolific woman writer in the United States.
Admirers spoke of her as a born storyteller. Ralph
Waldo Emerson, in the preface to his anthology,
Parnassus (1874), called her the ''greatest American
woman poet.''

In 1875, at the age of 45, she married William
Sharpless Jackson, a wealthy banker who relieved her
of financial worries and whom she had met the year
before at a Colorado resort. A Pennsylvania Quaker,
he ultimately became president of the Denver, Rio
Grande Western Railroad. Mrs. Jackson moved to
Colorado; thenceforth the West and its Indians were to
play an increasingly larger part in her life.

Although an adopted westerner, Mrs. Jackson remained at heart a New Englander and she occasionally
lost interest in isolated and still crudely remote Colorado. While at Boston in 1879 on one of her frequent
visits to the East, Mrs. Jackson attended a lecture that
was to become the turning point in her life. There she
heard the Ponca chieftain Standing Bear give an impassioned account of the sufferings of many dispos-
sessed Plains Indians. Curiously never interested in
Negro equality with whites, she was almost immediately
attracted to the cause of these Indians.

Standing Bear had brought his small protest delegation eastward at a time when the public was first begin-

ning to show concern over Indian matters. He asked that the Poncas be allowed to return to their ancestral lands in Dakota's Black Hills where a gold rush was underway. The federal government had removed some of the Poncas, in the dead of winter, into Nebraska. To solicit money with which to aid the starving, miserable Poncas, Standing Bear's party had journeyed to various cities of the East. His case was to make Indian history.

Soon Secretary of the Interior Carl Schurz, whose office was directly concerned with Indian affairs, became involved in the dispute. So did Helen Hunt Jackson, who helped form the Boston Indian Citizenship Association, a precursor of other Indian associations. Schurz, a distinguished public figure and a sincere friend of the Indians, was, nevertheless, flayed publically by Mrs. Jackson on the pages of the New York *Tribune*. She unfairly labeled Schurz a ''Blockhead,'' and made him out to be a mortal enemy of the Indians, as she tactlessly fought to clean out a swamp of indifference and misconception about them.

The time for such a crusade was generally favorable and Mrs. Jackson vowed to write a book that would expose the entire story of government maltreatment. Immersed in research for this book at New York's Astor Library, she found herself championing the cause not only of the Poncas but of the Utes and other Plains Indians threatened by governmental removal.

She particularly deplored persistent vacillations in official Indian policy. At one time the Interior Department took command of the Indians' fate, at another the War Department. Division of responsibility, although seemingly routine, produced effects similar to calculated brutality. The Indians, poised between two ways of life, were not firmly rooted in either. Their repeated uprootings by the government gave them little opportunity to achieve either cultural distinctiveness or assimilation into the American white culture.

While writing her Indian book Mrs. Jackson also circulated tracts and petitions, wrote letters to newspapers, and worked mightily to arouse public opinion on their behalf. She did not hesitate to take her cause to the many distinguished persons she knew.[5] In contrast to her friend, the shy Emily Dickinson, this worldly, modern woman had become a reformer. Whereas Emily was timorous, Helen grew increasingly fearless.

All this furious effort culminated, fittingly, in her *A Century of Dishonor* (1881), an acute arraignment of the government for cruelty toward its helpless wards. Directed toward a cynical and materialistic generation, she considered this book the best writing she had ever done. Much later she wrote Higginson from a California deathbed: "My *Century of Dishonor* and *Ramona* are the only things I have done for which I am glad now. The rest is of no moment. They will live on and they will bear fruit. They already have."[6]

A major thesis of *A Century of Dishonor* was that the United States had followed an outrageous Indian

---

[5] Men like Moorfield Storey, Bishop Hare, and Ethelbert Talbot joined her humanitarian crusade. She also persuaded the famous Boston divine Wendell Phillips to take up the Indian cause in addition to that of the Negroes, whom he had steadily championed.

[6] Quoted in Allan Nevins, "Helen Hunt Jackson, Sentimentalist vs. Realist," *American Scholar*, X (Summer, 1941), 276, The Right Reverend H. P. Whipple, a western bishop, wrote the preface and Amherst's President Julius H. Seelye its introduction.

policy in defiance of the basic principles of justice and of the laws of all nations. The book described maltreatment of the Indians from the period of the American Revolution. Focused first upon the Delawares and Cherokees, it went on to deplore the later sufferings of the Sioux, Nez Percés and Cheyennes. Mrs. Jackson's book was less a systematic history than a "record" of the awkward relations between the federal government and many important tribes. She found it startlingly easy to unearth a succession of broken treaties and many examples of inhumane treatment of the nation's 300,000 Indians.

Although Mrs. Jackson's book traces a record of perfidious cruelty in detail, it is structurally amorphous and its logical progression is impaired by "undeveloped and often unrelated fragments lacking in transitions and abruptly and choppily treated."[7] Yet, Mrs. Jackson could write with elegance and feeling. A decorous style, popular in that day, made her prose very marketable. Sophisticated modern readers, however, may not find her writing nearly so graceful, colorful or brilliant in tone as did her contemporaries.

Mrs. Jackson's own conception of *A Century of Dishonor* forms the best answer to its critics. In a letter to a friend she emphatically denies seeing it as a history: "To do that," she explained, "would take years and volumes." She preferred, rather, to call the book a "sketch." She stated: "I give an outline of the experiences of a tribe—broken treaties, removals, etc.—telling the history of each tribe straight through by itself. In this way, I am sure, this will be much more intelligible and interesting and effective. . . . My first chapter is

---

[7] Odell, 167.

simply a lawyer's brief. . . . I have been through all the law authorities in the Astor Library on these points. . . . All the heart and soul I possess have gone into it.''[8]

A Century of Dishonor was specifically directed toward the Congress of 1880, and Mrs. Jackson sent each legislator a copy. Printed in red on the cover of its second edition were the words:

> Look upon your hands! They are stained with the blood of your relations.
>
>   B. Franklin

In its appendices there appeared acrimonious correspondence with Schurz and other officials, details about outrages committed, treaty digests, and other indictments. The book presented a monumental plea to the nation to correct its record of Indian mistreatment.

Along with Indian Commissioner G. W. Manypenny's *Our Indian Wards* (1879), it shocked the public. These books called attention to the need for widespread reform within the Department of the Interior. Manypenny also leveled his attack upon the regular army, so frequently locked in jurisdictional discord about the Indians with the Department of the Interior. In some respects Manypenny's parallel defense of the Indians was more knowledgeable than Mrs. Jackson's. His studied pages, however, had nowhere near the same effect. Indeed, modern histories of the American Indians frequently omit his name but they could never do this with Mrs. Jackson. Although her impact was not immediate, cumulatively Mrs. Jackson's powerful message was scarcely lost. No one could ignore so massive

---

[8] Als., Helen Hunt Jackson to William Hayes Ward, n.d., ca., 1880, Huntington Library, San Marino, California.

an indictment of both civil and military authorities. About her book a recent interpreter writes: "Critics have damned her lack of balance, even suppression of facts that did not fit her preconceptions, but in *A Century of Dishonor* and *Ramona* she publicized the Indian cause as it had never been publicized before."[9]

There was, however, another point of view, one that was pro-settler. Anyone who had either sustained an Indian attack or lost a loved one in a western massacre, or who had fought savages with the cavalry obviously considered the Indian intractable and untrustworthy. For decades frontier army commanders like Generals Crook and Custer had frankly followed a "surrender-or-be-slaughtered" policy. Indian agents, government scouts, army officers, and the young Theodore Roosevelt (who fancied himself the ultimate authority on the West) were frequently anti-Indian. To Roosevelt, the Indian was "cruel beyond belief," a creature capable of great treachery, a "painted marauder," brutal, rapacious and a murderous savage. He believed both Mrs. Jackson's and Manypenny's books to be spiteful diatribes, however well intentioned. He favored, instead, the pro-white views expressed in Colonel Richard I. Dodge's *Our Wild Indians* (1882), J. P. Dunn's *Massacres of the Mountains* (1886), and, of course, his own *Winning of the West* (1889).

In our own day, historian Allan Nevins has also criticized Mrs. Jackson's attacks upon Secretary Schurz in particular. Nevins saw these jibes at a devoted public servant as those of a lachrymose sentimentalist. He believed that Mrs. Jackson, like the muckraking young reformers who followed her, overstated her case. In

---

[9] William T. Hagan, *American Indians* (Chicago, 1961), 123.

style she was more intuitive than analytical. Indeed, like other zealots, she lacked the power of self-criticism and became almost saccharine about her cause. Nevins called her writings "sentimental," presenting "but one aspect of a complex and difficult problem," and thereby oversimplifying and distorting it. "They are sentimental," he wrote, "in that they offer no constructive remedy whatever for the difficult problem they help to expose. They appeal solely to the emotions whereas these problems can be solved only by cold, careful, sustained use of the intellect." Yet, reform movements from the time of Savonarola to the Muckrakers have often been inspired by emotionally irreverent, indeed irrational, figures and Nevins himself concedes that American history too "owes much to our long list of sentimental books," including Mrs. Jackson's. Moreover, he acknowledged that within a year after the publication of *A Century of Dishonor,* the powerful Indian Rights Association was born. Nevins also observed that "the general agitation in which she played so prominent a part was largely responsible for the enactment in 1887 of the Dawes Act, the first comprehensive, constructive and altogether wise piece of legislation for the advancement of the Indians."[10] This law

---

[10] Nevins, 284. Constantly interspersed in Mrs. Jackson's correspondence with publishers is almost constant comment regarding Indian problems. At the end of 1879 Mrs. Jackson made impassioned pleas that they publish her pieces about Indian inequities. All around her there swirled a "thickening air" smoldering "with the smoke of this battle for the oppressed." She ranted in her letters against "that false-souled man, Carl Schurz" and about "the thieves who have been fattening on the seven millions a year spent on our Indian policy." Als., Helen Hunt Jackson to William Hayes Ward, Dec. 20, 1879, Jan. 27, 1880, Huntington Library.

allotted land directly to the Indians, provided for their citizenship, and abandoned the concept that they were independent nations, to be dealt with by treaty.

Mrs. Jackson continued her fight for the Indians even after her epic was published. From 1881 to 1885, years of restless travel for her, she made three visits to California, becoming interested in studying its Mission Indians and unearthing that state's pre-Yankee culture.

She found southern California charmingly warm-hearted. Its sleepy background stood in marked contrast to an aggressive culture about to overwhelm a provincial society. Unlike the western historian Hubert Howe Bancroft, who pontifically applauded the destruction of the old order by Anglo-Americans, she came to believe that this invasion had done a great wrong to California's simple Hispanic population as well as to its confused Indians.

In the middle 1880's, she turned her hand to a series of articles for *Century* magazine which dwelt upon this theme at length. At that time some 20,000 Indians lived near their former mission confines, often surrounded by semi-tropical orchards of orange and lemon, olives, walnut and fig trees. Cattle, horses, and sheep roamed far beyond crumbled mission walls that still enclosed clogged fountains, stunted palm trees, and weed-wild gardens. She found the aborigines in an equally unkempt, semi-barbaric state. Once again she encountered the old problem of forcible Indian removal by the government in order that invading whites could settle on the choicest lands. Mrs. Jackson's memory, with its fidelity for detail, made it possible for her later to reproduce in her *Ramona* many of the scenes she witnessed. All around her she recorded the twilight of a golden age about to be extinguished, whether on Indian *rancherías,* or missions, or on ranchos and in canyons that surrounded Los Angeles, hub of California's proud Arcadian past.

These observations did not serve only her literary purposes. Because of the furor created by Mrs. Jackson's *A Century of Dishonor,* in July, 1883 President Chester Arthur had appointed her a Commissioner of Indian Affairs. She was given the assignment to visit and report upon the condition of California's Mission Indians.

Traveling by two-horse, double-seated carriage with Abbot Kinney, another commissioner, she again visited the bulk of southern California's Indians throughout the old rancho and mission countryside. She talked to original settlers and directly intervened to prevent white squatters from pre-empting remote Indian lands. Even after breaking her leg, she wrote Emily Dickinson from Los Angeles in 1884 that she went out "every afternoon in an open carriage on roads where larks sing and flowers are in bloom. I can do everything I ever could—except walk!" she lamented. "I have found two Mexican women called Ramona, from whom I have bought Indian mortars."[11] Personally telegraphing Washington, she prevented illegal seizures of Indian land. In the process Mrs. Jackson's undeniable charges aroused the antipathy of anti-Indian Californians. She was roundly denounced for labeling various of the state's leaders as unscrupulous plunderers of Indian lands. She published the substance of her fifty-six-page

---

[11] Thomas H. Johnson, ed., *The Letters of Emily Dickinson,* III (Cambridge, 1958), 869. George Wharton James, *Through Ramona's Country* (Boston, 1909) is an effective literary reconstruction of the scenes used in Mrs. Jackson's later writings.

report to the Department of the Interior in an appendix to the second edition of *A Century of Dishonor,* reprinted at Boston in 1885.

During 1884, the last full year of her life, she drove herself unstintingly on behalf of the Indian cause. She had come to believe that her efforts in favor of California's natives had been depressingly unsuccessful. Despite her *A Century of Dishonor,* the mission Indians continued to be abused and even despised, not to speak of neglected. So she returned to fiction in order to indict the treachery of the whites and their government.

She began *Ramona* in New York during December, 1883 and concluded it the following spring. She told a friend that in *A Century of Dishonor* she "had tried to attack the people's conscience directly," whereas in *Ramona* she "had sugared my pill, and it remains to be seen if it will go down."[12] In 1886 the *North American Review* called this book "unquestionably the best novel yet produced by an American woman," ranking it with Harriet Beecher Stowe's *Uncle Tom's Cabin* as one of the two great ethical novels of the century.

Both of her "Indian books" captured large audiences and reached the hearts of persons with compassion for cultures submerged by the Anglo-Americans. In the case of *Ramona,* a romance whose protagonists are of Indian blood, its readers were captivated by beautiful and dramatic descriptions of the softer, more colorful Mediterranean civilization that stemmed from colonial Spain. The book quickly became famous far beyond its original didactic intentions. Even Nevins grants that *Ramona* occupies "a unique place in our

---

[12] Pollitt, 269; Nevins, 281.

literature and, for a *tour de force* in its field, still has
remarkable power.'' Although *Ramona* reconstructed
the Indian as a synthetic type that never was, its idyllic
insights into the Indian past and its appeal for justice
continued Mrs. Jackson's polemic, this time on behalf
of persons born into *two* cultures. Couched in overtones
of romanticism, *Ramona* (which she had planned to
entitle *In the Name of the Law*) depicted the decline
of California's quasi-fictional, patriarchial Spanish
dons as well as deplored the way in which their proud
Indian wards were driven to vagrancy, despair and
degeneracy, living ''like gypsies in brush huts.''[13]

When one compares the success of *Ramona* with that
of *A Century of Dishonor,* the superiority of imagina-
tive literature over non-fiction in arousing the public
is obvious. *Ramona* has gone through three hundred
printings; countless stage and screen versions testify to
its power. *A Century of Dishonor,* out of print since
the year of Mrs. Jackson's death in 1885, is a harsher
book, and considered by many, including Theodore
Roosevelt, as a strident, braying tract full of feminine
sentimentalism. Because *A Century of Dishonor* was
''written in good English,'' and because Mrs. Jackson
was ''intensely in earnest,'' Roosevelt thought her book
''capable of doing great harm.'' He continued emotionally: ''As a history it would be beneath criticism,
were it not that the high character of the author and
her excellent literary work'' led it to be repeatedly
quoted by a ''large class of amiable but maudlin
fanatics.''[14] As Nevins points out, Roosevelt was himself an ''unconscious sentimentalist'' about the white

[13] *Century,* 463.
[14] Theodore Roosevelt, *The Winning of the West,* I (New
York, 1926), 68–69, 81–82.

man. Although Roosevelt closed his eyes to the merits of *A Century of Dishonor,* one later critic believed it to be "one of the soundest and most exhaustive works" ever written about Indian rights.[15]

As to Mrs. Jackson's obvious pro-Indian bias, another authority states: "A balanced account of American Indian history would have attracted little attention." Once *A Century of Dishonor* had been written, the case against the government, he continues, was so clear that "later reformers could only repeat what she had said. . . ."[16] As to her veracity, another writer noted that "none of the hundreds of facts and incidents contained in her *Century of Dishonor* were ever successfully denied. Many of the recommendations offered by her are sound and could be applied with profit at the present time, although thirty years have elapsed since she laid down her pen."[17]

Today, eighty years later, at a time when there is renewed interest in civil rights, Mrs. Jackson would probably believe that Americans still have not sufficiently improved the lot of the minorities within our borders. The Indian population still suffers 45 per cent unemployment; 20 per cent of them are allegedly dying from malnutrition; and the Indians comprise the lowest national income group. Can we be self-congratulatory? Despite passage of the Dawes Act, the Indian problem

---

[15] Odell, 226; Nevins, 284.

[16] Loring Priest, *Uncle Sam's Stepchildren, the Reformation of United States Indian Policy, 1865–1887* (New Brunswick, N.J., 1942), 61–62.

[17] Warren K. Moorhead, *The American Indian in the United States* (Andover, Mass., 1914), 373. Old friend Emily Dickinson wrote of her: "Helen of Troy will die, but Helen of Colorado, never." Quoted in Louise Pound, "Biographical Accuracy and H.H.," *American Literature,* II (January, 1931), 420.

remains a blight upon our collective conscience. A passionate prodder of that conscience, Mrs. Jackson found herself at the vortex of a universal controversy: This is the problem of how an invading race should treat the invaded. Since the days of Rome, many nations, including our own, have sought to solve this baffling and tense issue, but so far in vain.

Helen Hunt Jackson had tried to make the issue unavoidable for Americans. A hater of oppression, she raised the question of humanitarian standards for treatment of subjugated peoples by those more technologically advanced. And that question will not down. She thought of herself as an "Indian Harriet Beecher Stowe" about whom she wrote: "If I can do one-hundredth part for the Indians as Mrs. Stowe did for the Negro, I will be thankful."[18]

Just before her death Mrs. Jackson wrote: "Hope has not yet died in my heart, though the time is very long, and bad men are in greater numbers in the Grand Council at Washington."[19] About her Allan Nevins has written: "We can point to her as eloquent evidence that at one period of our history a large body of Americans began to care, a large body began to be ashamed. And if her writings lacked constructive qualities they were not devoid of vision."[20]

Occidental College
January, 1965

---

[18] Helen Hunt Jackson to William Hayes Ward, January 1, 1884, Huntington Library.

[19] Helen Hunt Jackson to Mary Elizabeth Sheriff, July 17, 1885, Huntington Library.

[20] Nevins, 285.

AUTHOR'S NOTE.

ALL the quotations in this book, where the name of the authority is not cited, are from Official Reports of the War Department or the Department of the Interior.

The book gives, as its title indicates, only a sketch,* and not a history.

To write in full the history of any one of these Indian communities, of its forced migrations, wars, and miseries, would fill a volume by itself.

The history of the missionary labors of the different churches among the Indians would make another volume. It is the one bright spot on the dark record.

All this I have been forced to leave untouched, in strict adherence to my object, which has been simply to show our causes for national shame in the matter of our treatment of the Indians. It is a shame which the American nation ought not to lie under, for the American people, as a people, are not at heart unjust.

If there be one thing which they believe in more than any other, and mean that every man on this continent shall have, it is "fair play." And as soon as they fairly understand how cruelly it has been denied to the Indian, they will rise up and demand it for him.

HELEN HUNT JACKSON

---

* The book was originally published as *A Century of Dishonor: A Sketch of the United States Government's Dealings with Some of the Indian Tribes.* [Ed. Note]

A CENTURY OF DISHONOR.

CHAPTER I.

The question of the honorableness of the United States' dealings with the Indians turns largely on a much disputed and little understood point. What was the nature of the Indians' right to the country in which they were living when the continent of North America was discovered? Between the theory of some sentimentalists that the Indians were the real owners of the soil, and the theory of some politicians that they had no right of ownership whatever in it, there are innumerable grades and confusions of opinion. The only authority on the point must be the view and usage as accepted by the great discovering Powers at the time of discovery, and afterward in their disposition of the lands discovered.

Fortunately, an honest examination of these points leaves no doubt on the matter.

England, France, Spain, little Portugal—all quarrelling fiercely, and fighting with each other for the biggest share in the new continent—each claiming "sovereignty of the soil" by right of priority of discovery — all recognized the Indians' "right of occupancy" as a right; a right alienable in but two ways, either by purchase or by conquest.

All their discussions as to boundaries, from 1603 down to

1776, recognized this right and this principle. They reiterated, firstly, that discoverers had the right of sovereignty—a right in so far absolute that the discoverer was empowered by it not only to take possession of, but to grant, sell, and convey lands still occupied by Indians—and that for any nation to attempt to take possession of, grant, sell, or convey any such Indian-occupied lands while said lands were claimed by other nations under the right of discovery, was an infringement of rights, and just occasion of war; secondly, that all this granting, selling, conveying was to be understood to be "subject to the Indians' right of occupancy," which remained to be extinguished either through further purchase or through conquest by the grantee or purchaser.

Peters, in his preface to the seventh volume of the "United States Statutes at Large," says, "The history of America, from its discovery to the present day, proves the universal recognition of these principles."

Each discovering Power might regulate the relations between herself and the Indians; but as to the existence of the Indians' "right of occupancy," there was absolute unanimity among them. That there should have been unanimity regarding any one thing between them, is remarkable. It is impossible for us to realize what a sudden invitation to greed and discord lay in this fair, beautiful, unclaimed continent — eight millions of square miles of land—more than twice the size of all Europe itself. What a lure to-day would such another new continent prove! The fighting over it would be as fierce now as the fighting was then, and the "right of occupancy" of the natives would stand small chance of such unanimous recognition as the four Great Powers then justly gave it.

Of the fairness of holding that ultimate sovereignty belonged to the civilized discoverer, as against the savage barbarian, there is no manner nor ground of doubt. To question this is feeble sentimentalism. But to affirm and uphold this is not in any wise to overlook the lesser right which remained; as good, of its kind, and to its extent, as was the greater right to which, in the just nature of things, it was bound to give way.

It being clear, then, that the Indians' "right of occupancy" was a right recognized by all the great discovering Powers, acted upon by them in all their dispositions of lands here discovered, it remains next to inquire whether the United States Government, on taking its place among the nations, also recognized or accepted this Indian "right of occupancy" as an actual right. Upon this point, also, there is no doubt.

"By the treaty which concluded the War of our Revolution, Great Britain relinquished all claims not only to the government, but to the proprietary and territorial rights of the United States whose boundaries were fixed in the second Article. By this treaty the powers of the government and the right to soil which had previously been in Great Britain passed definitely to these States. We had before taken possession of them by declaring independence, but neither the declaration of independence nor the treaty confirming it could give us more than that which we before possessed, or to which Great Britain was before entitled. It has never been doubted that either the United States or the several States had a clear title to all the lands within the boundary-lines described in the treaty, subject only to the Indian right of occupancy, and that the exclusive right to extinguish that right was vested in that government which might constitutionally exercise it."*

"Subject to the Indian right of occupancy." It is noticeable how perpetually this phrase reappears. In their desire to define, assert, and enforce the greater right, the "right of sovereignty," the makers, interpreters, and recorders of law did not realize, probably, how clearly and equally they were defin-

---

* Peters, United States Statutes at Large, vol. vii.

ing, asserting, and enforcing the lesser right, the "right of occupancy."

Probably they did not so much as dream that a time would come when even this lesser right — this least of all rights, it would seem, which could be claimed by, or conceded to, an aboriginal inhabitant of a country, however savage—would be practically denied to our Indians. But if they had foreseen such a time, they could hardly have left more explicit testimony to meet the exigency.

"The United States have unequivocally acceded to that great and broad rule by which its civilized inhabitants now hold this country. They hold and assert in themselves the title by which it was acquired. They maintain, as all others have maintained, that discovery gave an exclusive right to extinguish the Indian title of occupancy, either by purchase or conquest, and gave also a right to such a degree of sovereignty as the circumstances of the people would allow them to exercise.

"The power now possessed by the United States to grant lands resided, while we were colonies, in the Crown or its grantees. The validity of the titles given by either has never been questioned in our courts. It has been exercised uniformly over territories in possession of the Indians. The existence of this power must negative the existence of any right which may conflict with and control it. An absolute title to lands cannot exist at the same time in different persons or in different governments. An absolute must be an exclusive title, or at least a title which excludes all others not compatible with it. All our institutions recognize the absolute title of the Crown, subject only to the Indian right of occupancy, and recognize the absolute title of the Crown to extinguish the right. This is incompatible with an absolute and complete title in the Indians."*

---

* Peters.

Certainly. But it is also "incompatible with an absolute and perfect title" in the white man! Here again, in their desire to define and enforce the greater right, by making it so clear that it included the lesser one, they equally define and enforce the lesser right as a thing to be included. The word "subject" is a strong participle when it is used legally. Provisions are made in wills, "subject to" a widow's right of dower, for instance, and the provisions cannot be carried out without the consent of the person to whom they are thus declared to be "subject." A title which is pronounced to be "subject to" anything or anybody cannot be said to be absolute till that subjection is removed.

There have been some definitions and limitations by high legal authority of the methods in which this Indian "right of occupancy" might be extinguished even by conquest.

"The title by conquest is acquired and maintained by force. The conqueror prescribes its limits. Humanity, however, acting on public opinion, has established as a general rule that the conquered shall not be wantonly oppressed, and that their condition shall remain as eligible as is compatible with the objects of the conquest. Usually they are incorporated with the victorious nation, and become subjects or citizens of the government with which they are connected. * * * When this incorporation is practicable. humanity demands, and a wise policy requires, that the rights of the conquered to property should remain unimpaired; that the new subjects should be governed as equitably as the old. * * * When the conquest is complete, and the conquered inhabitants can be blended with the conquerors, or safely governed as a distinct people, public opinion, which not even the conqueror can disregard, imposes these restraints upon him, and he cannot neglect them without injury to his fame, and hazard to his power."*

---

* Peters, United States Statutes at Large, vol. vii.

In the sadly famous case of the removal of the Cherokee tribe from Georgia, it is recorded as the opinion of our Supreme Court that "the Indians are acknowledged to have an unquestionable, and heretofore unquestioned, right to the lands they occupy until that right shall be extinguished by a voluntary cession to the Government." * * * "The Indian nations have always been considered as distinct independent political communities, retaining their original natural rights as the undisputed possessors of the soil, from time immemorial, with the single exception of that imposed by irresistible power, which excluded them from intercourse with any other European potentate than the first discoverer of the coast of the particular region claimed; and this was a restriction which those European potentates imposed on themselves as well as on the Indians. The very term 'nation,' so generally applied to them, means 'a people distinct from others.' The Constitution, by declaring treaties already made, as well as those to be made, to be the supreme law of the land, has adopted and sanctioned the previous treaties with the Indian nations, and consequently admits their rank among those powers who are capable of making treaties. The words 'treaty' and 'nation' are words of our own language, selected in our diplomatic and legislative proceedings by ourselves, having each a definite and well understood meaning. We have applied them to Indians as we have applied them to other nations of the earth. They are applied to all in the same sense."*

In another decision of the Supreme Court we find still greater emphasis put upon the Indian right of occupancy, by stating it as a right, the observance of which was stipulated for in treaties between the United States and other nations.

"When the United States acquired and took possession of the Floridas, the treaties which had been made with the Indian

---

* Worcester *vs.* State of Georgia, 6 Peters, 515.

tribes before the acquisition of the territory by Spain and Great Britain remained in force over all the ceded territory, as the law which regulated the relations with all the Indians who were parties to them, and were binding on the United States by the obligation they had assumed by the Louisiana treaty as a supreme law of the land.

"The treaties with Spain and England before the acquisition of Florida by the United States, which guaranteed to the Seminole Indians their lands, according to the right of property with which they possessed them, were adopted by the United States, who thus became the protectors of all the rights they (the Indians) had previously enjoyed, or could of right enjoy, under Great Britain or Spain, as individuals or nations, by any treaty to which the United States thus became parties in 1803. * * *

"The Indian right to the lands as property was not merely of possession; that of alienation was concomitant; both were equally secured, protected, and guaranteed by Great Britain and Spain, subject only to ratification and confirmation by the license, charter, or deed from the government representing the king." * * *

The laws made it necessary, when the Indians sold their lands, to have the deeds presented to the governor for confirmation. The sales by the Indians transferred the kind of right which they possessed; the ratification of the sale by the governor must be regarded as a relinquishment of the title of the Crown to the purchaser, and no instance is known of refusal of permission to sell, or of the rejection of an Indian sale.*

"The colonial charters, a great portion of the individual grants by the proprietary and royal governments, and a still greater portion by the States of the Union after the Revolu-

---

* United States *vs.* Clark, 9 Peters, 168.

tion, were made for lands within the Indian hunting-grounds. North Carolina and Virginia, to a great extent, paid their officers and soldiers of the Revolutionary War by such grants, and extinguished the arrears due the army by similar means. It was one of the great resources which sustained the war, not only by those States but by other States. The ultimate fee, encumbered with the right of occupancy, was in the Crown previous to the Revolution, and in the States afterward, and subject to grant. This right of occupancy was protected by the political power, and respected by the courts until extinguished." * * * "So the Supreme Court and the State courts have uniformly held."*

President Adams, in his Message of 1828, thus describes the policy of the United States toward the Indians at that time:

"At the establishment of the Federal Government the principle was adopted of considering them as foreign and independent powers, and also as proprietors of lands. As independent powers, we negotiated with them by treaties; as proprietors, we purchased of them all the land which we could prevail on them to sell; as brethren of the human race, rude and ignorant, we endeavored to bring them to the knowledge of religion and letters."

Kent says: "The European nations which, respectively, established colonies in America, assumed the ultimate dominion to be in themselves, and claimed the exclusive right to grant a title to the soil, subject only to the Indian right of occupancy. The natives were admitted to be the rightful occupants of the soil, with a *legal* as well as just claim to retain possession of it, and to use it according to their own discretion, though not to dispose of the soil at their own will, except to the government claiming the right of pre-emption." * * * "The United States adopted the same principle; and their exclusive right to

---

* Clark *vs.* Smith, 13 Peters.

extinguish the Indian title by purchase or conquest, and to grant the soil and exercise such a degree of sovereignty as circumstances required, has never been judicially questioned."

Kent also says, after giving the Supreme Court decision in the case of Johnson *vs.* M'Intosh: "The same court has since been repeatedly called upon to discuss and decide great questions concerning Indian rights and title, and the subject has of late become exceedingly grave and momentous, affecting the faith and the character, if not the tranquillity and safety, of the Government of the United States."

In Gardner's "Institutes of International Law" the respective rights to land of the Indians and the whites are thus summed up: "In our Union the aborigines had only a possessory title, and in the original thirteen States each owned in fee, *subject to the Indian right,* all ungranted lands within their respective limits; and beyond the States the residue of the ungranted lands were vested in fee in the United States, *subject to the Indian possessory* right, to the extent of the national limits."

Dr. Walker, in his "American Law," makes a still briefer summary: "The American doctrine on the subject of Indian title is briefly this: The Indians have no fee in the lands they occupy. The fee is in the Government. They cannot, of course, aliene them either to nations or individuals, the exclusive right of pre-emption being in the Government. Yet they have a qualified right of occupancy which can only be *extinguished by treaty, and upon fair compensation;* until which they are entitled to be protected in their possession."

"Abbott's Digest," one of the very latest authorities, reiterates the same principle: "The right of occupancy has been recognized in countless ways, among others by many decisions of courts and opinions of attorney-generals."

It being thus established that the Indian's "right of occupancy" in his lands was a right recognized by all the Great

Powers discovering this continent, and accepted by them as a right necessary to be extinguished either by purchase or conquest, and that the United States, as a nation, has also from the beginning recognized, accepted, and acted upon this theory, it is next in order to inquire whether the United States has dealt honorably or dishonorably by the Indians in this matter of their recognized " right of occupancy."

In regard to the actions of individuals there is rarely much room for discussion whether they be honorable or dishonorable, the standard of honor in men's conduct being, among the civilized, uniform, well understood, and undisputed. Stealing, for instance, is everywhere held to be dishonorable, as well as impolitic; lying, also, in all its forms; breaking of promises and betrayals of trust are scorned even among the most ignorant people. But when it comes to the discussion of the acts of nations, there seems to be less clearness of conception, less uniformity of standard of right and wrong, honor and dishonor. It is necessary, therefore, in charging a government or nation with dishonorable conduct, to show that its moral standard ought in nowise to differ from the moral standard of an individual; that what is cowardly, cruel, base in a man, is cowardly, cruel, base in a government or nation. To do this, it is only needful to look into the history of the accepted "Law of Nations," from the days of the Emperor Justinian until now.

The Roman jurisconsults employed as synonymous, says Wheaton, " the two expressions, ' jus gentium,' that law which is found among all the known nations of the earth, and 'jus naturale,' founded on the general nature of mankind; nevertheless, of these two forms of the same idea, the first ought to be considered as predominant, since it as well as the ' jus civile ' was a positive law, the origin and development of which must be sought for in history."

Nations being simply, as Vattel defines them, " societies of men united together," it is plain that, if there be such a thing as the "law of nature," which men as individuals are bound to obey, that law is also obligatory on the "societies" made up of men thus "united."

Hobbes divides the law of nature into that of man and that of States, saying, "The maxims of each of these laws are precisely the same; but as States, once established, assume personal properties, that which is termed the natural law when we speak of the duties of individuals is called the law of nations when applied to whole nations or States." The Emperor Justinian said, "The law of nations is common to the whole human race."

Grotius draws the distinction between the law of nature and the law of nations thus: "When several persons at different times and in various places maintain the same thing as certain, such coincidence of sentiment must be attributed to some general cause. Now, in the questions before us, that cause must necessarily be one or the other of these two—either a just consequence drawn from natural principles, or a universal consent; the former discovers to us the law of nature, and the latter the law of nations."

Vattel defines the "necessary law of nations" to be the "application of the law of nature to nations." He says: "It is 'necessary,' because nations are absolutely bound to observe it. This law contains the precepts prescribed by the law of nature to States, on whom that law is not less obligatory than on individuals; since States are composed of men, their resolutions are taken by men, and the law of nations is binding on all men, under whatever relation they act. This is the law which Grotius, and those who follow him, call the Internal Law of Nations, on account of its being obligatory on nations in the point of conscience."

Vattel says again: "Nations being composed of men naturally free and independent, and who before the establishment of civil societies lived together in the state of nature, nations or sovereign States are to be considered as so many free persons living together in the state of nature."

And again: "Since men are naturally equal, and a perfect equality prevails in their right and obligations as equally proceeding from nature, nations composed of men, and considered as so many free persons living together in the state of nature, are naturally equal, and inherit from nature the same obligations and rights. Power or weakness does not in this respect produce any difference. A dwarf is as much a man as a giant; a small republic no less a sovereign State than the most powerful kingdom."

In these two last sentences is touched the key-note of the true law of nations, as well as of the true law for individuals— justice. There is among some of the later writers on jurisprudence a certain fashion of condescending speech in their quotations from Vattel. As years have gone on, and States have grown more powerful, and their relations more complicated by reason of selfishness and riches, less and less has been said about the law of nature as a component and unalterable part of the law of nations. Fine subtleties of definition, of limitation have been attempted. Hundreds of pages are full of apparently learned discriminations between the parts of that law which are based on the law of nature and the parts which are based on the consent and usage of nations. But the two cannot be separated. No amount of legality of phrase can do away with the inalienable truth underlying it. Wheaton and President Woolsey to-day say, in effect, the same thing which Grotius said in 1615, and Vattel in 1758.

Says Wheaton: "International law, as understood among civilized nations, may be defined as consisting of those rules of conduct which reason deduces as consonant to justice from the nature of the society existing among independent nations."

President Woolsey says: "International law, in a wide and

abstract sense, would embrace those rules of intercourse between nations which are deduced from their rights and moral claims; or, in other words, it is the expression of the jural and moral relations of States to one another.

"If international law were not made up of rules for which reasons could be given satisfactory to man's intellectual and moral nature, if it were not built on principles of right, it would be even less of a science than is the code which governs the actions of polite society."

It is evident, therefore, that the one fundamental right, of which the "law of nations" is at once the expression and the guardian, is the right of every nation to just treatment from other nations, the right of even the smallest republic equally with "the most powerful kingdom." Just as the one fundamental right, of which civil law is the expression and guardian, is the right of each individual to just treatment from every other individual : a right indefeasible, inalienable, in nowise lessened by weakness or strengthened by power—as majestic in the person of "the dwarf" as in that of "the giant."

Of justice, Vattel says : "Justice is the basis of all society, the sure bond of all commerce. * * *

"All nations are under a strict obligation to cultivate justice toward each other, to observe it scrupulously and carefully, to abstain from anything that may violate it. * * *

"The right of refusing to submit to injustice, of resisting injustice by force if necessary, is part of the law of nature, and as such recognized by the law of nations.

"In vain would Nature give us a right to refuse submitting to injustice, in vain would she oblige others to be just in their dealings with us, if we could not lawfully make use of force when they refused to discharge this duty. The just would lie at the mercy of avarice and injustice, and all their rights would soon become useless. From the foregoing right arise, as two distinct branches, first, the right of a just defence, which belongs to every nation, or the right of making war against who-ever attacks her and her rights; and this is the foundation of defensive war. Secondly, the right to obtain justice by force, if we cannot obtain it otherwise, or to pursue our right by force of arms. This is the foundation of offensive war."

Justice is pledged by men to each other by means of promises or contracts; what promises and contracts are between men, treaties are between nations.

President Woolsey says: "A contract is one of the highest acts of human free-will: it is the will binding itself in regard to the future, and surrendering its right to change a certain expressed intention, so that it becomes, morally and jurally, a wrong to act otherwise.

"National contracts are even more solemn and sacred than private ones, on account of the great interests involved; of the deliberateness with which the obligations are assumed; of the permanence and generality of the obligations, measured by the national life, and including thousands of particular cases; and of each nation's calling, under God, to be a teacher of right to all, within and without its borders."

Vattel says: "It is a settled point in natural law that he who has made a promise to any one has conferred upon him a real right to require the thing promised; and, consequently, that the breach of a perfect promise is a violation of another person's right, and as evidently an act of injustice as it would be to rob a man of his property. * * *

"There would no longer be any security, no longer any commerce between mankind, if they did not think themselves obliged to keep faith with each other, and to perform their promises."

It is evident that the whole weight of the recognized and accepted law of nations is thrown on the side of justice between nation and nation, and is the recognized and accepted standard of the obligation involved in compacts between nation and nation.

We must look, then, among the accepted declarations of the
law of nations for the just and incontrovertible measure of the
shame of breaking national compacts, and of the wickedness of
the nations that dare to do it.

We shall go back to the earliest days of the world, and find
no dissent from, no qualification of the verdict of the infamy
of such acts. Livy says of leagues: "Leagues are such agreements as are made by the command of the supreme power, and
whereby the whole nation is made liable to the wrath of God
if they infringe it."

Grotius opens his "Admonition," in conclusion of the third
book of his famous "Rights of War and Peace," as follows:
"'For it is by faith,' saith Cicero, 'that not commonwealths
only, but that grand society of nations is maintained.' 'Take
away this,' saith Aristotle, 'and all human commerce fails.'
It is, therefore, an execrable thing to break faith on which so
many lives depend. 'It is,' saith Seneca, 'the best ornament
wherewith God hath beautified the rational soul; the strongest
support of human society, which ought so much the more inviolably to be kept by sovereign princes by how much they
may sin with greater license and impunity than other men.
Wherefore take away faith, and men are more fierce and cruel
than savage beasts, whose rage all men do horribly dread. Justice, indeed, in all other of her parts hath something that is
obscure; but that whereunto we engage our faith is of itself
clear and evident; yea, and to this very end do men pawn
their faith, that in their negotiations one with another all
doubts may be taken away, and every scruple removed. How
much more, then, doth it concern kings to keep their faith in-
violate, as well for conscience' sake as in regard to their honor
and reputation, wherein consists the authority of a kingdom.'"

Vattel says: "Treaties are no better than empty words, if
nations do not consider them as respectable engagements, as

rules which are to be inviolably observed by sovereigns, and held sacred throughout the whole earth.

"The faith of treaties—that firm and sincere resolution, that invariable constancy in fulfilling our engagements, of which we make profession in a treaty—is therefore to be held sacred and inviolable between the nations of the earth, whose safety and repose it secures; and if mankind be not wilfully deficient in their duty to themselves, infamy must ever be the portion of him who violates his faith. * * *

"He who violates his treaties, violates at the same time the law of nations, for he disregards the faith of treaties, that faith which the law of nations declares sacred; and, so far as dependent on him, he renders it vain and ineffectual. Doubly guilty, he does an injury to his ally, and he does an injury to all nations, and inflicts a wound on the great society of mankind. * * *

"On the observance and execution of treaties," said a respectable sovereign, "depends all the security which princes and States have with respect to each other, and no dependence could henceforward be placed in future conventions if the existing ones were not to be observed."

It is sometimes said, by those seeking to defend, or at least palliate, the United States Government's repeated disregard of its treaties with the Indians, that no Congress can be held responsible for the acts of the Congress preceding it, or can bind the Congress following it; or, in other words, that each Congress may, if it chooses, undo all that has been done by previous Congresses. However true this may be of some legislative acts, it is clearly not true, according to the principles of international law, of treaties.

On this point Vattel says: "Since public treaties, even those of a personal nature, concluded by a king, or by another sovereign who is invested with sufficient power, are treaties of State, and obligatory on the whole nation, real treaties, which were intended to subsist independently of the person who has concluded them, are undoubtedly binding on his successors; and the obligation which such treaties impose on the State passes successively to all her rulers as soon as they assume the public authority. The case is the same with respect to the rights acquired by those treaties. They are acquired for the State, and successively pass to her conductors."

Von Martens says: "Treaties, properly so called, are either personal or real. They are personal when their continuation in force depends on the person of the sovereign or his family, with whom they have been contracted. They are real when their duration depends on the State, independently of the person who contracts. Consequently, all treaties between republics must be real. All treaties made for a time specified or forever are real. * * *

"This division is of the greatest importance, because real treaties never cease to be obligatory, except in cases where all treaties become invalid. Every successor to the sovereignty, in virtue of whatever title he may succeed, is obliged to observe them without their being renewed at his accession."

Wheaton says: "They (treaties) continue to bind the State, whatever intervening changes may take place in its internal constitution or in the persons of its rulers. The State continues the same, notwithstanding such change, and consequently the treaty relating to national objects remains in force so long as the nation exists as an independent State."

There is no disagreement among authorities on this point. It is also said by some, seeking to defend or palliate the United States Government's continuous violations of its treaties with the Indians, that the practice of all nations has been and is to abrogate a treaty whenever it saw good reason for doing so. This is true; but the treaties have been done away with in one of two ways, either by a mutual and peaceful agreement to that effect between the parties who had made it—the treaty being considered in force until the consent of both parties to its abrogation had been given—or by a distinct avowal on the part of one nation of its intention no longer to abide by it, and to take, therefore, its chances of being made war upon in consequence. Neither of these courses has been pursued by the United States Government in its treaty-breaking with the Indians.

Vattel says, on the dissolution of treaties : " Treaties may be dissolved by mutual consent at the free-will of the contracting powers."

Grotius says : " If either party violate the League, the other party is freed ; because each Article of the League hath the form and virtue of a condition."

Kent says : " The violation of any one article of a treaty is a violation of the whole treaty. * * *

" It is a principle of universal jurisprudence that a compact cannot be rescinded by one party only, if the other party does not consent to rescind it, and does no act to destroy it. * * *

" To recommence a war by breach of the articles of peace, is deemed much more odious than to provoke a war by some new demand or aggression ; for the latter is simply injustice, but in the former case the party is guilty both of perfidy and injustice."

It is also said, with unanswerable irrelevancy, by some who seek to defend or palliate the United States Government's continuous violation of its treaties with the Indians, that it was, in the first place, absurd to make treaties with them at all, to consider them in any sense as treaty-making powers or nations. The logic of this assertion, made as a justification for the breaking of several hundred treaties, concluded at different times during the last hundred years, and broken as fast as concluded, seems almost equal to that of the celebrated defence in the case of the kettle, which was cracked when it was lent, whole when returned, and, in fact, was never borrowed at all. It would be a waste of words to reason with minds that can see in this position any shelter for the United States Government against the accusation of perfidy in its treaty relations with the Indians.

The statement is undoubtedly a true one, that the Indians, having been placed in the anomalous position as tribes, of "domestic dependent nations," and as individuals, in the still more anomalous position of adult "wards," have not legally possessed the treaty-making power. Our right to put them, or to consider them to be in those anomalous positions, might be successfully disputed; but they, helpless, having accepted such positions, did, no doubt, thereby lose their right to be treated with as nations. Nevertheless, that is neither here nor there now : as soon as our Government was established, it proceeded to treat with them as nations by name and designation, and with precisely the same forms and ratifications that it used in treating with other nations; and it continued to treat with them as nations by name and designation, and with continually increasing solemnity of asseveration of good intent and good faith, for nearly a century. The robbery, the cruelty which were done under the cloak of this hundred years of treaty-making and treaty-breaking, are greater than can be told. Neither mountains nor deserts stayed them; it took two seas to set their bounds.

In 1871, Congress, either ashamed of making treaties only to break them, or grudging the time, money, and paper it wasted, passed an act to the effect that no Indian tribe should hereafter be considered as a foreign nation with whom the United States might contract by treaty. There seems to have been at the time, in the minds of the men who passed this act, a certain shadowy sense of some obligation being involved in treaties; for they added to the act a proviso that it should not be construed as invalidating any treaties already made. But this sense of obligation must have been as short-lived as shadowy, and could have had no element of shame in it, since they forthwith proceeded, unabashed, to negotiate still more treaties with Indians, and break them; for instance, the so-called "Brunot Treaty" with the Ute Indians in Colorado, and one with the Crow Indians in Montana—both made in the summer of 1873. They were called at the time "conventions" or "agreements," and not "treaties;" but the difference is only in name.

They stated, in a succession of numbered articles, promises of payment of moneys, and surrenders and cessions of land, by both parties; were to be ratified by Congress before taking effect; and were understood by the Indians agreeing to them to be as binding as if they had been called treaties. The fact that no man's sense of justice openly revolted against such subterfuges, under the name of agreements, is only to be explained by the deterioration of the sense of honor in the nation. In the days of Grotius there were men who failed to see dishonor in a trick if profit came of it, and of such he wrote in words whose truth might sting to-day as, no doubt, it stung then:

"Whereas there are many that think it superfluous to require that justice from a free people or their governors which they exact daily from private men, the ground of this error is this: because these men respect nothing in the law but the profit that ariseth from it, which in private persons, being single and unable to defend themselves, is plain and evident; but for great cities, that seem to have within themselves all things necessary for their own well-being, it doth not so plainly appear that they have any need of that virtue called justice which respects strangers."

These extracts from unquestioned authorities on international law prove that we may hold nations to standards of justice and good faith as we hold men; that the standards are the same in each case; and that a nation that steals and lies and breaks promises, will no more be respected or unpunished than a man who steals and lies and breaks promises. It is possible to go still farther than this, and to show that a nation habitually guilty of such conduct might properly be dealt with therefor by other nations, by nations in nowise suffering on account of her bad faith, except as all nations suffer when the interests of human society are injured.

"The interest of human society," says Vattel, "would authorize all the other nations to form a confederacy, in order to humble and chastise the delinquent." * * * When a nation "regards no right as sacred, the safety of the human race requires that she should be repressed. To form and support an unjust pretension is not only doing an injury to the party whose interests are affected by that pretension; but to despise justice in general is doing an injury to all nations."

The history of the United States Government's repeated violations of faith with the Indians thus convicts us, as a nation, not only of having outraged the principles of justice, which are the basis of international law; and of having laid ourselves open to the accusation of both cruelty and perfidy; but of having made ourselves liable to all punishments which follow upon such sins—to arbitrary punishment at the hands of any civilized nation who might see fit to call us to account, and to that more certain natural punishment which, sooner or later, as surely comes from evil-doing as harvests come from sown seed.

To prove all this it is only necessary to study the history of any one of the Indian tribes. I propose to give in the following chapters merely outline sketches of the history of a few of them, not entering more into details than is necessary to show the repeated broken faith of the United States Government toward them. A full history of the wrongs they have suffered at the hands of the authorities, military and civil, and also of the citizens of this country, it would take years to write and volumes to hold.

There is but one hope of righting this wrong. It lies in appeal to the heart and the conscience of the American people. What the people demand, Congress will do. It has been—to our shame be it spoken—at the demand of part of the people that all these wrongs have been committed, these treaties broken, these robberies done, by the Government.

So long as there remains on our frontier one square mile of land occupied by a weak and helpless owner, there will be a strong and unscrupulous frontiersman ready to seize it, and a weak and unscrupulous politician, who can be hired for a vote or for money, to back him.

The only thing that can stay this is a mighty outspoken sentiment and purpose of the great body of the people. Right sentiment and right purpose in a Senator here and there, and a Representative here and there, are little more than straws which make momentary eddies, but do not obstruct the tide. The precedents of a century's unhindered and profitable robbery have mounted up into a very Gibraltar of defence and shelter to those who care for nothing but safety and gain. That such precedents should be held, and openly avowed as standards, is only one more infamy added to the list. Were such logic employed in the case of an individual man, how quick would all men see its enormity. Suppose that a man had had the misfortune to be born into a family whose name had been blackened by generations of criminals; that his father, his grandfather, and his great-grandfather before them had lived in prisons, and died on scaffolds, should that man say in his soul, "Go to! What is the use? I also will commit robbery and murder, and get the same gain by it which my family must have done?" Or shall he say in his soul, "God help me! I will do what may be within the power of one man, and the compass of one generation, to atone for the wickedness, and to make clean the name of my dishonored house!"

What an opportunity for the Congress of 1880 to cover itself with a lustre of glory, as the first to cut short our nation's record of cruelties and perjuries! the first to attempt to redeem the name of the United States from the stain of a century of dishonor!

CHAPTER II.

THE DELAWARES.

WHEN Hendrik Hudson anchored his ship, the *Half Moon*, off New York Island in 1609, the Delawares stood in great numbers on the shore to receive him, exclaiming, in their innocence, "Behold! the gods have come to visit us!"

More than a hundred years later, the traditions of this event were still current in the tribe. The aged Moravian missionary, Heckewelder, writing in 1818, says:

"I at one time, in April, 1787, was astonished when I heard one of their orators, a great chief of the Delawares,[1] Pachgantschilias by name, go over this ground, recapitulating the most extraordinary events which had before happened, and concluding in these words: 'I admit that there are good white men, but they bear no proportion to the bad; the bad must be the strongest, for they rule. They do what they please. They enslave those who are not of their color, although created by the same Great Spirit who created them. They would make slaves of us if they could; but as they cannot do it, they kill us. There is no faith to be placed in their words. They are not like the Indians, who are only enemies while at war, and are friends in peace. They will say to an Indian, "My friend; my brother!" They will take him by the hand, and, at the same moment, destroy him. And so you' (he was addressing himself to the Christian Indians at Gnadenbütten, Pennsylvania) 'will also be treated by them before long. Remember that

[1] Little writing exists on the Indians in Delaware, one of the tribes removed to the far West. See, however, Frederick W. Crumb, *Tom Quick, Early American* (Narrowsburg, N.Y., 1936) and Max Schrabisch, *Archaeology of the Delaware Valley* (Harrisburg, Pa., 1930).

this day I have warned you to beware of such friends as these. I know the Long-knives. They are not to be trusted.'"

The original name of the Delawares was Lenni Lenape, or " original people." They were also called by the Western tribes Wapenachki, " people at the rising of the sun." When the name " Delawares " was given to them by the whites, they at first resented it; but being told that they, and also one of their rivers, were thus named after a great English brave—Lord De la Warre—they were much pleased, and willingly took the name. Their lands stretched from the Hudson River to the Potomac. They were a noble-spirited but gentle people; much under the control of the arrogant and all-powerful Iroquois, who had put upon them the degradation of being called " women," and being forced to make war or give up land at the pleasure of their masters.

During William Penn's humane administration of the affairs of Pennsylvania, the Delawares were his most devoted friends. They called him Mignon, or Elder Brother.

" From his first arrival in their country," says Heckewelder, " a friendship was formed between them, which was to last as long as the sun should shine, and the rivers flow with water. That friendship would undoubtedly have continued to the end of time, had their good brother always remained among them."

In the French and Indian war of 1755 many of them fought on the side of the French against the English; and in the beginning of our Revolutionary war the majority of them sided with the English against us.

Most of the memorable Indian massacres which happened during this period were the result of either French or English influence. Neither nation was high-minded enough to scorn availing herself of savage allies to do bloody work which she would not have dared to risk national reputation by doing herself. This fact is too much overlooked in the habitual estimates of the barbarous ferocity of the Indian character as shown by those early massacres.

The United States' first treaty with the Delawares was made in 1778, at Fort Pitt. The parties to it were said to be "the United States and the Delaware Nation." It stipulates that there shall be peace, and that the troops of the United States may pass "through the country of the Delaware Nation," upon paying the full value of any supplies they may use. It further says that, "Whereas the enemies of the United States have endeavored by every artifice to possess the Indians with an opinion that it is our design to extirpate them, and take possession of their country; to obviate such false suggestions, the United States guarantee to said nation of Delawares, and their heirs, all their territorial rights in the fullest and most ample manner as bounded by former treaties."

The treaty also provides that, "should it for the future be found conducive for the mutual interest of both parties to invite any other tribes who have been friends to the interests of the United States to join the present confederation and form a State, whereof the Delaware Nation shall be the head," it shall be done; and the Delawares shall be entitled to send a representative to Congress.†

The Delawares agreed to send all the warriors they could spare to fight for us, and that there should be peace and perpetual friendship.

At this time the rest of the Ohio tribes, most of the New York tribes, and a large part of the Delawares were in arms on the British side. When the war of the Revolution was concluded, they were all forced to make peace as best they could with us; and in our first treaty we provided for the reinstating in the Delaware Nation of the chiefs and headmen who had

---

† It is superfluous to say that these provisions were never carried out.

made that old alliance with us; they having lost caste in their tribe for having fought on our side.

"It is agreed," says the final Article of the treaty, "that the Delaware chiefs, Kelelamand, or Lieut.-colonel Henry, Henque Pushees, or the Big Cat, and Wicocalind, or Captain White Eyes, who took up the hatchet for the United States, and their families, shall be received into the Delaware Nation in the same situation and rank as before the war, and enjoy their due portions of the lands given to the Wyandotte and Delaware nations in this treaty, as fully as if they had not taken part with America, or as any other person or persons in the said nations."

This Captain White Eyes had adhered to our cause in spite of great opposition from the hostile part of the tribe. At one time he was threatened with a violent death if he should dare to say one word for the American cause; but by spirited harangues he succeeded in keeping the enthusiasm of his own party centred around himself, and finally carrying them over to the side of the United States. Some of his speeches are on record, and are worthy to be remembered:

"If you will go out in this war," he said to them at one time, when the band were inclined to join the British, "you shall not go without me. I have taken peace measures, it is true, with the view of saving my tribe from destruction; but if you think me in the wrong, if you give more credit to runaway vagabonds than to your own friends—to a man, to a warrior, to a Delaware—if you insist on fighting the Americans—go! and I will go with you. And I will not go like the bear-hunter, who sets his dogs on the animal to be beaten about with his paws, while he keeps himself at a safe distance. No; I will lead you on; I will place myself in the front; I will fall with the first of you! You can do as you choose; but as for me, I will not survive my nation. I will not live to bewail the miserable destruction of a brave people, who deserved, as you do, a better fate."

Were there many speeches made by commanders to their troops in those revolutionary days with which these words do not compare favorably ?

This treaty, by which our faithful ally, Wicocalind, was reinstated in his tribal rank, was made at Fort M'Intosh in 1785. The Wyandottes, Chippewas, and Ottawas, as well as the Delawares, joined in it. They acknowledged themselves and all their tribes to be "under the protection of the United States, and of no other sovereign whatsoever." The United States Government reserved "the post of Detroit" and an outlying district around it; also, the post at Michilimackinac, with a surrounding district of twelve miles square, and some other reserves for trading-posts.

The Indians' lands were comprised within lines partly indicated by the Cuyahoga, Big Miami, and Ohio rivers and their branches; it fronted on Lake Erie; and if "any citizen of the United States," or "any other person not an Indian," attempted "to settle on any of the lands allotted to the Delaware and Wyandotte nations in this treaty"—the fifth Article of the treaty said—"the Indians may punish him as they please."

Michigan, Ohio, Indiana, Pennsylvania, all are largely made up of the lands which were by this first treaty given to the Indians.

Five years later, by another treaty at Fort Harmar, the provisions of this treaty were reiterated, the boundaries somewhat changed and more accurately defined. The privilege of hunting on all the lands reserved to the United States was promised to the Indians "without hinderance or molestation, so long as they behaved themselves peaceably;" and "that nothing may interrupt the peace and harmony now established between the United States and the aforesaid nations," it was promised in one of the articles that white men committing offences or murders on Indians should be punished in the same way as Indians committing such offences.

The year before this treaty Congress had resolved that "the sum of $20,000, in addition to the $14,000 already appropriated, be appropriated for defraying the expenses of the treaties which have been ordered, or which may be ordered to be held, in the present year, with the several Indian tribes in the Northern Department; and for extinguishing the Indian claims, the whole of the said $20,000, together with $6000 of the said $14,000, to be applied solely to the purpose of extinguishing Indian claims to the lands they have already ceded to the United States by obtaining regular conveyances for the same, and for extending a purchase beyond the limits hitherto fixed by treaty."

Here is one of the earliest records of the principle and method on which the United States Government first began its dealings with Indians. "Regular conveyances," "extinguishing claims" by "extending purchase." These are all the strictest of legal terms, and admit of no double interpretations.

The Indians had been much dissatisfied ever since the first treaties were made. They claimed that they had been made by a few only, representing a part of the tribe; and, in 1786, they had held a great council on the banks of the Detroit River, and sent a message to Congress, of which the following extracts will show the spirit.

They said: "It is now more than three years since peace was made between the King of Great Britain and you; but we, the Indians, were disappointed, finding ourselves not included in that peace according to our expectations, for we thought that its conclusion would have promoted a friendship between the United States and the Indians, and that we might enjoy that happiness that formerly subsisted between us and our Elder Brethren. We have received two very agreeable messages from the Thirteen United States. We also received a message from the king, whose war we were engaged in, desiring us to remain quiet, which we accordingly complied with. During this time of tranquillity we were deliberating the best method we could to form a lasting reconciliation with the Thirteen United States. * * * We are still of the same opinion as to the means which may tend to reconcile us to each other; and we are sorry to find, although we had the best thoughts in our minds during the before-mentioned period, mischief has nevertheless happened between you and us. We are still anxious of putting our plan of accommodation into execution, and we shall briefly inform you of the means that seem most probable to us of effecting a firm and lasting peace and reconciliation, the first step toward which should, in our opinion, be that all treaties carried on with the United States on our parts should be with the general will of the whole confederacy, and carried on in the most open manner, without any restraint on either side; and especially as landed matters are often the subject of our councils with you—a matter of the greatest importance and of general concern to us—in this case we hold it indisputably necessary that any cession of our lands should be made in the most public manner, and by the united voice of the confederacy, holding all partial treaties as void and of no effect. * * * We say, let us meet half-way, and let us pursue such steps as become upright and honest men. We beg that you will prevent your surveyors and other people from coming upon our side of the Ohio River."

These are touching words, when we remember that only the year before the United States had expressly told these Indians that if any white citizens attempted to settle on their lands they might "punish them as they pleased."

"We have told you before we wished to pursue just steps, and we are determined they shall appear just and reasonable in the eyes of the world. This is the determination of all the chiefs of our confederacy now assembled here, notwithstanding the accidents that have happened in our villages, even when in council, where several innocent chiefs were killed when absolutely engaged in promoting a peace with you, the Thirteen United States."

The next year the President instructed the governor of the territory northwest of the Ohio to "examine carefully into the real temper of the Indian tribes" in his department, and says: "The treaties which have been made may be examined, but must not be departed from, unless a change of boundary beneficial to the United States can be obtained." He says also: "You will not neglect any opportunity that may offer of extinguishing the Indian rights to the westward, *as far as the Mississippi*."

Beyond that river even the wildest dream of greed did not at that time look.

The President adds, moreover: "You may stipulate that any white persons going over the said boundaries without a license from the proper officers of the United States may be treated in such manner as the Indians may see fit."

I have not yet seen, in any accounts of the Indian hostilities on the North-western frontier during this period, any reference to those repeated permissions given by the United States to the Indians, to defend their lands as they saw fit. Probably the greater number of the pioneer settlers were as ignorant of these provisions in Indian treaties as are the greater number of American citizens to-day, who are honestly unaware—and being unaware, are therefore incredulous—that the Indians had either provocation or right to kill intruders on their lands.

At this time separate treaties were made with the Six Nations, and the governor says that these treaties were made separately because of the jealousy and hostility existing between them and the Delawares, Wyandottes, etc., which he is "not willing to lessen," because it weakens their power. "Indeed," he frankly adds, "it would not be very difficult, if circumstances required it, to set them at deadly variance."

Thus early in our history was the ingenious plan evolved of first maddening the Indians into war, and then falling upon them with exterminating punishment. The gentleman who has left on the official records of his country his claim to the first suggestion and recommendation of this method is "Arthur St. Clair, governor of the territory of the United States north-west of the Ohio River, and commissioner plenipotentiary of the United States of America for removing all causes of controversy, regulating trade, and settling boundaries with the Indian nations in the Northern Department."

Under all these conditions, it is not a matter of wonder that the frontier was a scene of perpetual devastation and bloodshed; and that, year by year, there grew stronger in the minds of the whites a terror and hatred of Indians; and in the minds of the Indians a stronger and stronger distrust and hatred of the whites.

The Delawares were, through the earlier part of these troubled times, friendly. In 1791 we find the Secretary of War recommending the commissioners sent to treat with the hostile Miamis and Wabash Indians to stop by the way with the friendly Delawares, and take some of their leading chiefs with them as allies. He says, "these tribes are our friends," and, as far as is known, "the treaties have been well observed by them."

But in 1792 we find them mentioned among the hostile tribes to whom was sent a message from the United States Government, containing the following extraordinary paragraphs:

"Brethren: The President of the United States entertains the opinion that the war which exists is an error and mistake on your parts. That you believe the United States want to deprive you of your lands, and drive you out of the country. *Be assured that this is not so;* on the contrary, that we should be greatly gratified with the opportunity of imparting to you all the blessings of civilized life; of teaching you to cultivate the earth, and raise corn; to raise oxen, sheep, and other domestic animals; to build comfortable houses; and to educate your children so as ever to dwell upon the land.

"Consult, therefore, upon the great object of peace; call in your parties, and enjoin a cessation of all further depredations; and as many of the principal chiefs as shall choose repair to Philadelphia, the seat of the Great Government, and there make a peace founded on the principles of justice and humanity. *Remember that no additional lands will be required of you, or any other tribe, to those that have been ceded by former treaties.*"

It was in this same year, also, that General Putnam said to them, in a speech at Post Vincennes: "The United States don't mean to wrong you out of your lands. They don't want to take away your lands by force. They want to do you justice." And the venerable missionary, Heckewelder, who had journeyed all the way from Bethlehem, Pennsylvania, to try to help bring about peace, said to them, "The great chief who has spoken to you is a good man. He loves you, and will always speak the truth to you. I wish you to listen to his words, and do as he desires you."

In 1793 a great council was held, to which came the chiefs and headmen of the Delawares, and of twelve other tribes, to meet commissioners of the United States, for one last effort to settle the vexed boundary question. The records of this council are profoundly touching. The Indians reiterated over and over the provisions of the old treaties which had established the Ohio River as one of their boundaries. Their words were not the words of ignorant barbarians, clumsily and doggedly holding to a point; they were the words of clear-headed, statesman-like rulers, insisting on the rights of their nations. As the days went on, and it became more and more clear that the United States commissioners would not

agree to the establishment of the boundary for which the Indians contended, the speeches of the chiefs grow sadder and
sadder.   Finally, in desperation, as a last hope, they propose to
the commissioners that all the money which the United States
offers to pay to them for their lands shall be given to the white
settlers to induce them to move away.   They say :

"Money to us is of no value, and to most of us unknown ;
and as no consideration whatever can induce us to sell the lands
on which we get sustenance for our women and children, we
hope we may be allowed to point out a mode by which your
settlers may be easily removed, and peace thereby obtained.

"We know that these settlers are poor, or they would never
have ventured to live in a country which has been in continual
trouble ever since they crossed the Ohio.   Divide, therefore,
this large sum of money which you have offered us among
these people ; give to each, also, a proportion of what you say
you would give to us annually, over and above this very large
sum of money, and we are persuaded they would most readily
accept of it in lieu of the lands you sold them.   If you add,
also, the great sums you must expend in raising and paying
armies with a view to force us to yield you our country, you
will certainly have more than sufficient for the purpose of re-
paying these settlers for all their labor and their improvements.

"You have talked to us about concessions.   It appears
strange that you should expect any from us, who have only
been defending our just rights against your invasions.   We
want peace.   Restore to us our country, and we shall be enemies no longer.

" * * * We desire you to consider, brothers, that our only
demand is the peaceable possession of a small part of our once
great country.   Look back and review the lands from whence
we have been driven to this spot.   We can retreat no farther,
because the country behind hardly affords food for its present

inhabitants, and we have therefore resolved to leave our bones in this small space to which we are now confined."

The commissioners replied that to make the Ohio River the boundary was now impossible; that they sincerely regretted that peace could not be made; but, "knowing the upright and liberal views of the United States," they trust that "impartial judges will not attribute the continuance of the war to them."

Notice was sent to the governor that the Indians "refused to make peace;" and General Anthony Wayne, a few weeks later, wrote to the Secretary of War, "The safety of the Western frontiers, the reputation of the legion, the dignity and interest of the nation—all forbid a retrograde manœuvre, or giving up one inch of ground we now possess, till the enemy are compelled to sue for peace."

The history of the campaigns that followed is to be found in many volumes treating of the pioneer life of Ohio and other North-western States. One letter of General Wayne's to the Secretary of War, in August, 1794, contains a paragraph which is interesting, as showing the habits and method of life of the people whom we at this time, by force of arms, drove out from their homes—homes which we had only a few years before solemnly guaranteed to them, even giving them permission to punish any white intruders there as they saw fit. By a feint of approaching Grand Glaize through the Miami villages, General Wayne surprised the settlement, and the Indians, being warned by a deserter, had barely time to flee for their lives. What General Wayne had intended to do may be inferred from this sentence in his letter: "I have good grounds to conclude that the defection of this villain prevented the enemy from receiving a fatal blow at this place when least expected."

However, he consoles himself by the fact that he has "gained possession of the grand emporium of the hostile Indians of the West without loss of blood. The very extensive

and highly cultivated fields and gardens show the work of
many hands. The margins of those beautiful rivers—the Miamis, of the Lake, and Au Glaize—appear like one continued
village for a number of miles, both above and below this place;
nor have I ever before beheld such immense fields of corn in
any part of America, from Canada to Florida."

All these villages were burnt, and all these cornfields destroyed; the Indians were followed up and defeated in a sharp
fight. The British agents did their best to keep them hostile,
and no inconsiderable aid was furnished to them from Canada.
But after a winter of suffering and hunger, and great vacillations of purpose, they finally decided to yield to the inevitable,
and in the summer of 1795 they are to be found once more
assembled in council, for the purpose of making a treaty; once
more to be told by the representatives of the United States
Government that "the heart of General Washington, the Great
Chief of America, wishes for nothing so much as peace and
brotherly love;" that "such is the justice and liberality of the
United States," that they will now a third time pay for lands;
and that they are "acting the part of a tender father to them
and their children in thus providing for them not only at present, but forever."

Eleven hundred and thirty Indians (eleven tribes, besides
the Delawares, being represented) were parties to this treaty.
By this treaty nearly two-thirds of the present State of Ohio
were ceded to the United States; and, in consideration of these
"cessions and relinquishments, and to manifest the liberality
of the United States as the great means of rendering this peace
strong and perpetual," the United States relinquished all claims
"to all other Indian lands northward of the River Ohio, eastward of the Mississippi, and westward and southward of the
Great Lakes and the waters uniting them, according to the
boundary line agreed upon by the United States and the King
of Great Britain, in the treaty of peace made between them

in the year 1783," with the exception of four tracts of land. But it was stated to the Indians that these reservations were not made "to annoy or impose the smallest degree of restraint on them in the quiet enjoyment and full possession of their lands," but simply to "connect the settlements of the people of the United States," and "to prove convenient and advantageous to the different tribes of Indians residing and hunting in their vicinity."

The fifth Article of the treaty is: "To prevent any misunderstanding about the Indian lands now relinquished by the United States, it is explicitly declared that the meaning of that relinquishment is this: that the Indian tribes who have a right to those lands are quietly to enjoy them—hunting, planting, and dwelling thereon *so long as they please* without any molestation from the United States; but when those tribes, or any of them, shall be disposed to sell their lands, or any part of them, they are to be sold only to the United States; and until such sale the United States will protect all the said Indian tribes in the quiet enjoyment of their lands against all citizens of the United States, and against all other white persons who intrude on the same."

The sixth Article reiterates the old pledge, proved by the last three years to be so worthless—that, "If any citizen of the United States, or any other white person or persons, shall presume to settle upon the lands now relinquished by the United States, such citizen or other person shall be out of the protection of the United States; and the Indian tribe on whose land the settlement may be made may drive off the settler, or punish him in such manner as they shall think fit."

The seventh Article gives the Indians the liberty "to hunt within the territory and lands which they have now ceded to the United States, without hinderance or molestation, so long as they demean themselves peaceably."

The United States agreed to pay to the Indians twenty

thousand dollars' worth of goods at once; and "henceforward, every year, forever, useful goods to the value of nine thousand five hundred dollars." Peace was declared to be "established" and "perpetual."

General Wayne told the Indians that they might believe him, for he had never, "in a public capacity, told a lie;" and one of the Indians said, with much more dignity, "The Great Spirit above hears us, and I trust we shall not endeavor to deceive each other."

In 1813, by a treaty at Vincennes, the bounds of the reservation of the Post of St. Vincennes were defined, and the Indians, "as a mark of their regard and attachment to the United States, relinquished to the United States the great salt spring on the Saline Creek."

In less than a year we made still another treaty with them for the extinguishment of their title to a tract of land between the Ohio and the Wabash rivers (which they sold to us for a ten years' annuity of three hundred dollars, which was to be "exclusively appropriated to ameliorating their condition and promoting their civilization"); and in one year more still another treaty, in which a still further cession of land was made for a permanent annuity of one thousand dollars.

In August of this year General Harrison writes to the Secretary of War that there are great dissensions between the Delawares and Miamis in regard to some of the ceded lands, the Miamis claiming that they had never consented to give them up. General Harrison observes the most exact neutrality in this matter, but says, "A knowledge of the value of land is fast gaining ground among the Indians," and negotiations are becoming in consequence much more difficult. In the course of this controversy, "one of the chiefs has said that he knew a great part of the land was worth six dollars an acre."

It is only ten years since one of the chiefs of these same tribes had said, "Money is to us of no value." However, they must be yet very far from having reached any true estimate of real values, as General Harrison adds: "From the best calculation I have been able to make, the tract now ceded contains at least two millions of acres, and embraces some of the finest lands in the Western country."

Cheap at one thousand dollars a year!—even with the negro man thrown in, which General Harrison tells the Secretary he has ordered Captain Wells to purchase, and present to the chief, The Turtle, and to draw on the United States Treasury for the amount paid for him.

Four years later (1809) General Harrison is instructed by the President "to take advantage of the most favorable moment for extinguishing the Indian title to the lands lying east of the Wabash, and adjoining south;" and the title was extinguished by the treaty of Fort Wayne—a little more money paid, and a great deal of land given up.

In 1814 we made a treaty, simply of peace and friendship, with the Delawares and several other tribes: they agreeing to fight faithfully on our side against the English, and we agreeing to "confirm and establish all the boundaries" as they had existed before the war.

In 1817 it was deemed advisable to make an effort to "extinguish the Indian title to all the lands claimed by them within the limits of the State of Ohio. Two commissioners were appointed, with great discretionary powers; and a treaty was concluded early in the autumn, by which there was ceded to the United States nearly all the land to which the Indians had claim in Ohio, a part of Indiana, and a part of Michigan. This treaty was said by the Secretary of War to be "the most important of any hitherto made with the Indians." "The extent of the cession far exceeded" his most sanguine expectations, and he had the honesty to admit that "there can be no real or well-founded objection to the amount of the compensation given for it, except that it is not an adequate one."

The commissioners who negotiated the treaty were apprehensive that they would be accused of having made too liberal terms with the Indians, and in their report to the department they enumerate apologetically the reasons which made it impossible for them to get the land cheaper. Mr. Cass says of the terms: "Under any circumstances, they will fall infinitely short of the pecuniary and political value of the country obtained."

The Indians, parties to this treaty, surrendered by it almost the last of their hunting-grounds, and would soon be driven to depending wholly upon the cultivation of the soil.

In 1818 the Delawares again ceded land to the United States—ceded all to which they laid claim in the State of Indiana—and the United States promised to provide for them "a country to reside in on the west side of the Mississippi," and "to guarantee to them the peaceable possession" of the same. They were to have four thousand dollars a year in addition to all the sums promised by previous treaties, and they were to be allowed to remain three years longer by sufferance in their present homes. The Government also agreed to pay them for their improvements on their lands, to give them a hundred and twenty horses, and a "sufficient number of pirogues to aid in transporting them to the west side of the Mississippi;" also provisions for the journey.

In 1829 a supplementary Article was added to this treaty. The United States Government began to show traces of compunction and pity. The Article says, "Whereas the Delaware Nation are now willing to remove," it is agreed upon that the country in the fork of the Kansas and Missouri rivers, selected for their home, "shall be conveyed and forever secured by the United States to the said Delaware Nation, as their permanent residence; and the United States hereby pledges the faith of the Government to guarantee to the said Delaware Nation, forever, the quiet and peaceable and undisturbed enjoyment of the same against the claims and assaults of all and every other people whatever."

An additional permanent annuity of one thousand dollars is promised; forty horses, "and the use of six wagons and ox-teams to assist in removing heavy articles," provisions for the journey, and one year's subsistence after they reach their new home; also the erection of a grist and saw mill within two years.

In 1833 the Secretary of War congratulated the country on the fact that "the country north of the Ohio, east of the Mississippi, including the States of Ohio, Indiana, Illinois, and the Territory of Michigan as far as the Fox and Wisconsin rivers," has been practically "cleared of the embarrassments of Indian relations," as there are not more than five thousand Indians, all told, left in this whole region.

The Commissioner of Indian Affairs in the same year says that it is "grateful to notice" how much the Indians' condition is "ameliorated under the policy of removal." He says that they, "protected by the strong arm of the Government, and dwelling on lands *distinctly* and permanently established as their own, enjoying a delightful climate and a fertile soil, turn their attention to the cultivation of the earth, and abandon the chase for the surer supply of domestic animals."

This commissioner apparently does not remember, perhaps never read, the records of the great fields of corn which the Delawares had on the Miami River in 1795, and how they returned twice that summer and replanted them, after General Wayne had cut down and burnt the young crops. They had "turned their attention to the cultivation of the soil" forty years ago, and that was what came of it. We shall see how much better worth while it may be for them to plant corn in their new "permanent home," than it was in their last one.

The printed records of Indian Affairs for the first forty years of this century are meagre and unsatisfactory. Had the

practice prevailed then, as at the present time, of printing full
annual reports for the different tribes, it would be possible to
know much which is now forever locked up in the traditions
and the memories of the Indians themselves. For ten years
after the making of this last quoted treaty, there is little official mention of the Delawares by name, beyond the mention
in the fiscal reports of the sums paid to them as annuities and
for education. In 1833 the commissioner says, "The agent for
the Delawares and Shawnees states that he was shown cloth
that was spun and wove, and shirts and other clothing made
by the Indian girls."

In 1838 the Delawares are reported as cultivating one thousand five hundred acres of land in grain and vegetables, and
raising a great many hogs, cattle, and horses. "They are a
brave, enterprising people," and "at peace with all neighboring
Indians."

Parties of them frequently make excursions into the Rocky
Mountains after beaver, and return with a rich reward, sometimes as much as one thousand dollars to an individual; but
their money is soon spent, chiefly for ardent spirits. The
agent says: "The only hinderance now in the way of the
Delawares, Shawnees, and Kickapoos is ardent spirits. * * *
These whiskey traffickers, who seem void of all conscience,
rob and murder many of these Indians; I say rob—they will
get them drunk, and then take their horses, guns, or blankets
off their backs, regardless of how quick they may freeze to
death; I say they murder—if not directly, indirectly, they
furnish the weapon—they make them drunk, and, when drunk,
they kill their fellow-beings. Some freeze to death when drunk;
several drunken Indians have been drowned in the Missouri
River this season, aiming to cross when drunk."

In 1844 the chiefs of the Delawares met together, and prepared a remarkable document, which was forwarded to the
Secretary of War. In this paper they requested that all the

school funds to which they were entitled by treaty provisions might be paid to the Indian Manual Labor School near the Fort Leavenworth Agency; might be pledged to that school for ten years to come, and that they might therefor be guaranteed the education and subsistence of Delaware children, not exceeding fifty at any one time. It came out, in course of this negotiation, that two thousand dollars were due them on arrearages of their school fund.

The Secretary acceded to this request, but imposed five conditions upon it, of which the fourth seems worth chronicling, as an indication of the helplessness of the Delawares in the matter of the disposition of their own money : "The interest to be paid annually when it may suit the Treasury; and this ratification to be subject to withdrawal, and the agreement itself to rescission, and to be annulled at the pleasure of the Department."

In 1845 the Delawares "raise a sufficiency to subsist on. The women do a large portion of the work on the farms. In many families, however, the women do not work on the farm. They raise corn, pumpkins, beans, pease, cabbages, potatoes, and many kinds of garden vegetables. Some few raise wheat and oats. They have lately had built, out of their own means, a good saw and grist mill, with two run of stones, one for corn and the other for wheat. There is a constant stream, called the Stranger, in their country that affords excellent water privileges. On this stream their mills are built."

At this time they are waiting with much anxiety to see if their "Great Father" will punish the Sioux, who have at two different times attacked them, and murdered in all some thirty men. "They say they do not wish to offend and disobey their Great Father, and before they attempt to revenge themselves they will wait and see if their Great Father will compel the Sioux to make reparation."

In 1848 "almost every family is well supplied with farming-stock; and they have raised abundance of corn, some wheat, potatoes, oats, and garden vegetables; have made butter and cheese; and raised fruit, etc., etc. They dwell in good log-cabins, and some have extremely neat houses, well furnished. They have their outhouses, stables, well-fenced lots, and some have good barns." There are seventy scholars in one school alone that are taught by the Friends; and the teacher reports: "It is truly astonishing to see the rapidity with which they acquire knowledge. The boys work on the farm part of the time, and soon learn how to do what they are set at. The girls spend a part of their time in doing housework, sewing, etc. Many of them do the sewing of their own, and some of the clothes of the other children."

In 1853 the Delawares are recorded as being "among the most remarkable of our colonized tribes. By their intrepidity and varied enterprise they are distinguished in a high degree. Besides being industrious farmers and herdsmen, they hunt and trade all over the interior of the continent, carrying their traffic beyond the Great Salt Lake, and exposing themselves to a thousand perils."

Their agent gives, in his report for this year, a graphic account of an incident such as has only too often occurred on our frontier. "A small party of Delawares, consisting of a man, his squaw, and a lad about eighteen years of age, recently returning from the mountains, with the avails and profits of a successful hunt and traffic, after they had commenced their journey homeward the second day the man sickened and died. Before he died he directed his squaw and the young man to hasten home with their horses and mules—thirteen in number —their money (four hundred and forty-five dollars), besides many other articles of value. After a few days' travel, near some of the forts on the Arkansas, they were overtaken by four white men, deserters from the United States Army—three on foot, and one riding a mule. The squaw and young man loaned each of the men on foot a horse or mule to ride, and furnished them with provisions. They all travelled on friendly together for some six or seven days, till they arrived at Cottonwood Creek, thirty-five or forty miles west of Council Grove. One evening, while resting, the young man was killed by these men; and the squaw was also supposed by these wretches to be dead, having had her throat cut badly and her head fractured. The two were then dragged off in the grass, supposed to be dead. The men gathered the mules, horses, money, guns, blankets—all that they supposed of value—and made for Jackson County, Missouri, where they disposed of the stock as best they could, and three of them took steamer for St. Louis. The squaw, on the day after, resuscitated; and soon discovering that her companion had been killed, and everything they possessed had disappeared, she, in her feeble and dangerous condition, took the road to Council Grove. The fifth day, she says, she was overtaken by a Kaw Indian, and brought into Council Grove, where the traders had every attention paid her, and sent a runner to the Delaware traders and myself, and we soon succeeded in capturing one of the men in Liberty, Clay County, Missouri, where he confessed the whole tragedy — the murder, robbing, etc. The three others had left for St. Louis. A telegraphic despatch to St. Louis, however, had the desired effect, and the three men were taken and brought back to Liberty, where, on trial before two justices of the peace, they were committed for trial in the District Court of the United States for the State of Missouri. As feeble as the squaw was, I was under the necessity of having her taken to Liberty as a witness. She readily recognized and pointed out in a large crowd of persons three of the prisoners. I have caused four of the recovered mules and horses to be turned over to the unfortunate squaw. I expect to recover two or three more; the balance, I am of opinion, will never be obtained."

In the report of the Indian Commissioner for this year there is also a paragraph which should not be omitted from this sketch: "The present seems to be an appropriate occasion for calling the attention of Congress to certain treaty stipulations with various Indian tribes which the Government, for a number of years, has failed to execute. In consideration of the cession of their lands to the United States"—by some nine tribes of the Mississippi and Missouri regions, among whom were the Delawares—"it was stipulated on the part of the Government that certain sums should be paid to said tribes, amounting in the aggregate to $2,396,600, and that the same should be invested in safe and profitable stocks, yielding an interest of not less than five per cent. per annum.

"Owing, however, to the embarrassed condition of the Treasury, it was deemed advisable by Congress, in lieu of making the investments, to appropriate from year to year a sum equal to the annual interest at five per cent. on the several amounts required to be invested. On this amount the Government has already paid from its treasury $1,742,240 — a sum which is now equal to two-thirds of the principal, and will in a few years be equal to the whole, if the practice of appropriating the interest be continued. As there is no limitation to the period of these payments, such a policy indefinitely continued would prove a most costly one to the Government. At the end of every twenty years it will have paid from the public treasury by way of interest the full amount of the stipulated investments. * * * The public finances are in a prosperous condition. Instead of fiscal embarrassment, there is now a redundancy of money, and one of the vexed questions of the day is, What shall be done with the surplus in the Treasury? Considering the premises, it seems to be quite clear that so much thereof as may be necessary for the purpose should be promptly applied to the fulfilment of our treaty obligations."

In 1854 the influx of white settlers into Kansas was so great, it became evident that the Indian reservations there could not be kept intact; and the Delawares made a large cession of their lands back to the United States, to be restored to the public domain. For this they were to receive ten thousand dollars. The sixth Article of this treaty provided for the giving of annuities to their chiefs. "The Delawares feel now, as heretofore, grateful to their old chiefs for their long and faithful services. In former treaties, when their means were scanty, they provided by small life annuities for the wants of the chiefs, some of whom are now receiving them. These chiefs are poor, and the Delawares believe it their duty to keep them from want in their old age." The sum of ten thousand dollars, therefore, was to be paid to their five chiefs—two hundred and fifty dollars a year each.

Article second provided that the President should cause the land now reserved for their permanent home to be surveyed at any time when they desired it, in the same manner as the ceded country was being surveyed for the white settlers.

In the following year their agent writes thus of the results which have followed the opening of this large tract to white settlers: "The Indians have experienced enough to shake their confidence in the laws which govern the white race. The irruptions of intruders on their trust lands, their bloody dissensions among themselves, outbreaks of party, etc., must necessarily, to these unsophisticated people, have presented our system of government in an unfavorable light.

"Numerous wrongs have been perpetrated on many parts of the reserve; the white men have wasted their most valuable timber with an unsparing hand; the trust lands have been greatly injured in consequence of the settlements made thereon. The Indians have complained, but to no purpose. I have found it useless to threaten legal proceedings.* * * The Government is bound in good faith to protect this people. * * *

The agricultural portion of this tribe have done well this season; abundant crops of corn promise them a supply of food for the ensuing year."

The simple-minded trustingness of these people is astonishing. Even now they assent to an Article in this treaty which says that, as the means arising from the sale of all this land they had given up would be more than they could use, the remainder should be "from time to time invested by the President of the United States in safe and profitable stocks; the principal to remain unimpaired, and the interest to be applied annually for the civilization, education, and religious culture of the Delaware people, and such other objects of a beneficial character as in his judgment are proper and necessary." Another Article stipulates that, if any of the Delawares are worthless or idle, the President can withhold their share of the moneys.

Article fifteenth says, gravely, "The primary object of this instrument being to advance the interests and welfare of the Delaware people, it is agreed that, if it prove insufficient to effect these ends from causes which cannot now be foreseen, Congress may hereafter make such farther provision, by law not inconsistent herewith, as experience may prove to be necessary to promote the interests, peace, and happiness of the Delaware people."

In 1860 the United States made its next treaty with the Delawares, in which they consented to give the Leavenworth, Pawnee, and Western Railroad Company right of way and certain lands in their reserve. In 1861 another treaty, in which, as the railway company had not paid, and was not able to pay, the $286,742 which it had promised to pay the Delawares, the President authorized the Commissioners of Indian Affairs to take the bonds of said railroad for that amount, and a mortgage on one hundred thousand acres of the land which the Indians had sold to the railway company.

There was another very curious bit of legislation in regard to the Delawares this year, viz., an Act of Congress authorizing the Secretary of the Treasury to enter on his books $423,990 26 to the credit of the Delawares; being the amount of bonds which the United States had invested for the Delawares in State bonds of Missouri, Tennessee, and North Carolina, and which had been stolen while in the custody of Jacob Thompson, late Secretary of the Interior, in whose department they had been deposited for safe-keeping. (At the same time there were stolen $66,735 belonging to the Iowas, and $169,686 75 belonging to the confederated bands of Kaskaskias, Peorias, Piankeshaws, and Keas.)

In this year the Commissioner of Indian Affairs visited the Delawares, and reported them well advanced in civilization, in possession of comfortable dwellings and farms, with personal property averaging one thousand dollars to an individual. Many of them were traders, and travelled even to the boundaries of California.

In 1862 two regiments of Delawares and Osages enlisted as soldiers in an expedition to the Indian Territory, under Colonel Weer, who says of them: "The Indian soldiers have far exceeded the most sanguine expectations. They bore the brunt of the fighting done by the expedition, and, had they been properly sustained, would have effectually ended the sway of the rebels in the Indian Territory."

There was during this year a terrible condition of affairs in Kansas and the Indian Territory. The Indians were largely on the side of the rebels; yet, as the Indian Commissioner said in his report for this year—a paragraph which is certainly a species of Irish bull—"While the rebelling of a large portion of most of the tribes abrogates treaty obligations, and places them at our mercy, the very important fact should not be forgotten that the Government first wholly failed to keep its treaty stipulations with them in protecting them." "By withdrawing all the troops from the forts in the Indian Territory," it left them "at the mercy of the rebels." That is, we first broke the treaty; and then their subsequent failure to observe it "placed them at our mercy!"

"It is," he says, "a well-known fact that in many instances self-preservation compelled them to make the best terms they could with the rebels; and that this is the case has been proved by a large number of them joining our army as soon as a sufficient force had penetrated their country to make it safe for them to do so."

The Delawares enlisted, in 1862, one hundred and seventy men in the Union army, and this out of a population of only two hundred males between the ages of eighteen and forty-five. There was probably no instance in the whole country of such a ratio of volunteers as this. They were reported as being in the army "tractable, sober, watchful, and obedient to the commands of their superiors." They officered their own companies, and the use of spirituous liquors was strictly prohibited among them—a fact the more remarkable, as drunkenness was one of their chief vices at home.

Already, however, the "interests" of the white settlers in Kansas were beginning to be clearly in opposition to the interests of the Indians. "Circumscribed as they are, and closely surrounded by white settlements, I can see nothing in the future for them but destruction," says the commissioner. "I think it is for the interest of the Indians that they be removed to some other locality as soon as possible."

"Several of them have from fifty to one hundred acres of land in cultivation, with comfortable dwellings, barns, and out-houses. * * * All the families are domiciled in houses. * * * Their crops of corn will yield largely. Nearly every family will have a sufficiency for their own consumption, and many of the larger farmers a surplus. * * * There are but few Delaware children of the age of twelve or fourteen that cannot read."

Here is a community of a thousand people, larger than many of the farming villages in New England, for instance, "the average of personal property amounting to one thousand dollars;" all living in their own houses, cultivating from fifty to one hundred acres of land, nearly all the children in schools, and yet it is for their "interest to be moved!" The last sentence of the following paragraph tells the story :

"When peace is restored to our country, a removal of all the Indians in Kansas will certainly be advantageous to them as well as to the State."

In 1863 their agent writes: "Since the question of the removal of the Indians from Kansas has been agitated, improvements have been much retarded among the Delawares and other Indians in Kansas.

"I think they are sufficiently prepared to make new treaties with the Government, * * * having in view settlement in the Southern country of those who elect to emigrate, compensation for the homes they relinquish, and a permission to remain in their present homes for all who are opposed to leaving Kansas."

At this time, "one-half the adult population are in the volunteer service of the United States. They make the best of soldiers, and are highly valued by their officers. * * * No State in the Union has furnished so many men for our armies, from the same ratio of population, as has the Delaware tribe. * * * The tribe has 3900 acres of land under cultivation, in corn, wheat, oats, and potatoes." (And yet one-half the adult men are away !)

In this year the Delawares, being "sufficiently prepared" to make new treaties looking to their removal out of the way of the white settlers in Kansas, petitioned the United States Government to permit them to take eight hundred dollars of their annuity funds to pay the expense of sending a delegation of their chiefs to the Rocky Mountains, to see if they could find there a country which would answer for their new home. The commissioner advises that they should not be allowed to go there, but to the Indian Territory, of which he says, "The geographical situation is such that its occupation by lawless whites can be more easily prevented than any other portion of the country." "By common consent, this appears to be recognized as the Indian country, and I have strong hopes that it will eventually prove for them a prosperous and happy home."

In 1864 their agent writes that the greater part of the personal property owned by the Delawares is in stock, "which is constantly being preyed upon by the whites, until it has become so reduced that it is difficult to obtain a good animal in the nation." He says he is unable, for the want of proper information, to determine what amount they had at the beginning of the year, but believes, from observation, "that it has undergone a depletion to the extent of twenty thousand dollars in the past year."

What a picture of a distressed community! The men away at war, old men, women, and children working the farms, and twenty thousand dollars of stock stolen from them in one year!

In 1865 a large proportion of those who had enlisted in the United States Army were mustered out, and returned home. The agent says: "It affords me great pleasure to chronicle the continued loyalty of this tribe during the past four years; and, as events tend westward, they evince every disposition to aid the Government by contributing their knowledge of the country to the officers of the army, and rendering such services thereto as they are qualified to perform."

They "have distinguished themselves in many instances in the conflicts on the borders;" nevertheless, in this same year, these discharged soldiers were prohibited by the Government from carrying revolvers. When the commissioner instructed the agent to disarm them, the agent very properly replied, stating the difficulties in the case: "Firstly, what disposition is to be made of weapons taken forcibly from these Indians? Secondly, many of these Indians are intelligent, only using weapons when any well-disposed white person would have done so; and if one class is disarmed, all must be;" on which the commissioner so modified his order as to say that "peaceably disposed Indians" might keep the usual weapons used by them in hunting; but whenever they visited agencies or towns they must deliver up all weapons to the agent, who would receipt for them, and return them "at proper times." This order is to be enforced, if possible, by an "appeal to their better judgment."

There are no records of the practical working of this order. Very possibly it fell at once, by its own weight, into the already large category of dead-letter laws in regard to Indians. It is impossible to imagine an Indian who had served four years as an officer in the army (for the Delawares officered their own companies) submitting to be disarmed by an agent on any day when he might need to go to Atchison on business. Probably even that "appeal to his better judgment" which the commissioner recommends, would only draw from him a very forcible statement to the effect that any man who went about in Kansas at that time unarmed was a fool.

In 1866 the Indian Commissioner reports that "the State of Kansas is fast being filled by an energetic population who appreciate good land; and as the Indian reservations were selected as being the best in the State, but *one result can be expected to follow.*

"Most of the Indians are anxious to move to the Indian country south of Kansas, where white settlers cannot interfere with them.

"Intermingled as the Kansas reservations are with the public lands, and surrounded in most cases by white settlers who too often act on the principle that an Indian has no rights that a white man is bound to respect, they are injured and annoyed in many ways. Their stock are stolen, their fences broken down, their timber destroyed, their young men plied with whiskey, their women debauched; so that, while the uncivilized are kept in a worse than savage state, having the crimes of civilization forced upon them, those farther advanced, and disposed to honest industry, are discouraged beyond endurance."

In spite of all this the Delawares raised, in 1866, 72,000 bushels of grain, 13,000 bushels of potatoes, and owned 5000 head of cattle.

In July of this year a treaty was made with them, providing for the removal to the Indian Territory of all who should not decide to become citizens of Kansas, and the sale of their lands. The superintendent of the Fort Leavenworth Agency writes at this time: "The running of the Union Pacific Railroad through the Delawares' diminished reserve has been a source of grievous annoyance and damage to the Delawares, as has also an organization styled the Delaware Lumber Company. Out of these two companies grew much complaint and investigation, resulting in the appointment of a special agent to sell to the railroad the timber required for the construction of the road, and no more. The Delaware Lumber Company being thus restricted" (i. e., being prevented from helping themselves to the Indians' timber), immediately "gave up their business, and stopped their mills," but not before they had damaged the Indians' property to the amount of twenty-eight thousand dollars.

Twenty thousand dollars' worth of stock and twenty-eight thousand dollars' worth of timber having been stolen in two years from this little village of farmers, no wonder they are "sufficiently prepared to move." Other causes have conspired also to render them in haste to be gone. The perpetual expectation of being obliged to remove had unsettled the whole community, and made them indifferent to effort and improvement. The return of their young men from the war had also had a demoralizing effect. Drunken frays were not uncommon, in which deadly weapons were used, spite of the Department's regulations for disarming all Indians.

In July of this year the Delaware chiefs, distressed by this state of affairs, drew up for their nation a code of laws which compare favorably with the laws of so-called civilized States.

In 1867 the Delawares are said to be "very impatient to be gone from their reserve, in order to build houses this autumn for winter use, and to be fencing fields for the ensuing year at their new reserve." The annuities due them in April of this year have not been paid till autumn, and this has delayed their movements. Many of the young men are still away, acting as scouts and guides in the army. In the course of this year and the next the whole tribe moved by detachments to their new home. "Those who removed during the winter went to work in a laudable manner, and made their improvements—many building comfortable houses and raising respectable crops" the first season. They are said to be now in a fair way to be better off than ever before. They have "given up their tribal organization and become Cherokee citizens. They report that they are well pleased with their new homes; and, being separated from the many temptations by which they were surrounded in their old reservation, are learning to appreciate the many benefits to be derived from leading a temperate, industrious, and consequently a prosperous and happy life."

In 1869 it is said that, "as soon as the final arrangement relative to their funds is perfected, they will lose their nationality and become identified with the Cherokees."

In 1870 we find nearly all the Delawares in Indian Territory; but it seems that, owing to a carelessly surveyed boundary, some three hundred of them had settled down on lands which were outside the Cherokee Reservation, and had been assigned by the Government to the Osages. This unfortunate three hundred, therefore, are removed again; this time to the lands of the Peorias, where they ask permission to establish themselves. But in the mean time, as they had made previous arrangements with the Cherokees, and all their funds had been transferred to the Cherokee Nation, it is thought to be " very unfortunate that they should be thus obliged to seek a new home;" and it is said to be " quite desirable that the parties in interest should reconcile their unsettled affairs to mutual advantage."

We are too much inclined to read these records carelessly, without trying to picture to ourselves the condition of affairs which they represent. It has come to be such an accepted thing in the history and fate of the Indian that he is to be always pushed on, always in advance of what is called the march of civilization, that to the average mind statements of these repeated removals come with no startling force, and suggest no vivid picture of details, only a sort of reassertion of an abstract general principle. But pausing to consider for a moment what such statements actually mean and involve; imagining such processes applied to some particular town or village that we happen to be intimately acquainted with, we can soon come to a new realization of the full bearing and import of them; such uprooting, such perplexity, such loss, such confusion and uncertainty, inflicted once on any community of white people anywhere in our land, would be considered quite enough to destroy its energies and blight its prospects for years. It may very well be questioned whether any of our small communities would have recovered from such successive shocks, changes, and forced migrations, as soon and as well as have many of these Indian tribes. It is very certain that they would not have submitted to them as patiently.

After this we find in the Official Reports no distinctive mention of the Delawares by name, except of a few who had been for some time living in the Indian Territory, and were not included in the treaty provisions at the time of the removal from Kansas. This little handful—eighty-one in number—is all that now remain to bear the name of that strong and friendly people to whom, a little more than one hundred years ago, we promised that they should be our brothers forever, and be entitled to a representation in our Congress.

This band of Delawares is associated with six other dwindled remnants of tribes — the Caddoes, Ionies, Wichitas, Towaconies, Wacoes, Keechies, and Comanches—on the Wichita Agency, in Indian Territory.

They are all reported as being " peaceable, well disposed," and " actively engaged in agricultural pursuits."

Of the Delawares it is said, in 1878, that they were not able to cultivate so much land as they had intended to during that year, " on account of loss of stock by horse-thieves."

Even here, it seems, in that " Indian country south of Kansas, where " (as they were told) " white settlers could not interfere with them," enemies lie in wait for them, as of old, to rob and destroy ; even here the Government is, as before, unable to protect them ; and in all probability, the tragedies of 1866 and 1867 will before long be re-enacted with still sadder results.

CHAPTER III.

THE CHEYENNES.

OUR first treaty with the Cheyennes[2] was made in 1825, at the mouth of the Teton River. It was merely a treaty of amity and friendship, and acknowledgment on the part of the Cheyennes of the "supremacy" of the United States. Two years before this, President Monroe reported the "Chayenes" to be "a tribe of three thousand two hundred and fifty souls, dwelling and hunting on a river of the same name, a western tributary of the Missouri, a little above the Great Bend." Ten years later, Catlin, the famous painter of Indians, met a "Shienne" chief and squaw among the Sioux, and painted their portraits. He says, "The Shiennes are a small tribe of about three thousand in number, living neighbors to the Sioux on the west of them, between the Black Hills and the Rocky Mountains. There is no finer race of men than these in North America, and none superior in stature, except the Osages: scarcely a man in the tribe full grown who is less than six feet in height." They are "the richest in horses of any tribe on the continent; living where the greatest herds of wild horses are grazing on the prairies, which they catch in great numbers, and sell to the Sioux, Mandans, and other tribes, as well as to the fur-traders.

"These people are the most desperate set of warriors and horsemen, having carried on almost unceasing wars with the Pawnees and Blackfeet. The chief was clothed in a handsome dress of deer-skins, very neatly garnished with broad bands of porcupine-quill work down the sleeves of his shirt and leg-

[2] Regarding the Cheyennes, consult Donald J. Berthong, *The Southern Cheyennes* (Norman, Oklahoma, 1963) and George B. Grinnell, *The Fighting Cheyennes* (New York, 1915). See also Grinnell's *The Cheyenne Indians* (2 vols., New Haven, 1923).

gings. The woman was comely, and beautifully dressed. Her dress of the mountain-sheepskin tastefully ornamented with quills and beads, and her hair plaited in large braids that hung down on her breast."

In 1837 the agent for the "Sioux, Cheyennes, and Poncas" reports that "all these Indians live exclusively by the chase;" and that seems to be the sum and substance of his information about them. He adds, also, that these remote wandering tribes have a great fear of the border tribes, and wish to avoid them. In 1838 the Cheyennes are reported as carrying on trade at a post on the Arkansas River near the Santa Fe road, but still depending on the chase.

In 1842 they are spoken of as a "wandering tribe on the Platte;" and in the same year, Mr. D. D. Mitchell, Supt. of Indian Affairs, with his head-quarters at St. Louis, writes: "Generations will pass away before this territory" [the territory in which the wild tribes of the Upper Mississippi were then wandering] "becomes much more circumscribed; for if we draw a line running north and south, so as to cross the Missouri about the mouth of the Vermilion River, we shall designate the limits beyond which civilized men are never likely to settle. At this point the Creator seems to have said to the tides of emigration that are annually rolling toward the West, 'Thus far shalt thou go, and no farther.' At all events, if they go beyond this, they will never stop on the east side of the Rocky Mountains. The utter destitution of timber, the sterility of sandy soil, together with the coldness and dryness of the climate, furnish obstacles which not even Yankee enterprise is likely to overcome. A beneficent Creator seems to have intended this dreary region as an asylum for the Indians, when the force of circumstances shall have driven them from the last acre of the fertile soil which they once possessed. Here no inducements are offered to the ever-restless Saxon breed to erect their huts. * * * The time may arrive when the whole of the Western Indians will be forced to seek a resting-place in this Great American Desert; and this, in all probability, will form a new era in the history of this singular and ill-fated race. They will remain a wandering, half civilized, though happy people. 'Their flocks and herds will cover a thousand hills,' and will furnish beef and mutton for a portion of the dense population of whites that will swarm in the more fertile sections of the great valley of the Mississippi."

This line, recommended by Mr. Mitchell, runs just east of Dakota, through the extreme eastern portion of Nebraska, a little to the east of the middle of Kansas, through the middle of Indian Territory and Texas, to the Gulf of Mexico.   Montana, Idaho, Colorado, and New Mexico, all lie west of it.

The records of the War Department for 1846 contain an interesting account of a visit made to all the wild tribes of the Upper Missouri Agency—the Yankton Sioux, the Arrikarees, Mandans, Assinaboines, Arapahoes, Cheyennes, and others.   In reply to the agent's remonstrances with one of the Sioux chiefs in regard to their perpetual warring with each other, the chief " was very laconic and decided, remarking ' that if their great-grandfather desired them to cease to war with their enemies, why did he not send each of them a petticoat, and make squaws of them at once ?' "   This same chief refused to allow the boys of his tribe to go to the Choctaw schools, saying, " They would return, as the few did who went to St. Louis, drunkards, or die on the way."

The Cheyennes and other Indians living on the Platte complained bitterly of the passage of the emigrants through their country. They said they ought to be compensated for the right of way, and that the emigrants should be restricted by law and the presence of a military force from burning the grass, and from unnecessary destruction of game. They were systematically plundered and demoralized by traders. Whiskey was to be had without difficulty; sugar and coffee were sold at one dollar a pound; ten-cent calico at one dollar a yard; corn at seventy-five cents a gallon, and higher.

In 1847 a law was passed by Congress forbidding the introduction of whiskey into the Indian country, and even the partial enforcement of this law had a most happy effect. Foremost among those to acknowledge the benefits of it were the traders themselves, who said that the Indians' demand for substantial articles of trade was augmented two hundred per cent.: "They enjoy much better health, look much better, and are better people. * * * You now rarely ever hear of a murder committed, whereas when whiskey was plenty in that country murder was a daily occurrence." These Indians themselves were said to be "opposed to the introduction of ardent spirits into their country; * * * but, like almost all other Indians, will use it if you give it to them, and when under its influence are dangerous and troublesome." There were at this time nearly forty-six thousand of these Upper Missouri Indians. Five bands of them—"the Sioux, Cheyennes, Gros Ventres, Mandans, and Poncas"—were "excellent Indians, devotedly attached to the white man," living "in peace and friendship with our Government," and "entitled to the special favor and good opinion of the Department for their uniform good conduct and pacific relations."

In 1848 it was estimated from the returns made by traders that the trade of this agency amounted to $400,000. Among the items were 25,000 buffalo tongues. In consequence of this prosperity on the part of the Indians, there was a partial cessation of hostilities on the whites; but it was still a perilous journey to cross the plains, and in 1849 the necessity for making some sort of treaty stipulations with all these wild tribes begins to be forced emphatically upon the attention of the United States Government. A safe highway across the continent must be opened. It is a noticeable thing, however, that, even as late as this in the history of our diplomatic relations with the Indian, his right to a certain control as well as occupancy of the soil was instinctively recognized. The Secretary of the Interior, in his report for 1849, says: " The wild tribes of Indians who have their hunting-grounds in the great prairie through which our emigrants to California pass, have, during the year, been more than usually pacific. They have suffered our people to pass through their country with little interruption, though they travelled in great numbers, and consumed on their route much grass and game. For these the Indians expect compensation, and their claim is just."

The Secretary, therefore, concurs in the recommendation of the Commissioner of Indian Affairs that treaties be negotiated with these tribes, stipulating for the right of way through their country, and the use of grass and game, paying them therefor small annuities in useful articles of merchandise, and agricultural implements, and instruction. "The right of way"— "through their country." A great deal is conceded, covered, and conveyed by such phrases as these. If they mean anything, they mean all that the Indians ever claimed.

The Indians were supposed to be influenced to this peaceableness and good-will more by a hope of rewards and gifts than by a wholesome fear of the power of the Government; and it was proposed to take a delegation of chiefs to Washington, " in order that they may acquire some knowledge of our greatness and strength, which will make a salutary impression on them, and through them on their brethren," and " will tend to influence them to continue peaceful relations."

It begins to dawn upon the Government's perception that peace is cheaper as well as kinder than war. " We never can whip them into friendship," says one of the superintendents of the Upper Missouri Agency. A treaty " can do no harm, and the expense would be less than that of a six months' war. * * * Justice as well as policy requires that we should make some remuneration for the damages these Indians sustain in consequence of the destruction of their game, timber, etc., by the whites passing through their country."

"Their game, timber," "their country," again. The perpetual recurrence of this possessive pronoun, and of such phrases as these in all that the Government has said about the Indians, and in all that it has said to them, is very significant.

In 1850 the Indian Commission writes that "it is much to be regretted that no appropriation was made at the last session of Congress for negotiating treaties with the wild tribes of the plains. These Indians have long held undisputed possession of this extensive region; and, regarding it as their own, they consider themselves entitled to compensation not only for the right of way through their territory, but for the great and injurious destruction of game, grass, and timber committed by our troops and emigrants."

The bill providing for the negotiation of these treaties was passed unanimously by the Senate, but "the unhappy difficulties existing on the subject of slavery" delayed it in the House until it was too late to be carried into effect.

All the tribes had been informed of this pending bill, and were looking forward to it with great interest and anxiety. In 1849 they had all expressed themselves as "very anxious to be instructed in agriculture and the civilized arts." Already the buffalo herds were thinning and disappearing. From time immemorial the buffalo had furnished them food, clothing, and shelter; with its disappearance, starvation stared them in the face, and they knew it. There can be no doubt that at this time all the wild tribes of the Upper Missouri region — the Sioux, Cheyennes, Arapahoes—were ready and anxious to establish friendly relations with the United States Government, and to enter into some arrangement by which some means of future subsistence, and some certainty of lands enough to live on, could be secured to them. Meantime they hunted with greater diligence than ever; and in this one year alone had sold to the fur-traders within the limits of one agency $330,000 worth of buffalo - robes, and "furs, peltries, and miscellaneous goods to the amount of $60,000. What they thus receive for their furs, robes, etc., would be ample for their support," says Hatton, " were it not that they have to give such exorbitant prices for what they purchase from the whites."

In the winter and spring of 1850 all these tribes were visited by an agent of the Government. He reported them as "friendly disposed," but very impatient to come to some understanding about the right of way. " This is what the Indians want, and what they are anxious about; having been told long since, and so often repeated by travellers passing (who care little about the consequences of promises so they slip through safely and unmolested themselves), that their 'Great Father' would soon reward them liberally for the right of way, the destruction of timber, game, etc., as well as for any kindness shown Americans passing through their country."

In the summer of 1851 this much desired treaty was made. Seven of the prairie and mountain tribes gathered in great force at Fort Laramie. The report of this council contains some interesting and noticeable points.

" We were eighteen days encamped together, during which time the Indians conducted themselves in a manner that excited the admiration and surprise of every one. The different tribes, although hereditary enemies, interchanged daily visits, both in their individual and national capacities; smoked and feasted together; exchanged presents; adopted each other's children, according to their own customs; and did all that was held sacred or solemn in the eyes of these Indians to prove the sincerity of their peaceful and friendly intentions, both among themselves and with the citizens of the United States lawfully residing among them or passing through the country."

By this treaty the Indians formally conceded to the United States the right to establish roads, military or otherwise, throughout the Indian country, " so far as they claim or exercise ownership over it."

They agreed " to maintain peaceful relations among themselves, and to abstain from all depredations upon whites passing through their country, and to make restitution for any damages or loss that a white man shall sustain by the acts of their people."

For all the damages which they had suffered up to that time in consequence of the passing of the whites through their country, they accepted the presents then received as payment in full.

An annuity of $50,000 a year for fifty years to come was promised to them. This was the price of the " right of way."

" Fifty thousand dollars for a limited period of years is a small amount to be distributed among at least fifty thousand Indians, especially when we consider that we have taken away, or are rapidly taking away from them all means of support," says one of the makers of this treaty. There would probably be no dissent from this opinion. A dollar a year, even assured to one for fifty years, seems hardly an adequate compensation for the surrender of all other " means of support."

The report continues : " Viewing the treaty in all its provisions, I am clearly of opinion that it is the best that could have been made for both parties. I am, moreover, of the opinion that it will be observed and carried out in as good faith on the part of the Indians as it will on the part of the United States and the white people thereof. There was an earnest solemnity and a deep conviction of the necessity of adopting some such measures evident in the conduct and manners of the Indians throughout the whole council. On leaving for their respective homes, and bidding each other adieu, they gave the strongest possible evidence of their friendly intentions for the future, and the mutual confidence and good faith which they had in each other. Invitations were freely given and as freely accepted by each of the tribes to interchange visits, talk, and smoke together like brothers, upon ground where they had

never before met except for the purpose of scalping each other.
This, to my mind, was conclusive evidence of the sincerity of
the Indians, and nothing but bad management or some un-
toward misfortune ever can break it."

The Secretary of the Interior, in his report for this year,
speaks with satisfaction of the treaties negotiated with Indians
during the year, and says: "It cannot be denied that most of
the depredations committed by the Indians on our frontiers
are the offspring of dire necessity. The advance of our population compels them to relinquish their fertile lands, and seek
refuge in sterile regions which furnish neither corn nor game:
impelled by hunger, they seize the horses, mules, and cattle of
the pioneers, to relieve their wants and satisfy the cravings of
nature. They are immediately pursued, and, when overtaken,
severely punished. This creates a feeling of revenge on their
part, which seeks its gratification in outrages on the persons
and property of peaceable inhabitants. The whole country
then becomes excited, and a desolating war, attended with a
vast sacrifice of blood and treasure, ensues. This, it is believed,
is a true history of the origin of most of our Indian hostilities.

"All history admonishes us of the difficulty of civilizing a
wandering race who live mainly upon game. To tame a savage you must tie him down to the soil. You must make him
understand the value of property, and the benefits of its separate ownership. You must appeal to those selfish principles
implanted by Divine Providence in the nature of man for the
wisest purposes, and make them minister to civilization and
refinement. You must encourage the appropriation of lands
by individuals; attach them to their homes by the ties of interest; teach them the uses of agriculture and the arts of
peace; * * * and they should be taught to look forward to
the day when they may be elevated to the dignity of American
citizenship.

"By means like these we shall soon reap our reward in the

suppression of Indian depredations; in the diminution of the expenses of the Department of War; in a valuable addition to our productive population; in the increase of our agriculture and commerce; and in the proud consciousness that we have removed from our national escutcheon the stain left on it by our acknowledged injustice to the Indian race."

We find the Cheyennes, therefore, in 1851, pledged to peace and good-will toward their Indian neighbors, and to the white emigrants pouring through their country. For this conceded right of way they are to have a dollar a year apiece, in "goods and animals;" and it is supposed that they will be able to eke out this support by hunting buffaloes, which are still not extinct.

In 1852 the Commissioner of Indian Affairs writes: "Notwithstanding the mountain and prairie Indians continue to suffer from the vast number of emigrants who pass through their country, destroying their means of support, and scattering disease and death among them, yet those who were parties to the treaty concluded at Fort Laramie, in the fall of 1851, have been true to their obligations, and have remained at peace among themselves and with the whites."

And the superintendent writes: "Congress made a very liberal appropriation of $100,000 to make a treaty with the prairie and mountain tribes. A very satisfactory treaty was made with them last fall at Fort Laramie, the conditions of which, on their part, have been faithfully observed—no depredations having been committed during the past season by any of the tribes parties to the Fort Laramie treaty. The Senate amended the treaty, substituting *fifteen* instead of *fifty* years as the period for which they were to have received an annual supply of goods, animals, etc., at the discretion of the President. This modification of the treaty I think very proper, as the condition of these wandering hordes will be entirely changed during the next fifteen years. The treaty, however, should have been sent

back to the Indians for the purpose of obtaining their sanction
to the modification, as was done in the case of the Sioux treaty
negotiated by Commissioners Ramsey and Lea. It is hoped
this oversight will be corrected as early as practicable next
spring, otherwise the large amounts already expended will have
been uselessly wasted, and the Indians far more dissatisfied
than ever."

To comment on the bad faith of this action on the part of
Congress would be a waste of words; but its impolicy is so
glaring that one's astonishment cannot keep silent—its impolicy
and also its incredible niggardliness. A dollar apiece a year,
"in goods, animals," etc., those Indians had been promised that
they should have for fifty years. It must have been patent
to the meanest intellect that this was little to pay each year
to any one man from whom we were taking away, as the commissioner said, "his means of support." But, unluckily for the
Indians, there were fifty thousand of them. It entered into
some thrifty Congressman's head to multiply fifty by fifty,
and the aggregate terrified everybody. This was much more
likely to have been the cause of the amendment than the cause
assigned by the superintendent, viz., the probable change of
localities of all the "wandering hordes" in the next fifteen
years. No doubt it would be troublesome to the last degree
to distribute fifty thousand dollars, "in goods, animals," etc., to
fifty thousand Indians wandering over the entire Upper Missouri region; but no more troublesome, surely, in the sixteenth
year than in the fifteenth. The sophistry is too transparent;
it does not in the least gloss over the fact that, within the first
year after the making of our first treaty of any moment with
these tribes—while they to a man, the whole fifty thousand of
them, kept their faith with us—we broke ours with them in
the meanest of ways—robbing them of more than two-thirds
of the money we had promised to pay.

All the tribes "promptly" assented to this amendment, however; so says the Annual Report of the Indian Commissioner for 1853; and adds that, with a single exception, they have maintained friendly relations among themselves, and "manifested an increasing confidence in and kindness toward the whites."

Some of them have begun to raise corn, beans, pumpkins, etc., but depend chiefly on the hunt for their support. But the agent who was sent to distribute to them their annuities, and to secure their assent to the amendment to the treaty, reports: "The Cheyennes and the Arapahoes, and many of the Sioux, are actually in a starving state. They are in abject want of food half the year, and their reliance for that scanty supply, in the rapid decrease of the buffalo, is fast disappearing. The travel upon the roads drives them off, or else confines them to a narrow path during the period of emigration, and the different tribes are forced to contend with hostile nations in seeking support for their villages. Their women are pinched with want, and their children constantly crying with hunger. Their arms, moreover, are unfitted to the pursuit of smaller game, and thus the lapse of a few years presents only the prospect of a gradual famine." And in spite of such suffering, these Indians commit no depredations, and show increasing confidence in and kindness toward the whites.

This agent, who has passed many years among the Indians, speaks with great feeling of the sad prospect staring them in the face. He says: "But one course remains which promises any permanent relief to them, or any lasting benefit to the country in which they dwell; that is, simply to make such modifications in the 'intercourse' laws as will invite the residence of traders among them, and open the whole Indian Territory for settlement. Trade is the only civilizer of the Indian. It has been the precursor of all civilization heretofore, and it will be of all hereafter. It teaches the Indian the value of other things besides the spoils of the chase, and offers to him other pursuits and excitements than those of war. All obstructions to its freedom, therefore, only operate injuriously. * * * The Indians would soon lose their nomadic character, and forget the relations of tribes. * * * And this, while it would avoid the cruel necessity of our present policy—to wit, extinction — would make them an element in the population, and sharer in the prosperity of the country." He says of the "system of removals, and congregating tribes in small parcels of territory," that it has "eventuated injuriously on those who have been subjected to it. It is the legalized murder of a whole nation. It is expensive, vicious, and inhuman, and producing these consequences, and these alone. The custom, being judged by its fruits, should not be persisted in."

It is in the face of such statements, such protests as these, that the United States Government has gone steadily on with its policy, so called, in regard to the treatment of the Indian.

In 1854 the report from the Upper Missouri region is still of peace and fidelity on the part of all the Indians who joined in the Fort Laramie treaty. "Not a single instance of murder, robbery, or other depredation has been committed by them, either on the neighboring tribes parties to the treaty or on whites. This is the more remarkable, as before the treaty they were foremost in the van of thieves and robbers—always at war, pillaging whoever they met, and annoying their own traders in their own forts."

In the summer of this year the Cheyennes began to be dissatisfied and impertinent. At a gathering of the northern band at Fort Laramie, one of the chiefs demanded that the travel over the Platte road should be stopped. He also, if the interpreter was to be relied on, said that next year the Government must send them out one thousand white women for wives. The Southern Cheyennes had given up to their agent some Mexican prisoners whom they had taken in the spring, and this act, it was supposed, had seemed to the northern band a needless interference on the part of the United States. Moreover, it was a matter constantly open to the observation of all friendly Indians that the hostiles, who were continually plundering and attacking emigrant trains, made, on the whole, more profit out of war than they made out of peace. On the North Platte road during this year the Pawnees alone had stolen several thousands of dollars' worth of goods; and, in addition to this, there was the pressure of public sentiment—a thing which is as powerful among Indians as among whites. It was popular to be on the war-path: the whites were invaders; it was brave and creditable to slay them. Taking all these things into account, it was only to be wondered at that these Cheyennes, Arapahoes, and Sioux kept to the provisions of their treaty at all. Nevertheless, the Cheyennes, Arapahoes,[3] and some bands of the Sioux continued peaceable and friendly; and in 1855 they begged to be supplied with a farmer to teach them how to farm; also with a blacksmith. Their agent strongly recommends that this be done, saying that there is not "in the whole Indian country a more favorable location for a farm for grazing stock and game than the South Platte. In a very short period of time the Arapahoes and Cheyennes would become fixed and settled, and a part of each tribe—the old women and men—would become agriculturists; rude, it is true, yet sufficiently skilful to raise corn, potatoes, and beans, and dwell in cabins or fixed habitations."

In the summer of 1856 the Cheyennes were, by a disastrous accident, forced into the position of hostiles. A small war-band went out to attack the Pawnees; they were in camp near the North Platte road: as the mail-wagon was passing, two of the Cheyennes ran toward it to beg tobacco. The mail-carrier, terrified, fired on them, and the Indians fired back, wounding him; the chiefs rushed out, stopped the firing, explained the matter, and then severely flogged the Indians who had returned the mail-carrier's fire. But the mischief had been done.

[3] Regarding the Arapahoes see United States Government, *Treaty Between the United States and the Arapaho and Cheyenne Indians of the Upper Arkansas River* (Washington, 1861); George A. Dorsey, *The Arapaho Sun Dance* (Chicago, 1903).

The mail-carrier reported his having been fired at by a Cheyenne Indian, and the next day troops from Fort Kearny at
tacked the Indians and killed six of the war-party. The rest
refused to fight, and ran away, leaving their camp and all it
contained. The war-party, thoroughly exasperated, attacked
an emigrant train, killed two men and a child, and took one
woman captive. The next day they killed her, because she
could not ride on horseback and keep up with them. Within
a short time two more small war-parties had left the band, attacked trains, and killed two men, two women, and a child.
The chiefs at first could not restrain them, but in September
they sent a delegation to the agency to ask their agent's assistance and advice. They said that the war-party was now completely under their control, and they wished to know what
they could do. They implored the Great Father not to be angry with them, "for they could not control the war-party when
they saw their friends killed by soldiers after they had thrown
down their bows and arrows and begged for life."

In October the agent reported that the Cheyennes were
"perfectly quiet and peaceable, and entirely within control,
and obedient to authority." The chiefs had organized a
sort of police, whose duty was to kill any war-parties that
might attempt to leave the camp.

Through the winter the Cheyennes remained in the south
and south-eastern parts of the agency, and strictly observed the
conditions which their agent had imposed upon them. In the
following August, however, a military force under General
Sumner was sent out "to demand from the tribe the perpetrators of their late outrages on the whites, and ample security for
their good conduct." The Cheyennes were reported by General Sumner as showing no disposition to yield to these demands; he therefore attacked them, burnt their village to the
ground, and destroyed their winter supplies—some fifteen or
twenty thousand pounds of buffalo meat.

Of how they lived, and where, during the winter following this fight, there is little record. In the next year's reports the Cheyennes are said to be very anxious for a new treaty, which will assign to them a country in which they can dwell safely. "They said they had learned a lesson last summer in their fight with General Sumner—that it was useless to contend with the white man, who would soon with his villages occupy the whole prairie. They wanted peace; and as the buffalo—their principal dependence for food and clothing (which even now they were compelled to seek many miles from home, where their natural enemies, the Pawnee and Osage, roamed), would soon disappear entirely, they hoped their Great Father, the white chief at Washington, would listen to them, and give them a home where they might be provided for and protected against the encroachments of their white brothers, until at least they had been taught to cultivate the soil and other arts of civilized life. They have often desired ploughs and hoes, and to be taught their use."

The next year's records show the Government itself aware that some measures must be taken to provide for these troublesome wild tribes of the prairie: almost more perplexing in time of peace than in time of war is the problem of the disposition to be made of them. Agents and superintendents alike are pressing on the Government's attention the facts and the bearing of the rapid settling of the Indian lands by the whites; the precariousness of peaceful relations; the dangers of Indian wars. The Indians themselves are deeply anxious and disturbed.

"They have heard that all of the Indian tribes to the eastward of them have ceded their lands to the United States, except small reservations; and hence, by an Indian's reasoning, in a few years these tribes will emigrate farther west, and, as a matter of necessity, occupy the hunting-grounds of the wild tribes."

When the agent of the Upper Platte Agency tried to reason on this subject with one of the Sioux chiefs, the chief said: "When I was a young man, and I am not yet fifty, I travelled with my people through the country of the Sac and Fox tribe, to the great water Minne Toukah (Mississippi), where I saw corn growing, but no white people; continuing eastward, we came to the Rock River valley, and saw the Winnebagoes, but no white people. We then came to the Fox River valley, and thence to the Great Lake (Lake Michigan), where we found a few white people in the Pottawattomie country. Thence we returned to the Sioux country at the Great Falls of Irara (St. Anthony), and had a feast of green corn with our relations, who resided there. Afterward we visited the pipe-clay quarry in the country of the Yankton Sioux, and made a feast to the 'Great Medicine,' and danced the 'sun dance,' and then returned to our hunting-grounds on the prairie. And now our Father tells us the white man will never settle on our lands, and kill our game; but see! the whites cover all of those lands I have just described, and also the lands of the Poncas, Omahas, and Pawnees. On the South Platte the white people are finding gold, and the Cheyennes and Arapahoes have no longer any hunting-grounds. Our country has become very small, and before our children are grown up we shall have no game."

In the autumn of this year (1859) an agent was sent to hold a council with the Cheyennes and Arapahoes, and tell them of the wish of the Government that they should "assume a fixed residence, and occupy themselves in agriculture. This they at once received with favor, and declared with great unanimity to be acceptable to them. They expected and asked that the Department shall supply them with what is necessary to establish themselves permanently. * * * Both these tribes had scrupulously maintained peaceful relations with the whites, and with other Indian tribes, notwithstanding the many causes of irritation growing out of the occupation of the gold region, and the emigration to it through their hunting-grounds, which are no longer reliable as a certain source of food to them."

It was estimated that during the summer of 1859 over sixty thousand emigrants crossed these plains in their central belt. The trains of vehicles and cattle were frequent and valuable in proportion; and post lines and private expresses were in constant motion.

In 1860 a commissioner was sent out to hold a council with the Cheyennes and Arapahoes at Bent's Fort, on the Upper Arkansas, and make a treaty with them. The Arapahoes were fully represented; but there were present only two prominent chiefs of the Cheyennes — Black Kettle and White Antelope. (White Antelope was one of the chiefs brutally murdered five years later in the Chivington massacre in Colorado.) As it was impossible for the rest of the Cheyennes to reach the Fort in less than twenty days, and the commissioner could not wait so long, Black Kettle and White Antelope wished it to be distinctly understood that they pledged only themselves and their own bands.

The commissioner says: " I informed them as to the object of my visit, and gave them to understand that their Great Father had heard with delight of their peaceful disposition, although they were almost in the midst of the hostile tribes. They expressed great pleasure on learning that their Great Father had heard of their good conduct, and requested me to say, in return, that they intended in every respect to conform to the wishes of the Government. I then presented to them a diagram of the country assigned them, by their treaty of 1851, as their hunting-grounds, which they seemed to understand perfectly, and were enabled without difficulty to give each initial point. In fact, they exhibited a degree of intelligence seldom to be found among tribes where no effort has been made to civilize them. I stated to them that it was the intention of their Great Father to reduce the area of their present reservation, and that they should settle down and betake themselves to agriculture, and eventually abandon the chase as a means of support. They informed me that such was their wish; and that they had been aware for some time that they would be compelled to do so: that game was growing more scarce every year, and that they had also noticed the approach of whites, and felt that they must soon, in a great measure, conform to their habits. * * * It has not fallen to my lot to visit any Indians who seem more disposed to yield to the wishes of the Government than the Cheyennes and Arapahoes. Notwithstanding they are fully aware of the rich mines discovered in their country, they are disposed to yield up their claims without any reluctance. They certainly deserve the fostering hand of the Government, and should be liberally encouraged in their new sphere of life."

This treaty was concluded in February of the next year, at Fort Wise. The chiefs of the Cheyennes and Arapahoes there "ceded and relinquished" all the lands to which they had any claim, "wherever situated," except a certain tract whose boundaries were defined. The land relinquished included lands in Kansas and Nebraska, and all of that part of Colorado which is north of the Arkansas, and east of the Rocky Mountains.

The Cheyennes and Arapahoes, in "consideration of their kind treatment by the citizens of Denver and the adjoining towns," "respectfully requested," in the eleventh Article of this treaty, that the United States would permit the proprietors of these towns to enter their lands at the minimum price of one dollar and twenty-five cents an acre. This Article was struck out by the Senate, and the Indians consented to the amendment; but the proof of their good-will and gratitude remained on record, nevertheless.

The desire of the Government to make farmers of these Indians was reiterated in this treaty, and evidenced by pledges of purchase of stock, agricultural implements, etc.; mills, also, and mechanic shops they were to have, and an annuity of $30,000 a year for fifteen years. There was this clause, however, in an article of the treaty, "Their annuities may, at the discretion of the President of the United States, be discontinued entirely should said Indians fail to make reasonable and satisfactory efforts to improve and advance their condition; in which case such other provision shall be made for them as the President and Congress may judge to be suitable or proper." Could there be a more complete signing away than this of all benefits provided for by the treaty?

Lands were to be assigned to them "in severalty," and certificates were to be issued by the Commissioner of Indian Affairs, specifying the names of individuals; and that the "said tracts were set apart for the exclusive use and benefit of the assignees and their heirs." Each Indian was to have forty acres of land, "to include in every case, as far as practicable, a reasonable portion of timber and water."

The tenth Article of the treaty provided that the annuities now paid to the Arapahoes and Cheyennes should be continued to them until the stipulations of such treaties or articles of agreement should be fulfilled; and the seventh Article provided that the President, with the assent of Congress, should have power to modify or change any "of the provisions of former treaties" "in such manner and to whatever extent" he might judge it to be necessary and expedient for their best interests.

Could a community of people be delivered up more completely bound and at the mercy of a government? Some of the bands of the Cheyennes who were not represented at this council were much dissatisfied with the treaty, as evidently they had great reason to be. And as time went on, all the bands became dissatisfied. Two years later we find that, instead of their being settled on those farms "in severalty," the survey of their lands has been just completed, and that "a contract will soon be made for the construction of a ditch for the purpose of irrigating their arable land." "It is to be hoped," the Superintendent of the Colorado Agency writes, that "when suitable preparations for their subsistence by agriculture and grazing are made, these tribes will gradually cease their roaming, and become permanently settled." It would seem highly probable that under those conditions the half-starved creatures would be only too glad to cease to roam. It is now ten years since they were reported to be in a condition of miserable starvation every winter, trying to raise a little corn here and there, and begging to have a farmer and a blacksmith sent out to them. They are now divided and subdivided into small bands, hunting the buffalo wherever they can find him, and going in small parties because there are no longer large herds of buffaloes to be found anywhere. The Governor of Colorado says, in his report for 1863, that "these extensive subdivisions of the tribes caused great difficulty in ascertaining the really guilty parties in the commission of offences." Depredations and hostilities are being frequently committed, but it is manifestly unjust to hold the whole tribe responsible for the acts of a few.

Things grew rapidly worse in Colorado. Those "preparations for their subsistence by agriculture and grazing"—which it took so much room to tell in the treaty—not having been made; the farmer, and the blacksmith, and the grist-mill not having arrived; the contract not having been even let for the irrigating-ditch, without which no man can raise any crops in Colorado, not even on arable lands—many of the Cheyennes and Arapahoes took to a system of pilfering reprisals from emigrant trains, and in the fights resulting from this effort to steal they committed many terrible murders. All the tribes on the plains were more or less engaged in these outrages; and it was evident, before midsummer of 1864, that the Government must interfere with a strong hand to protect the emigrants and

Western settlers—to protect them from the consequences of its own bad faith with the Indians. The Governor of Colorado called for military aid, and for authority to make a campaign against the Indians, which was given him. But as there was no doubt that many of the Indians were still peaceable and loyal, and he desired to avoid every possibility of their sharing in the punishment of the guilty, he issued a proclamation in June, requesting all who were friendly to come to places which he designated, where they were to be assured of safety and protection. This proclamation was sent to all the Indians of the plains. In consequence of it, several bands of friendly Arapahoes and Cheyennes came to Fort Lyon, and were there received by the officer in charge, rationed, and assured of safety. Here there occurred, on the 29th of November, one of the foulest massacres which the world has seen. This camp of friendly Indians was surprised at daybreak, and men, women, and children were butchered in cold blood. Most of those who escaped fled to the north, and, joining other bands of the tribe, proceeded at once to take most fearful, and, it must be said, natural revenge. A terrible war followed. Some of them confederated with the Sioux, and waged relentless war on all the emigrant routes across the plains. These hostilities were bitter in proportion to the bitterness of resentment felt by the refugees from this massacre. " It will be long before faith in the honor and humanity of the whites can be re-established in the minds of these barbarians," says an official report, " and the last Indian who escaped from the brutal scene at Sand Creek will probably have died before its effects will have disappeared."

In October of the next year some of the bands, having first had their safety assured by an old and tried friend, I. H. Leavenworth, Indian Agent for the Upper Arkansas, gathered together to hold a council with United States Commissioners on the Little Arkansas. The commissioners were empowered by the President to restore to the survivors of the Sand Creek massacre full value for all the property then destroyed; "to make reparation," so far as possible. To each woman who had lost a husband there they gave one hundred and sixty acres of land; to each child who had lost a parent, the same. Probably even an Indian woman would consider one hundred and sixty acres of land a poor equivalent for a murdered husband; but the offers were accepted in good part by the tribe, and there is nothing in all the history of this patient race more pathetic than the calm and reasonable language employed by some of these Cheyenne and Arapahoe chiefs at this council. Said Black Kettle, the chief over whose lodge the American flag, with a white flag tied below, was floating at the time of the massacre, "I once thought that I was the only man that persevered to be the friend of the white man; but since they have come and cleaned out our lodges, horses, and everything else, it is hard for me to believe white men any more. * * * All my friends, the Indians that are holding back, they are afraid to come in; are afraid that they will be betrayed as I have been. I am not afraid of white men, but come and take you by the hand." Elsewhere, Black Kettle spoke of Colonel Chivington's troops as "that fool-band of soldiers that cleared out our lodges, and killed our women and children. This is hard on us." With a magnanimity and common-sense which white men would have done well to imitate in their judgments of the Indians, he recognized that it would be absurd, as well as unjust, to hold all white men in distrust on account of the acts of that "fool-band of soldiers."*

---

* Gen. Harney, on being asked by Bishop Whipple if Black Kettle were a hostile Indian, replied, laying his hand on his heart, "I have worn this uniform fifty-five years. He was as true a friend of the white man as I am."

By the terms of this treaty, a new reservation was to be set apart for the Cheyennes and Arapahoes; hostile acts on either side were to be settled by arbitration; no whites were to be allowed on the reservation; a large tract of country was to be "relinquished" by the Indians, but they were "expressly permitted to reside upon and range at pleasure throughout the unsettled portions of that part of the country they claim as originally theirs." The United States reserved the right to build roads and establish forts in the reservation, and pledged itself to pay "annually, for the period of forty years," certain sums of money to each person in the tribe: twenty dollars a head till they were settled on their reservation; after that, forty dollars a head. To this end an accurate annual census of the Indians was promised at the time of the annuity payment in the spring.

The Indians went away from this council full of hope and satisfaction. Their oldest friends, Colonel Bent and Kit Carson, were among the commissioners, and they felt that at last they had a treaty they could trust. Their old reservation in Colorado (to which they probably could never have been induced to return) was restored to the public domain of that territory, and they hoped in their new home for greater safety and peace. The Apaches, who had heretofore been allied with the Kiowas and Comanches, were now allied with them, and to have the benefits of the new treaty. A small portion of the tribe—chiefly young men of a turbulent nature—still held aloof, and refused to come under the treaty provisions. One riotous band, called the Dog Soldiers, were especially refractory; but, before the end of the next year, they also decided to go southward and join the rest of the tribe on the new reservation. Occasional hostilities took place in the course of the winter, one of which it is worth while to relate, the incident is so typical a one.

On the 21st of February a son of one Mr. Boggs was killed and scalped by a party of four Cheyenne Indians about six miles east of Fort Dodge, on the Arkansas River. On investigation, it appeared that Mr. Boggs had gone to the Indian camp without any authority, and had there traded off eleven one-dollar bills for ten-dollar bills. The Indian on whom this trick had been played found Mr. Boggs out, went to him, and demanded reparation; and, in the altercation and fight which ensued, Mr. Boggs's son was killed. This story is given in the official report of Lieutenant-colonel Gordon, U.S.A., and Colonel Gordon adds, "I think this case needs no further comment."

The Cheyennes did not long remain at peace; in the summer the Senate had added to this last treaty an amendment requiring their new reservation to be entirely "outside the State of Kansas, and not within any Indian territory, except on consent of the tribes interested." As the reservation had been partly in Kansas, and partly on the lands of the Cherokees, this amendment left them literally without any home whatever. Under these circumstances, the young men of the tribe soon began to join again with other hostile Indians in committing depredations and hostilities along the great mail-routes on the plains. Again they were visited with summary and apparently deserved vengeance by the United States troops, and in the summer of 1867 a Cheyenne village numbering three hundred lodges was burnt by United States soldiers under General Hancock. Fortunately the women and children had all fled on the first news of the approach of the army. Soon after this another council was held with them, and once more the precarious peace was confirmed by treaty; but was almost immediately broken again in consequence of the failure of the Government to comply with the treaty provisions. That some members of these tribes had also failed to keep to the treaty provisions is undoubtedly true, but by far the greater part of them were loyal and peaceable. "The substantial cause of this war," however, was acknowledged by the Indian Bureau itself to be "the fact that the Department, for want of appropriations, was compelled to stop their supplies, and to permit them to recur to the chase for subsistence."

In 1868 "the country bounded east by the State of Arkansas, south by Texas, north by Kansas, and west by the hundredth meridian of longitude, was set apart for the exclusive use of the Cheyennes, Arapahoes, Kiowas, and Comanches, and such other bands as might be located there by proper authority;" and the whole was declared to constitute " a military district," under command of Major-general Hazen, U.S.A. In October of the same year Major Wynkoop, who had been the faithful friend of the Cheyennes and Arapahoes ever since the days of Sand Creek, published his last protest in their behalf, in a letter to the Commissioner of Indian Affairs. He says that the failure of the Government to fulfil treaty provisions in the matter of supplies forced them to resort to hunting again ; and then the refusal of the Government to give them the arms and ammunition promised in the treaty, left them without any means of securing the game; hence the depredations. The chiefs had promised to deliver up the guilty ones to Major Wynkoop, " but before sufficient time had elapsed for them to fulfil their promises the troops were in the field, and the Indians in flight. * * * Even after the majority of the Cheyennes had been forced to take the war-path, in consequence of the bad acts of some of their nation, several bands of the Cheyennes, and the whole Arapahoe tribe, could have been kept at peace had proper action been taken at the time ; but now all the Indians of the Upper Arkansas are engaged in the struggle."*

In 1869 many Arapahoes and Cheyennes had made their way to Montana, and were living with the Gros Ventres ; most of those who remained at the south were quiet, and seemed to be disposed to observe the provisions of the treaty, but were earnestly imploring to be moved farther to the north, where they might hunt buffalo.

---

* On October 27th of this year Black Kettle and his entire band were killed by Gen. Custer's command at Antelope Hills, on the Wichita River.

In 1870, under the care of an agent of the Society of Friends, the improvement of the Southern Cheyennes was remarkable. Buildings were put up, land was broken and planted, and the agent reports that, "with proper care on the part of the Government," there will not be any "serious trouble" with the tribe, although there are still some "restless spirits" among them.

In 1872 the Cheyennes and Arapahoes are reported as "allied to the Government in the maintenance of peace on the border. Very strong inducements have been made by the raiding bands of Kiowas, at critical times in the past two years, to join them in hostile alliance in raids against the whites; but all such appeals have been rejected, and, as a tribe, they have remained loyal and peaceful."

Thirty lodges of the Northern Cheyennes returned this year and joined their tribe, but many of them were still roaming among the Northern Sioux. In 1874 there were said to be over three thousand of these Northern Cheyennes and Arapahoes at the Red Cloud Agency. The Government refused any longer to permit them to stay there; and, after repeated protests, and expressions of unwillingness to move, they at last consented to go to the Indian Territory. But their removal was deferred, on account of the unsettled state of the Southern Cheyennes. Early in the spring troubles had broken out among them, in consequence of a raid of horse-thieves on their reservation. The chief, Little Robe, lost forty-three head of valuable ponies. These ponies were offered for sale in Dodge City, Kansas, where Little Robe's son, with a small band of young men, made an unsuccessful effort to reclaim them. Failing in this, the band, on their way back, stole the first stock they came to; were pursued by the Kansas farmers, the stock recaptured, and Little Robe's son badly wounded. This was sufficient to bring on a general war against white men in the whole region; and the history of the next few months was a history of murders and outrages by Cheyennes, Kiowas, Osages, and Comanches. Sixty lodges of the Cheyennes took refuge under the protection of the United States troops at the agency, and the old problem returned again, how to punish the guilty without harming the innocent. A vigorous military campaign was carried on under General Miles against the hostiles until, in the spring of 1875, the main body surrendered. Wretched, half starved, more than half naked, without lodges, ponies—a more pitiable sight was never seen than this band of Indians. It was inconceivable how they had so long held out; nothing but a well-nigh indomitable pride and inextinguishable hatred of the whites and sense of wrongs could have supported them. It was decided that thirty-three of the most desperate ones should be sent as prisoners to St. Augustine, Florida; but before the selection was completed a general stampede among the surrendered braves took place, resulting in the final escape of some four hundred. They held their ground from two P. M. until dark against three companies of cavalry and two Gatlin guns, and, "under cover of an extremely dark and stormy night, escaped, leaving only three dead on the field." It is impossible not to admire such bravery as this. The Report of the Indian Bureau for 1875 says of the condition of affairs at this agency at this time: "The friendly Cheyennes have had their loyalty put to the severest test by comparing their own condition with that of the full-fed and warmly-housed captives of the War Department. Notwithstanding all privations, they have been unswerving in their friendship, and ever ready to assist the agent in maintaining order, and compelling the Northern Cheyennes who have visited the agency to submit to a count." In consequence of the hostilities, they were obliged to remain close to the agency in camp—a hardship that could hardly be endured, and resulted in serious suffering. Their rations were not enough to subsist them, and yet, being cut off from hunting, they were entirely dependent on them. And even these inadequate rations did not arrive when they were due. Their agent writes, in 1875 : "On last year's flour contract not a single pound was received until the fourteenth day of First Month, 1875, when six months of cold weather and many privations had passed, notwithstanding the many protestations and urgent appeals from the agent."

The now thoroughly subjugated Cheyennes went to work with a will. In one short year they are reported as so anxious to cultivate the ground that, when they could not secure the use of a plough or hoe, they used "axes, sticks of wood, and their hands, in preparing the ground, planting and cultivating their garden spots."

The Northern Cheyennes are still on the Red Cloud Agency, and are reported as restless and troublesome.

In 1877 they were all removed to the Cheyenne and Arapahoe Agency, in Indian Territory. The Reports of the Department say that they asked to be taken there. The winter of 1866 and the summer of 1867 were seasons of great activity and interest at this agency. In the autumn they went off on a grand buffalo hunt, accompanied by a small detail of troops from Fort Reno. Early in the winter white horse-thieves began to make raids on their ponies, and stole so many that many of the Indians were obliged to depend on their friends' ponies to help them return home. Two hundred and sixty in all were stolen—carried, as usual, to Dodge City and sold. A few were recovered; but the loss to the Indians was estimated at two thousand nine hundred dollars. "Such losses are very discouraging to the Indians," writes their agent, and are "but a repetition of the old story that brought on the war of 1874."

In midsummer of this year the "Cheyenne and Arapahoe Transportation Company" was formed: forty wagons were sent out, with harness, by the Government; the Indians furnished the horses; and on the 19th of July the Indians set out in their new *rôle* of "freighters" of their own supplies. They went to Wichita, Kansas—one hundred and sixty-five miles—in six days, with their ponies; loaded sixty-five thousand pounds of supplies into the wagons, and made the return trip in two weeks, all things being delivered in good condition.

This experiment was thoroughly tested; and its results are notable among the many unheeded refutations of the constantly repeated assertion that Indians will not work. The agent of the Cheyennes and the Arapahoes, testifying before a Senate Committee in 1879, says: "We have run a wagon train, driven by Indians, to Wichita, for three years and over, and have never had a drunken Indian yet."

"Do they waste their money, or bring it home?"

"They almost invariably spend it for saddles or clothing, or something of use to them that is not furnished by the Government. * * * They have never stolen an ounce of sugar, coffee, or anything else: they have been careful not to injure or waste anything, and have delivered everything in good faith."

The agent reports not a single case of drunkenness during the year. The manual labor and boarding-school has one hundred and thirteen scholars in it, "all it can accommodate." The children earned four hundred dollars in the year by work of one sort and another, and have "expended the money as judiciously as would white children of their ages." They bought calico, cotton cloth, shoes, hats, several head of cattle, and one horse. They also "bought many delicacies for their friends in camp who were sick and in need."

"One Cheyenne woman tanned robes, traded them for twenty-five two-year-old heifers, and gave them to her daughter in the school. * * * The boys have one hundred and twenty acres of corn under cultivation, ten acres of potatoes, broom-corn, sugar-cane, peanuts, melons, and a good variety of vegetables. They are entitled to one-half the crop for cultivating it."

This is a marvellous report of the change wrought in a people in only two years' time. It proves that the misdemeanors, the hostilities of 1874 and 1875, had been largely forced on them by circumstances.

The winter of 1877 and summer of 1878 were terrible seasons for the Cheyennes. Their fall hunt had proved unsuccessful. Indians from other reservations had hunted the ground over before them, and driven the buffalo off; and the Cheyennes made their way home again in straggling parties, destitute and hungry. Their agent reports that the result of this hunt has clearly proved that "in the future the Indian must rely on tilling the ground as the principal means of support; and if this conviction can be firmly established, the greatest obstacle to advancement in agriculture will be overcome. With the buffalo gone, and their pony herds being constantly decimated by the inroads of horse-thieves, they must soon adopt, in all its varieties, the way of the white man. * * * The usual amount of horse-stealing has prevailed, and the few cases of successful pursuit have only increased the boldness of the thieves and the number of the thefts. Until some other system of law is introduced we cannot hope for a cessation of this grievance."

The ration allowed to these Indians is reported as being "reduced and insufficient," and the small sums they have been able to earn by selling buffalo-hides are said to have been "of material assistance" to them in "supplementing" this ration. But in this year there have been sold only $657 worth of skins by the Cheyennes and Arapahoes together. In 1876 they sold $17,600 worth. Here is a falling off enough to cause very great suffering in a little community of five thousand people. But this was only the beginning of their troubles. The summer proved one of unusual heat. Extreme heat, chills and fever, and "a reduced and insufficient ration," all combined, resulted in an amount of sickness heart-rending to read of. "It is no exaggerated estimate," says the agent, "to place the number of sick people on the reservation at two thousand. Many deaths occurred which might have been obviated had there been a proper supply of anti-malarial remedies at hand. * * * Hundreds applying for treatment have been refused medicine."

The Northern Cheyennes grew more and more restless and unhappy. "In council and elsewhere they profess an intense desire to be sent North, where they say they will settle down as the others have done," says the report; adding, with an obtuseness which is inexplicable, that "no difference has been made in the treatment of the Indians," but that the "compliance" of these Northern Cheyennes has been "of an entirely different nature from that of the other Indians," and that it may be "necessary in the future to compel what so far we have been unable to effect by kindness and appeal to their better natures."

If it is "an appeal to men's better natures" to remove them by force from a healthful Northern climate, which they love and thrive in, to a malarial Southern one, where they are struck down by chills and fever — refuse them medicine which can combat chills and fever, and finally starve them—then, indeed, might be said to have been most forcible appeals made to the "better natures" of these Northern Cheyennes. What might have been predicted followed.

Early in the autumn, after this terrible summer, a band of some three hundred of these Northern Cheyennes took the desperate step of running off and attempting to make their way back to Dakota. They were pursued, fought desperately, but were finally overpowered, and surrendered. They surrendered, however, only on the condition that they should be taken to Dakota. They were unanimous in declaring that they would rather die than go back to the Indian Territory. This was nothing more, in fact, than saying that they would rather die by bullets than of chills and fever and starvation.

These Indians were taken to Fort Robinson, Nebraska. Here they were confined as prisoners of war, and held subject to the orders of the Department of the Interior. The department was informed of the Indians' determination never to be taken back alive to Indian Territory. The army officers in charge reiterated these statements, and implored the department to permit them to remain at the North; but it was of no avail. Orders came—explicit, repeated, finally stern—insisting on the return of these Indians to their agency. The commanding officer at Fort Robinson has been censured severely for the course he pursued in his effort to carry out those orders. It is difficult to see what else he could have done, except to have resigned his post. He could not take three hundred Indians by sheer brute force and carry them hundreds of miles, especially when they were so desperate that they had broken up the iron stoves in their quarters, and wrought and twisted them into weapons with which to resist. He thought perhaps he could starve them into submission. He stopped the issue of food; he also stopped the issue of fuel to them. It was midwinter; the mercury froze in that month at Fort Robinson. At the end of two days he asked the Indians to let their women and children come out that he might feed them. Not a woman would come out. On the night of the fourth day— or, according to some accounts, the sixth—these starving, freezing Indians broke prison, overpowered the guards, and fled, carrying their women and children with them. They held the pursuing troops at bay for several days; finally made a last stand in a deep ravine, and were shot down—men, women, and children together. Out of the whole band there were left alive some fifty women and children and seven men, who, having been confined in another part of the fort, had not had the good fortune to share in this outbreak and meet their death in the ravine. These, with their wives and children, were sent to Fort Leavenworth, to be put in prison; the men to be tried for murders committed in their skirmishes in Kansas on their way to the north. Red Cloud, a Sioux chief, came to Fort Robinson immediately after this massacre, and entreated to be allowed to take the Cheyenne widows and orphans into his tribe to be cared for. The Government, therefore, kindly permitted twenty-two Cheyenne widows and thirty-two Cheyenne children— many of them orphans—to be received into the band of the Ogallalla Sioux.

An attempt was made by the Commissioner of Indian Affairs, in his Report for 1879, to show by tables and figures that these Indians were not starving at the time of their flight from Indian Territory. The attempt only redounded to his own disgrace; it being proved, by the testimony given by a former clerk of the Indian Bureau before the Senate committee appointed to investigate the case of the Northern Cheyennes, that the commissioner had been guilty of absolute dishonesty in his estimates, and that the quantity of beef actually issued to the Cheyenne Agency was hundreds of pounds less than he had reported it, and that the Indians were actually, as they had claimed, " starving."

The testimony given before this committee by some of the Cheyenne prisoners themselves is heart-rending. One must have a callous heart who can read it unmoved.

When asked by Senator Morgan, " Did you ever really suffer from hunger?" one of the chiefs replied, " We were *always* hungry; we *never* had enough. When they that were sick once in awhile felt as though they could eat something, we had nothing to give them."

" Did you not go out on the plains sometimes and hunt buffalo, with the consent of the agent?"

" We went out on a buffalo-hunt, and nearly starved while out; we could not find any buffalo hardly; we could hardly get back with our ponies; we had to kill a good many of our ponies to eat, to save ourselves from starving."

"How many children got sick and died?"

"Between the fall of 1877 and 1878 we lost fifty children. A great many of our finest young men died, as well as many women."

"Old Crow," a chief who served faithfully as Indian scout and ally under General Crook for years, said: "I did not feel like doing anything for awhile, because I had no heart. I did not want to be in this country. I was all the time wanting to get back to the better country where I was born, and where my children are buried, and where my mother and sister yet live. So I have laid in my lodge most of the time with nothing to think about but that, and the affair up north at Fort Robinson, and my relatives and friends who were killed there. But now I feel as though, if I had a wagon and a horse or two, and some land, I would try to work. If I had something, so that I could do something, I might not think so much about these other things. As it is now, I feel as though I would just as soon be asleep with the rest."

The wife of one of the chiefs confined at Fort Leavenworth testified before the committee as follows: "The main thing I complained of was that we didn't get enough to eat; my children nearly starved to death; then sickness came, and there was nothing good for them to eat; for a long time the most they had to eat was corn-meal and salt. Three or four children died every day for awhile, and that frightened us."

(This testimony was taken at Fort Reno, in Indian Territory.)

When asked if there were anything she would like to say to the committee, the poor woman replied: "I wish you would do what you can to get my husband released. I am very poor here, and do not know what is to become of me. If he were released he would come down here, and we would live together quietly, and do no harm to anybody, and make no trouble. But I should never get over my desire to get back north; I should always want to get back where my children were born, and died, and were buried. That country is better than this in every respect. * * * There is plenty of good, cool water there—pure water—while here the water is not good. It is not hot there, nor so sickly. Are you going where my husband is? Can you tell when he is likely to be released?"

The Senators were obliged to reply to her that they were not going where her husband was, and they could not tell when he would be released.

In view of the accounts of the sickness and suffering of these Indians in 1877 and 1878, the reports made in 1879 of the industry and progress at the Cheyenne and Arapahoe Agency are almost incredible. The school children have, by their earnings, bought one hundred head of cattle; 451,000 pounds of freight have been transported by the Indians during the year; they have also worked at making brick, chopping wood, making hay, hauling wood, and splitting and hauling rails; and have earned thereby $7121 25. Two of the girls of the school have been promoted to the position of assistant teachers; and the United States mail contractor between this agency and Fort Elliott, in Texas—a distance of one hundred and sixty-five miles—has operated almost exclusively with full-blooded Indians: "there has been no report of breach of trust on the part of any Indians connected with this trust, and the contractor expresses his entire approval of their conduct."

It is stated also that there was not sufficient clothing to furnish each Indian with a warm suit of clothing, " as promised by the treaty," and that, " by reference to official correspondence, the fact is established that the Cheyennes and Arapahoes are judged as having no legal rights to any lands, having forfeited their treaty reservation by a failure to settle thereon," and their " present reservation not having been, as yet, confirmed by Congress. Inasmuch as the Indians fully understood, and were assured that this reservation was given to them in lieu of their treaty reservation, and have commenced farming in the belief that there was no uncertainty about the matter, it is but common justice that definite action be had at an early day, securing to them what is their right."

It would seem that there could be found nowhere in the melancholy record of the experiences of our Indians a more glaring instance of confused multiplication of injustices than this. The Cheyennes were pursued and slain for venturing to leave this very reservation, which, it appears, is not their reservation at all, and they have no legal right to it. Are there any words to fitly characterize such treatment as this from a great, powerful, rich nation, to a handful of helpless people?

CHAPTER IV.

THE NEZ PERCÉS.

BOUNDED on the north, south, and east by snow-topped mountains, and on the west by shining waters; holding in its rocky passes the sources of six great rivers; bearing on its slopes and plains measureless forests of pine and cedar and spruce; its meadows gardens of summer bloom and fruit, and treasure-houses of fertility,—lies Oregon: wide, healthful, beautiful, abundant, and inviting, no wonder it was coveted and fought for.

When Lewis and Clarke visited it, eighty years ago, they found living there many tribes of Indians, numbering in all, at the lowest estimates, between twenty and thirty thousand; of all these tribes the Nez Percés [4] were the richest, noblest, and most gentle.

To the Cayuses, one of the most warlike of these tribes, Messrs. Lewis and Clarke presented an American flag, telling them it was an emblem of peace. The gay coloring and beauty of the flag, allied to this significance, made a deep impression on the poetic minds of these savages. They set the flag up in a beautiful valley called the Grande Ronde — a fertile basin some twenty-five miles in diameter, surrounded by high walls of basaltic rock, and watered by a branch of the Snake River: around this flag they met their old enemies the Shoshones, and swore to keep perpetual peace with them; and the spot became consecrated to an annual meeting of the tribes—a sort of fair, where the Cayuse, Nez Percé, and Walla Walla Indians came every summer and traded their roots, skins, elk and buffalo

[4] Regarding the Nez Percés, consult Francis Haines, *The Nez Percés, Tribesmen of the Columbia Plateau* (Norman, Oklahoma, 1955).

meats, for salmon and horses, with the Shoshones. It was a beautiful spot, nearly circular, luxuriantly covered with grass, the hill wall around it thick grown with evergreen trees, chiefly larch. The Indians called it Karpkarp, which being translated is "Balm of Gilead."

The life of these Indians was a peculiar one. Most of them had several homes, and as they lived only a part of the year in each, were frequently spoken of by travellers as nomadic tribes, while in fact they were as wedded to their homes as any civilized inhabitants of the world; and their wanderings were as systematic as the removals of wealthy city people from town homes to country places. If a man were rich enough, and fond enough of change, to have a winter house in New York, a house for the summer in Newport, and one for autumn in the White Mountains, nobody would think of calling him a nomad; still less if he made these successive changes annually, with perfect regularity, owing to opportunities which were offered him at regularly recurring intervals in these different places to earn his living; which was the case with the Oregon Indians.

As soon as the snow disappears in the spring there is in certain localities, ready for gathering, the "pohpoh"—a small bulb, like an onion. This is succeeded by the "spatlam," and the "spatlam" by the "cammass" or "ithwa," a root like a parsnip, which they make into fine meal. In midsummer come the salmon in countless shoals up the rivers. August is the month for berries, of which they dry great quantities for winter use. In September salmon again—coming down stream now, exhausted and ready to die, but in sufficiently good condition to be dried for the winter. In October comes the "mesani," another root of importance in the Indian larder. After this they must depend on deer, bears, small game, and wildfowl. When all these resources fail, there is a kind of lichen growing on the trees, of which they can eat enough to keep themselves from starving, though its nutritive qualities are very small. Thus each season had its duty and its appointed place of abode, and year after year the same month found them in the same spot.

In 1833 a delegation from these Oregon Indians went to St. Louis, and through Mr. Catlin, the artist, made known their object, which was "to inquire for the truth of a representation which they said some white men had made among them, that our religion was better than theirs, and that they would all be lost if they did not embrace it." Two members of this delegation were Nez Percés—"Hee-oh'ks-te-kin" and "H'co-a-h'co-a-h'cotes-min," or "Rabbit-skin Leggings," and "No Horns on his Head." Their portraits are to be found in "Catlin's American Indians." One of these died on his way home; but the other journeyed his thousands of miles safely back, and bore to his tribe the news "that the report which they had heard was well founded, and that good and religious men would soon come among them to teach this religion, so that they could all understand and have the benefits of it."

Two years later the Methodist Episcopal Society and the American Board both sent missionaries to Oregon. Before this the religion of the fur-traders was the only white man's religion that the Indians had had the opportunity of observing. Eleven different companies and expeditions, besides the Hudson's Bay and the North-west Companies, had been established in their country, and the Indians had become only too familiar with their standards and methods. It was not many years after the arrival of the missionaries in Oregon that a traveller there gave the following account of his experience with a Nez Percé guide:

"Creekie (so he was named) was a very kind man; he turned my worn-out animals loose, and loaded my packs on his own; gave me a splendid horse to ride, and intimated by significant gestures that we would go a short distance that afternoon. I gave my assent, and we were soon on our way; hav-

ing ridden about ten miles, we camped for the night. I noticed, during the ride, a degree of forbearance toward each other which I had never before observed in that race. When we
halted for the night the two boys were behind; they had been
frolicking with their horses, and, as the darkness came on, lost
the trail. It was a half-hour before they made their appearance, and during this time the parents manifested the most
anxious solicitude for them. One of them was but three years
old, and was lashed to the horse he rode; the other only seven
years of age—young pilots in the wilderness at night. But
the elder, true to the sagacity of his race, had taken his course,
and struck the brook on which we were encamped within three
hundred yards of us. The pride of the parents at this feat,
and their ardent attachment to the children, were perceptible
in the pleasure with which they received them at their even-
ning fire, and heard the relation of their childish adventures.
The weather was so pleasant that no tent was spread. The
willows were bent, and the buffalo-robes spread over them.
Underneath were laid other robes, on which my Indian host
seated himself, with his wife and children on one side and
myself on the other. A fire burnt brightly in front. Water
was brought, and the evening ablutions having been performed,
the wife presented a dish of meat to her husband and one to
myself. There was a pause. The woman seated herself between her children. The Indian then bowed his head and
prayed to God. A wandering savage in Oregon, calling on
Jehovah in the name of Jesus Christ! After the prayer he
gave meat to his children and passed the dish to his wife.
While eating, the frequent repetition of the words Jehovah and
Jesus Christ, in the most reverential manner, led me to suppose that they were conversing on religious topics, and thus
they passed an hour. Meanwhile the exceeding weariness of a
long day's travel admonished me to seek rest. I had slumber-
ed I know not how long, when a strain of music awoke me.

The Indian family was engaged in its evening devotions. They were singing a hymn in the Nez Percés language. Having finished, they all knelt and bowed their faces on the buffalo-robe, and Creekie prayed long and fervently. Afterward they sung another hymn, and retired. To hospitality, family affection, and devotion, Creekie added honesty and cleanliness to a great degree, manifesting by these fruits, so contrary to the nature and habits of his race, the beautiful influence of the work of grace on the heart."

The earliest mention of the Nez Percés in the official records of the Indian Bureau is in the year 1843. In that year an agent was sent out to investigate the condition of the Oregon tribes, and he reports as follows: "The only tribes from which much is to be hoped, or anything to be feared in this part of Oregon, are the Walla Wallas, Cayuses, and Nez Percés, inhabiting a district on the Columbia and its tributaries, commencing two hundred and forty miles from its mouth, and stretching four hundred and eighty miles in the interior."

The Nez Percés, living farther inland, "inhabit a beautiful grazing district, not surpassed by any I have seen for verdure, water privileges, climate, or health. This tribe forms an honorable exception to the general Indian character—being more noble, industrious, sensible, and better disposed toward the whites and their improvements in the arts and sciences; and though brave as Cæsar, the whites have nothing to dread at their hands in case of their dealing out to them what they conceive to be right and equitable."

When this agent arrived at the missionary station among the Nez Percés, he was met there by a large body of the Indians with twenty-two of their chiefs. The missionaries received him "with joyful countenances and glad hearts;" the Indians, "with civility, gravity, and dignified reserve."

He addressed them at length, explaining to them the kind intentions of the Government toward them. They listened

with "gravity, fixed attention, and decorum." Finally an aged
chief, ninety years of age, arose and said: "I speak to-day;
perhaps to-morrow I die. I am the oldest chief of the tribe.
I was the high chief when your great brothers, Lewis and
Clarke, visited this country. They visited me, and honored me
with their friendship and counsel. I showed them my numerous wounds, received in bloody battle with the Snakes. They
told me it was not good; it was better to be at peace; gave
me a flag of truce; I held it up high. We met, and talked,
but never fought again. Clarke pointed to this day—to you
and this occasion. We have long waited in expectation; sent
three of our sons to Red River school to prepare for it; two
of them sleep with their fathers; the other is here, and can be
ears, mouth, and pen for us. I can say no more; I am quickly tired; my voice and limbs tremble. I am glad I live to see
you and this day; but I shall soon be still and quiet in
death."

At this council the Nez Percés elected a head chief named
Ellis, and adopted the following Code of Laws:

Art. 1. Whoever wilfully takes life shall be hung.

Art. 2. Whoever burns a dwelling-house shall be hung.

Art. 3. Whoever burns an out-building shall be imprisoned six months,
receive fifty lashes, and pay all damages.

Art. 4. Whoever carelessly burns a house or any property shall pay
damages.

Art. 5. If any one enter a dwelling without permission of the occupant,
the chiefs shall punish him as they think proper. Public rooms are ex-
cepted.

Art. 6. If any one steal, he shall pay back twofold; and if it be the
value of a beaver-skin or less, he shall receive twenty-five lashes; and if
the value is over a beaver-skin, he shall pay back twofold, and receive
fifty lashes.

Art. 7. If any one take a horse and ride it, without permission, or take
any article and use it, without liberty, he shall pay for the use of it, and
receive from twenty to fifty lashes, as the chief shall direct.

Art. 8. If any one enter a field and injure the crops, or throw down the fence, so that cattle or horses go in and do damage, he shall pay all damages, and receive twenty-five lashes for every offence.

Art. 9. Those only may keep dogs who travel or live among the game. If a dog kill a lamb, calf, or any domestic animal, the owner shall pay the damage, and kill the dog.

Art. 10. If an Indian raise a gun or other weapon against a white man, it shall be reported to the chiefs, and they shall punish him. If a white man do the same to an Indian, it shall be reported to Dr. White, and he shall punish or redress it.

Art. 11. If an Indian break these laws, he shall be punished by his chiefs; if a white man break them, he shall be reported to the agent, and punished at his instance.

These laws, the agent says, he "proposed one by one, leaving them as free to reject as to accept. They were greatly pleased with all proposed, but wished a heavier penalty to some, and suggested the dog-law, which was annexed."

In a history of Oregon written by one W. H. Gray, of Astoria, we find this Indian agent spoken of as a "notorious blockhead." Mr. Gray's methods of mention of all persons toward whom he has antagonism or dislike are violent and undignified, and do not redound either to his credit as a writer or his credibility as a witness. But it is impossible to avoid the impression that in this instance he was not far from the truth. Surely one cannot read, without mingled horror and incredulity, this programme of the whipping-post, offered as one of the first instalments of the United States Government's "kind intentions" toward these Indians; one of the first practical illustrations given them of the kind of civilization the United States Government would recommend and introduce.

We are not surprised to read in another narrative of affairs in Oregon, a little later, that "the Indians want pay for being whipped, the same as they did for praying—to please the missionaries—during the great revival of 1839. * * * Some of the influential men in the tribe desired to know of what benefit this whipping-system was going to be to them. They said they were willing it should continue, provided they were to receive shirts and pants and blankets as a reward for being whipped. They had been whipped a good many times, and had got nothing for it, and it had done them no good. If this state of things was to continue, it was all good for nothing, and they would throw it away."

The Secretary of War does not appear to have seen this aspect of his agent's original efforts in the line of jurisprudence. He says of the report which includes this astounding code, merely that "it furnishes some deeply interesting and curious details respecting certain of the Indian tribes in that remote part of our territories," and that the conduct of the Nez Percés on the occasion of this important meeting "impresses one most agreeably."

A report submitted at the same time by the Rev. Mr. Spaulding, who had lived six years as missionary among the Nez Percés, is much pleasanter reading. He says that "nearly all the principal men and chiefs are members of the school; that they are as industrious in their schools as on their farms. They cultivate their lands with much skill and to good advantage, and many more would do so if they had the means. About one hundred are printing their own books with the pen. This keeps up a deep interest, as they daily have new lessons to print; and what they print must be committed to memory as soon as possible. A good number are now so far advanced in reading and printing as to render much assistance in teaching. Their books are taken home at night, and every lodge becomes a school-room. Their lessons are Scripture lessons; no others (except the laws) seem to interest them."

Even this missionary seems to have fallen under some strange glamour on the subject of the whipping-code; for he adds: "The laws which you so happily prepared, and which were unanimously adopted by the people, I have printed in the form of a small school-book. A great number of the school now read them fluently."

In the next year's report of the Secretary of War we read that "the Nez Percé tribe have adopted a few simple and plain laws as their code, which will teach them self-restraint, and is the beginning of government on their part." The Secretary also thinks it "very remarkable that there should so soon be several well supported, well attended, and well conducted schools in Oregon." (Not at all remarkable, considering that the Congregationalists, the Methodist Episcopalians, and the Roman Catholics have all had missionaries at work there for eight years.)

In 1846, the Nez Percés, with the rest of the Oregon tribes, disappear from the official records of the Indian Bureau. "It will be necessary to make some provision for conducting our relations with the Indian tribes west of the Rocky Mountains," it is said; but, "the whole subject having been laid before Congress, it was not deemed advisable to continue a service that was circumscribed in its objects, and originally designed to be temporary." The founder of the whipping-post in Oregon was therefore relieved from his duties, and it is to be hoped his laws speedily fell into disuse. The next year all the Protestant missions in Oregon were abandoned, in consequence of the frightful massacre by the Cayuses of the missionary families living among them. But the Nez Percés, though deprived of their teaching, did not give up the faith and the practice they had taught them. Six years later General Benjamin Alvord bore the following testimony to their religious character:

"In the spring of 1853 a white man, who had passed the previous winter in the country of the Nez Percés, came to the military post at the Dalles, and on being questioned as to the manners and customs of the tribe, he said that he wintered with a band of several hundred in number, and that the whole party assembled every evening and morning for prayer, the exercises being conducted by one of themselves in their own language. He stated that on Sunday they assembled for ex· hortation and worship."

In 1851 a superintendent and three agents were appointed for Indian service in Oregon. Treaties were negotiated with some of the tribes, but they were not ratified, and in 1853 there was, in consequence, a wide-spread dissatisfaction among all the Indians in the region. "They have become distrustful of all promises made them by the United States," says the Oregon superintendent, "and believe the design of the Government is to defer doing anything for them till they have wasted away. The settlement of the whites on the tracts which they regarded as secured to them by solemn treaty stipulations, results in frequent misunderstandings between them and the settlers, and occasions and augments bitter animosities and resentments. I am in almost daily receipt of complaints and petitions for a redress of wrongs from both parties."

Governor Stevens, of Washington Territory, in charge of the Northern Pacific Railroad Explorations and Survey, wrote, this year, "These hitherto neglected tribes, whose progress from the wild wanderers of the plains to kind and hospitable neighbors is personally known to you, are entitled, by every consideration of justice and humanity, to the fatherly care of the Government."

In Governor Stevens's report is to be found a comprehensive and intelligible account of all the Indian tribes in Oregon and Washington Territory. The greater part of the Nez Percés' country was now within the limits of Washington Territory, only a few bands remaining in Oregon. They were estimated to number at least eighteen hundred, and were said to be a "rich and powerful tribe, owning many horses." Every year they crossed the mountains to hunt buffalo on the plains of the Missouri.

In 1855 there was a general outbreak of hostilities on the part of the Oregon Indians. Tribe after tribe, even among those who had been considered friendly, fell into the ranks of the hostiles, and some base acts of treachery were committed. The Oregon settlers, menaced with danger on all sides, became naturally so excited and terrified that their actions were hasty and ill-advised. "They are without discipline, without order, and similar to madmen," says one official report. "Every day they run off the horses and the cattle of the friendly Indians I will soon no longer be able to restrain the friendly Indians. They are indignant at conduct so unworthy of the whites, who have made so many promises to respect and protect them if they remain faithful friends. I am very sure, if the volunteers are not arrested in their brigand actions, our Indians will save themselves by flying to the homes of their relations, the Nez Percés, who have promised them help; and then all these Indians of Oregon would join in the common defence until they be entirely exterminated."

It is difficult to do full justice to the moral courage which is shown by Indians who remain friendly to whites under such circumstances as these. The traditions of their race, the powerful influence of public sentiment among their relatives and friends, and, in addition, terror for their own lives—all combine in times of such outbreaks to draw even the friendliest tribes into sympathy and co-operation with those who are making war on whites.

At this time the hostile Indians in Oregon sent word to the Nez Percés, "Join us in the war against the whites, or we will wipe you out." They said, "We have made the whites run out of the country, and we will now make the friendly Indians do the same."

"What can the friendly Indians do?" wrote the colonel of a company of Washington Territory Volunteers; "they have no ammunition, and the whites will give them none; and the hostiles say to them, 'We have plenty; come and join us, and save your lives.'   The Nez Percés are very much alarmed; they say, 'We have no ammunition to defend ourselves with if we are attacked.'"

The Oregon superintendent writes to General Wool (in command at this time of the Department of the Pacific), imploring him to send troops to Oregon to protect both friendly Indians and white settlers, and to enable this department to maintain guarantees secured to these Indians by treaty stipulations.   He says that the friendly Indians are "willing to submit to almost any sacrifice to obtain peace, but there may be a point beyond which they could not be induced to go without a struggle."

This outbreak terminated after some sharp fighting, and about equal losses on both sides, in what the Oregon superintendent calls "a sort of armistice," which left the Indians "much emboldened," with the impression on their minds that they have the "ability to contend successfully against the entire white race."

Moreover, "the non-ratification of the treaties heretofore made to extinguish their title to the lands necessary for the occupancy and use of our citizens, seems to have produced no little disappointment; and the continued extension of our settlements into their territory, without any compensation being made to them, is a constant source of dissatisfaction and hostile feeling.

"It cannot be expected that Indians situated like those in Oregon and Washington Territory, occupying extensive sections of country where, from the game and otherwise, they derive a comfortable support, will quietly and peaceably submit, without any equivalent, to be deprived of their homes and possessions, and to be driven off to some other locality where they cannot find their usual means of subsistence.   Such a proceeding is not only contrary to our policy hitherto, but is repugnant alike to the dictates of humanity and the principles of natural justice.

"The principle of recognizing and respecting the usufruct right of the Indians to the lands occupied by them has not been so strictly adhered to in the case of the tribes in the Territories of Oregon and Washington. When a territorial government was first provided for Oregon—which then embraced the present Territory of Washington—strong inducements were held out to our people to emigrate and settle there without the usual arrangements being made in advance for the extinguishment of the title of the Indians who occupied and claimed the lands. Intruded upon, ousted of their homes and possessions without any compensation, and deprived in most cases of their accustomed means of support, without any arrangement having been made to enable them to establish and maintain themselves in other locations, it is not a matter of surprise that they have committed many depredations upon our citizens, and been exasperated to frequent acts of hostility."

As was to be expected, the armistice proved of no avail; and in 1858 the unfortunate Territories had another Indian war on their hands. In this war we find the Nez Percés fighting on the side of the United States against the hostile Indians. One of the detachments of United States troops was saved from destruction only by taking refuge with them. Nearly destitute of ammunition, and surrounded by hundreds of hostile Indians, the little company escaped by night; and "after a ride of ninety miles mostly at a gallop, and without a rest, reached Snake River," where they were met by this friendly tribe, who "received them with open arms, succored the wounded men, and crossed in safety the whole command over the difficult and dangerous river."

The officer in command of the Nez Percé band writes as follows, in his report to the Indian Commissioner:

"Allow me, my dear sir, while this general war is going on, to point you to at least a few green spots where the ravages of war do not as yet extend, and which thus far are untainted and unaffected, with a view of so retaining them that we may hereafter point to them as oases in this desert of war. These green spots are the Nez Percés, the Flat-heads, and Pend d'Oreilles. In this connection I refer with grateful pride to an act of Colonel Wright, which embodies views and motives which, endorsed and carried out by the Government, must redound to his credit and praise, and be the means of building up, at no distant day, a bold, brave, warlike, and numerous people.

"Before leaving Walla-Walla, Colonel Wright assembled the Nez Percé people, told them his object was to war with and punish our enemies; but as this great people were and ever had been our friends, he wanted their friendship to be as enduring as the mountains around which they lived; and in order that no difference of views or difficulty might arise, that their mutual promises should be recorded."

With this view he there made a treaty of friendship with them, and thirty of the bravest warriors and chiefs at once marshalled themselves to accompany him against the enemy.

When Colonel Wright asked these Indians what they wanted, "their reply was worthy of a noble race—'Peace, ploughs, and schools.'" At this time they had no agent appointed to attend to their welfare; they were raising wheat, corn, and vegetables with the rude means at their command, and still preserved the faith and many of the practices taught them by the missionaries thirteen years before.

In 1859 peace was again established in Oregon, and the Indians "considered as conquered." The treaties of 1855 were ratified by the Senate, and this fact went far to restore tranquillity in the territories. Congress was implored by the superintendents to realize "the importance of making the appropriations for fulfilling those treaty stipulations at the earliest practicable moment;" that it may "prevent the recurrence of another savage war, necessarily bloody and devastating to our settlements, extended under the authority and sanction of our Government." With marvellous self-restraint, the superintendents do not enforce their appeals by a reference to the fact that, if the treaties had been fulfilled in the outset, all the hostilities of the last four years might probably have been avoided.

The reservation secured to the Nez Percés was a fine tract of country, one hundred miles long and sixty in width—well watered, timbered, and of great natural resources. Already the Indians had begun to practice irrigation in their fields; had large herds of horses, and were beginning to give attention to improving the breed. Some of them could read and write their own language, and many of them professed Christianity, and were exemplary in their conduct—a most remarkable fact, proving the depth of the impression the missionary teachings must have made. The majority of them wore the American costume, and showed "their progress in civilization by attaching little value to the gewgaws and trinkets which so generally captivate the savage."

In less than two years the peace of this noble tribe was again invaded; this time by a deadly foe—the greed of gold. In 1861 there were said to be no less than ten thousand miners in the Nez Percé country prospecting for gold. Now arose the question, What will the Government do? Will it protect the rights of the Indians or not?

"To attempt to restrain miners would be like attempting to restrain the whirlwind," writes the superintendent of Washington Territory; and he confesses that, "seeing the utter impossibility of preventing miners from going to the mines," he has refrained from taking any steps which, by a certain want of success, would tend to weaken the force of the law.

For the next few years the Nez Percés saw with dismay the steady stream of settlers pouring into their country. That they did not resist it by force is marvellous, and can only be explained by the power of a truly Christian spirit.

"Their reservation was overrun by the enterprising miners; treaty stipulations were disregarded and trampled under foot; towns were established thereon, and all the means that cupidity could invent or disloyalty achieve were resorted to to shake their confidence in the Government. They were disturbed in the peaceable possession of what they regarded as their vested rights, sacredly secured by treaty. They were informed that the Government was destroyed, and that whatever treaties were made would never be carried out. All resistance on their part proved unavailing, and inquietude and discontent predominated among them," says the Governor of Idaho, in 1865. Shortly after, by the organization of that new Territory, the Nez Percés' reservation had been removed from the jurisdiction of Washington Territory to that of Idaho.

A powerful party was organized in the tribe, advocating the forming of a league with the Crows and Blackfeet against the whites. The non-arrival of promised supplies; the non-payment of promised moneys; the unchecked influx of miners throughout the reservation, put strong weapons into the hands of these disaffected ones. But the chiefs "remained firm and unwavering in their devotion to the Government and the laws. They are intelligent—their head chief, Sawyer, particularly so —and tell their people to still wait patiently." And yet, at this very time, there was due from the United States Government to this chief Sawyer six hundred and twenty-five dollars! He had for six months been suffering for the commonest necessaries of life, and had been driven to disposing of his vouchers at fifty cents on the dollar to purchase necessaries. The warriors also, who fought for us so well in 1856, were still unpaid; although in the seventh article of the treaty of 1863 it had been agreed that "the claims of certain members of the Nez Percé tribe against the Government, for services rendered and horses furnished by them to the Oregon Mounted Volunteers, as appears by certificates issued by W. H. Fauntleroy, Acting Regimental Quartermaster, and commanding Oregon Volunteers, on the 6th of March, 1856, at Camp Cornelius, and amounting to $4665, shall be paid to them in full in gold coin."

How many communities of white men would remain peaceable, loyal, and friendly under such a strain as this?

In 1866 the Indian Bureau report of the state of our diplomatic relations with the Nez Percés is that the treaty concluded with them in 1863 was ratified by the Senate, " with an amendment which awaited the action of the Indians. The ratification of this treaty has been delayed for several years for various reasons, partly arising from successive changes in the Superintendent of Indian Affairs in Idaho, whose varying opinions on the subject of the treaty have caused doubts in the minds of senators. A later treaty had been made, but, on careful consideration of the subject, it was deemed advisable to carry into effect that of 1863. The Nez Percés claimed title to a very large district of country comprised in what are now organized as Oregon, Washington, and Idaho, but principally within the latter Territory; and already a large white population is pressing upon them in the search for gold. They are peaceable, industrious, and friendly, and altogether one of the most promising of the tribes west of the Rocky Mountains, having profited largely by the labors of missionaries among them."

By the treaty ratified in this year they give up "all their lands except a reservation defined by certain natural boundaries, and agree to remove to this reservation within one year. Where they have improvements on lands outside of it, such improvements are to be appraised and paid for. The tillable lands are to be surveyed into tracts of twenty acres each, and allotted to such Indians as desire to hold lands in severalty. The Government is to continue the annuities due under former treaties, and, in addition, pay the tribe, or expend for them for certain specific purposes having their improvement in view, the sum of $262,500, and a moderate sum is devoted to homes and salaries for chiefs. The right of way is secured through the reservation, and the Government undertakes to reserve all important springs and watering-places for public use."

In this same year the Governor of Idaho writes, in his annual report to the Department of the Interior: "Prominent among the tribes of Northern Idaho stand the Nez Percés, a majority of whom boast that they have ever been the faithful friends of the white man. But a few over half of the entire tribe of the Nez Percés are under treaty. The fidelity of those under treaty, even under the most discouraging circumstances, must commend itself to the favorable consideration of the Department. The non-payment of their annuities has had its natural effect on the minds of some of those under treaty; but their confiding head chief, Sawyer, remains unmoved, and on all occasions is found the faithful apologist for any failure of the Government. Could this tribe have been kept aloof from the contaminating vices of white men, and had it been in the power of the Government promptly to comply with the stipulations of the treaty of 1855, there can be no doubt but that their condition at this time would have been a most prosperous one, and that the whole of the Nez Percé nation would by this time have been willing to come under treaty, and settle on the reservation with those already there."

In 1867 the patience of the Nez Percés is beginning to show signs of wearing out. The Governor of Idaho writes: "This disaffection is great, and serious trouble is imminent. It could all be settled by prompt payment by the Government of their just dues; but if delayed too long I greatly fear open hostilities. They have been patient, but promises and explanations are losing force with them now. * * * Their grievances are urged with such earnestness that even Sawyer, who has always been our apologist, has in a measure abandoned his pacific policy, and asks boldly that we do them justice. * * * Even now it may not be too late; but, if neglected, war may be reasonably expected. Should the Nez Percés strike a blow, all over our Territory and around our boundaries will blaze the signal-fires and gleam the tomahawks of the savages—Kootenays, Pen d'Oreilles, Cœur d'Alenes, Blackfeet, Flat-heads, Spokanes, Pelouses, Bannocks, and Shoshones will be involved."

This disaffection, says the agent, "began to show itself soon after the visit of George C. Haigh, Esq., special agent, last December, to obtain their assent to the amendments to the treaty of June 9th, 1863—the non-ratification of that treaty had gone on so long, and promises made them by Governor Lyon that it would not be ratified, and that he was authorized to make a new treaty with them by which they would retain all of their country, as given them under the treaty of 1851, except the site of the town of Lewiston. They had also been informed in March, 1866, that Governor Lyon would be here in the June following, to pay them back-annuities due under the treaty of 1855. The failure to carry out these promises, and the idea they have that the stipulations of the treaty of 1863 will be carried out in the same manner, is one of the causes of their bad feeling. It showed itself plainly at the council lately held, and is on the increase. If there is the same delay in carrying out the stipulations of the treaty of 1863 that there has been in that of 1855, some of the chiefs with their bands will join the hostile Indians. There are many things it is impossible to explain to them. They cannot understand why the $1185 that was promised by Governor Lyon to the Indian laborers on the church is not paid. He told them when the walls were up they should receive their pay. These laborers were poor men, and such inducements were held out to them that they commenced the work in good faith, with the full expectation of receiving their pay when their labors ceased."

The head chief Sawyer's pay is still in arrears. For the last quarter of 1863, and the first and second of 1864, he has received no pay. No wonder he has ceased to be the "apologist" of the Government, which four years ago promised him an annuity of $500 a year.

Spite of this increasing disaffection the Nez Percés are industrious and prosperous. They raised in this year 15,000 bushels of wheat. "Many of them carried their wheat to be ground to the mills, while many sold the grain to packers for feed, while much of it is boiled whole for food. Some few of the better class have had their wheat ground, and sold the flour in the mining-camps at lower prices than packers could lay it down in the camps. Some have small pack-trains running through the summer; one in particular, Cru-cru-lu-ye, runs some fifteen animals; he sometimes packs for whites, and again runs on his own account. A Clearwater Station merchant a short time ago informed me of his buying some oats of Cru-cru-lu-ye last fall. After the grain had been weighed, and emptied out of the sacks, the Indian brought the empty sacks to the scales to have them weighed, and the tare deducted, saying he only wanted pay for the oats. Their sales of melons, tomatoes, corn, potatoes, squashes, green pease, etc., during the summer, in the different towns and mining-camps, bring in some $2000 to $3000. Their stock of horses and cattle is increasing fast, and with the benefits to be derived from good American stallions, and good bulls and cows, to be distributed to them under the stipulations of the treaty of 1863, they will rapidly increase in wealth."

In 1869 their reservation is still unsurveyed, and when the Indians claim that white settlers are establishing themselves inside the lines there is no way of proving it, and the agent says all he can do is to promise that "the white man's heart shall be better;" and thus the matter will rest until another disturbance arises, when the same complaints are made, and the same answers given as before—that "the white man's heart shall be better, and the boundary-line shall be surveyed."

Other treaty stipulations are still unfulfilled; and the non-treaty party, while entirely peaceable, is very strong, and immovably opposed to treaties.

In 1870, seven years after it was promised, the long deferred survey of the reservation was made. The superintendent and the agent both remonstrated, but in vain, against the manner in which it was done; and three years later a Board of Special Commissioners, appointed to inquire into the condition of the Indians in Idaho, examined the fence put up at that time, and reported that it was "a most scandalous fraud. It is a post-and-board fence. The posts are not well set. Much of the lumber is deficient in width and length. The posts are not dressed. The lumber laps at any joint where it may chance to meet, whether on the posts or between them, and the boards are not jointed on the posts where they meet; they are lapped and fastened generally with one nail, so that they are falling down rapidly. The lumber was cut on the reservation. The contract price of the fence was very high; the fencing done in places of no value to any one, for the reason that water cannot be had for irrigation. The Government cannot be a party to such frauds on the people who intrust it with their property."

In this year a commission was sent to Oregon to hold council with the band of Nez Percés occupying Wallowa Valley, in Oregon, "with a view to their removal, if practicable, to the Nez Percé Reservation in Idaho. They reported this removal to be impracticable, and the Wallowa Valley has been withdrawn from sale, and set apart for their use and occupation by Executive order."*

This commission report that one of the most troublesome questions in the way of the Government's control of Indian af-

---

* Report of the Secretary of the Interior for 1873.

fairs in Idaho is the contest between the Catholic and Protestant churches. This strife is a great detriment to the Indians. To illustrate this, they quote Chief Joseph's[5] reason for not wishing schools on his reservation. He was the chief of the non-treaty band of Nez Percés occupying the Wallowa Valley, in Oregon:

"Do you want schools and school-houses on the Wallowa Reservation?" asked the commissioners.

Joseph. "No, we do not want schools or school-houses on the Wallowa Reservation."

Com. "Why do you not want schools?"

Joseph. "They will teach us to have churches."

Com. "Do you not want churches?"

Joseph. "No, we do not want churches."

Com. "Why do you not want churches?"

Joseph. "They will teach us to quarrel about God, as the Catholics and Protestants do on the Nez Percé Reservation, and at other places. We do not want to learn that. We may quarrel with men sometimes about things on this earth, but we never quarrel about God. We do not want to learn that."

Great excitement prevailed among the settlers in Oregon at the cession of the Wallowa Valley to the Indians. The presence of United States soldiers prevented any outbreak; but the resentment of the whites was very strong, and threats were openly made that the Indians should not be permitted to occupy it; and in 1875 the Commissioner of Indian Affairs writes:

"The settlements made in the Wallowa Valley, which has for years been the pasture-ground of the large herds of horses owned by Joseph's band, will occasion more or less trouble between this band and the whites, until Joseph is induced or compelled to settle on his reservation."

It is only two years since this valley was set apart by Executive order for the use and occupation of these Indians; already

[5] Regarding the tragic Chief Joseph of the Nez Percés consult Lucullus V. McWhorter, *Hear Me My Chiefs!* (Caldwell, Idaho, 1952) and Chester A. Fee, *Chief Joseph* (New York, 1936).

the Department is contemplating "compelling" them to leave
it and go to the reservation in Idaho. There were stormy
scenes there also during this year. Suits were brought against
all the employés of the Lapwai Agency, and a claim set up for
all the lands of the agency, and for many of the Indian farms,
by one Langford, representing the old claim of the missionaries,
to whom a large tract of ground had been ceded some thirty
years before. He attempted to take forcible possession of the
place, and was ejected finally by military force, after the decision of the Attorney-general had been given that his claim
was invalid.

The Indian Bureau recommended a revocation of the executive order giving the Wallowa Valley to Joseph and his band.
In June of this year President Grant revoked the order, and
in the autumn a commission was sent out "to visit these Indians, with a view to secure their permanent settlement on the
reservation, their early entrance on a civilized life, and to adjust
the difficulties then existing between them and the settlers."

It is worth while to study with some care the reasons which
this commission gave to Chief Joseph why the Wallowa Valley, which had been given to him by Executive order in 1873,
must be taken away from him by Executive order in 1875:

"Owing to the coldness of the climate, it is not a suitable
location for an Indian reservation. * * * It is now in part settled by white squatters for grazing purposes. * * * The President claimed that he extinguished the Indian title to it by the
treaty of 1863. * * * It is embraced within the limits of the
State of Oregon. * * * The State of Oregon could not probably be induced to cede the jurisdiction of the valley to the
United States for an Indian reservation. * * * In the conflicts
which might arise in the future, as in the past, between him
and the whites, the President might not be able to justify or
defend him. * * * A part of the valley had already been surveyed and opened to settlement: * * * if, by some arrange·

ment, the white settlers in the valley could be induced to leave it, others would come."

To all these statements Joseph replied that he "asked nothing of the President. He was able to take care of himself. He did not desire Wallowa Valley as a reservation, for that would subject him and his band to the will of, and dependence on, another, and to laws not of their own making. He was disposed to live peaceably. He and his band had suffered wrong rather than do wrong. One of their number was wickedly slain by a white man during the last summer, but he would not avenge his death."

"The serious and feeling manner in which he uttered these sentiments was impressive," the commissioners say, and they proceeded to reply to him "that the President was not disposed to deprive him of any just right, or govern him by his individual will, but merely subject him to the same just and equal laws by which he himself as well as all his people were ruled."

What does it mean when commissioners sent by the President to induce a band of Indians to go on a reservation to live, tell them that they shall be subjected on that reservation "merely to the same just and equal laws" by which the President and "all his people are ruled?" And still more, what is the explanation of their being so apparently unaware of the enormity of the lie that they leave it on official record, signed by their names in full? It is only explained, as thousands of other things in the history of our dealings with the Indians are only to be explained, by the habitual indifference, carelessness, and inattention with which questions relative to Indian affairs and legislation thereon are handled and disposed of, in whatever way seems easiest and shortest for the time being. The members of this commission knew perfectly well that the instant Joseph and his band moved on to the reservation they became subject to laws totally different from those by which the President and "all his people were ruled," and neither "just" nor "equal:" laws forbidding them to go beyond certain bounds without a pass from the agent; laws making them really just as much prisoners as convicts in a prison—the only difference being that the reservation is an unwalled out-of-door prison; laws giving that agent power to summon military power at any moment, to enforce any command he might choose to lay on them, and to shoot them if they refused to obey.* "The same just and equal laws by which the President himself and all his people are ruled!" Truly it is a psychological phenomenon that four men should be found willing to leave it on record under their own signatures that they said this thing.

Farther on in the same report there is an enumeration of some of the experiences which the Nez Percés who are on the Idaho Reservation have had of the advantages of living there, and of the manner in which the Government has fulfilled its promises by which it induced them to go there; undoubtedly these were all as well known to Chief Joseph as to the commissioners. For twenty-two years he had had an opportunity to study the workings of the reservation policy. They say:

"During an interview held with the agent and the treaty Indians, for the purpose of ascertaining whether there were sufficient unoccupied tillable lands for Joseph's band on the reservation, and for the further purpose of securing their co-operation to aid us in inducing Joseph to come upon the reservation, facts were brought to our attention of a failure on the part of the Government to fulfil its treaty stipulations with these Indians. The commission therefore deem it their duty to call the attention of the Government to this subject.

"1st. Article second of the treaty of June 9th, 1863, provides that no white man—excepting such as may be employed by the

---

* Witness the murder of Big Snake at Fort Reno, Indian Territory, in the summer of 1879.

Indian Department—shall be permitted to reside upon the reservation without permission of the tribe, and the superintendent and the agent. Nevertheless, four white men are occupying or claiming large tracts on the reservation.

"It is clearly the duty of the Government to adjust and quiet these claims, and remove the parties from the reservation. Each day's delay to fulfil this treaty stipulation adds to the distrust of the Indians in the good faith of the Government.

" 2d. Article third of the same treaty of 1863 provides for the survey of the land suitable for cultivation into lots of twenty acres each ; while a survey is reported to have been early made, no measures were then, or have been since, taken to adjust farm limits to the lines of the surveyed lots.

" 3d. Rules and regulations for continuing the possession of these lots and the improvements thereon in the families of deceased Indians, have not been prescribed, as required by the treaty.

"4th. It is also provided that certificates or deeds for such tracts shall be issued to individual Indians.

" The failure of the Government to comply with this important provision of the treaty causes much uneasiness among the Indians, who are little inclined to spend their labor and means in improving ground held by the uncertain tenure of the pleasure of an agent.

" 5th. Article seventh of the treaty provides for a payment of four thousand six hundred and sixty-five dollars in gold coin to them for services and horses furnished the Oregon Mounted Volunteers in 1856. It is asserted by the Indians that this provision of the treaty has hitherto been disregarded by the Government."

The commissioners say that "every consideration of justice and equity, as well as expediency, demands from the Government a faithful and literal compliance with all its treaty obligations toward the Indians. A failure to do this is looked upon as bad faith, and can be productive of only bad results."

At last Chief Joseph consented to remove from the Wallowa Valley with his band, and go to the Lapwai Reservation. The incidents of the council in which this consent was finally wrung from him, are left on record in Chief Joseph's own words, in an article written by him (through an interpreter) and published in the *North American Review* in 1874. It is a remarkable contribution to Indian history.

It drew out a reply from General O. O. Howard, who called his paper "The true History of the Wallowa Campaign;" published in the *North American Review* two months after Chief Joseph's paper.

Between the accounts given by General Howard and by Chief Joseph of the events preceding the Nez Percé war, there are noticeable discrepancies.

General Howard says that he listened to the "oft-repeated dreamer nonsense of the chief, 'Too-hool-hool-suit,' with no impatience, but finally said to him : 'Twenty times over I hear that the earth is your mother, and about the chieftainship of the earth. I want to hear it no more.'"

Chief Joseph says: "General Howard lost his temper, and said 'Shut up! I don't want to hear any more of such talk.'

"Too-hool-hool-suit answered, 'Who are you, that you ask us to talk, and then tell me I sha'n't talk? Are you the Great Spirit? Did you make the world?'"

General Howard, quoting from his record at the time, says: "The rough old fellow, in his most provoking tone, says something in a short sentence, looking fiercely at me. The interpreter quickly says: 'He demands what person pretends to divide this land, and put me on it?' In the most decided voice I said, 'I am the man. I stand here for the President, and there is no spirit, bad or good, that will hinder me.   My orders are plain, and will be executed.' "

Chief Joseph says: " General Howard replied, ' You are an impudent fellow, and I will put you in the guard-house,' and then ordered a soldier to arrest him."

General Howard says: " After telling the Indians that this bad advice would be their ruin, I asked the chiefs to go with me to look at their land. ' The old man (Too-hool-hool-suit) shall not go. I will leave him with Colonel Perry.' He says, ' Do you want to scare me with reference to my body?' I said, ' I will leave your body with Colonel Perry.' I then arose and led him out of the council, and gave him into the charge of Colonel Perry."

Chief Joseph says: " Too-hool-hool-suit made no resistance. He asked General Howard, ' Is that your order? I don't care. I have expressed my heart to you. I have nothing to take back. I have spoken for my country. You can arrest me, but you cannot change me, or make me take back what I have said.' The soldiers came forward and seized my friend, and took him to the guard - house. My men whispered among themselves whether they should let this thing be done. I counselled them to submit. * * * Too-hool-hool-suit was prisoner for five days before he was released."

General Howard, it will be observed, does not use the word " arrested," but as he says, later, " Too-hool-hool-suit was released on the pledge of Looking-glass and White Bird, and on his own earnest promise to behave better," it is plain that Chief Joseph did not misstate the facts. This Indian chief, therefore, was put under military arrest, and confined for five days, for uttering what General Howard calls a " tirade " in a council to which the Indians had been asked to come for the purpose of consultation and expression of sentiment.

Does not Chief Joseph speak common-sense, as well as natural feeling, in saying, " I turned to my people and said, ' The arrest of Too-hool-hool-suit was wrong, but we will not resent the insult. We were invited to this council to express our hearts, and we have done so.'"

If such and so swift penalty as this, for "tirades" in council, were the law of our land, especially in the District of Columbia, it would be "no just cause of complaint" when Indians suffer it. But considering the frequency, length, and safety of "tirades" in all parts of America, it seems unjust not to permit Indians to deliver them. However, they do come under the head of "spontaneous productions of the soil;" and an Indian on a reservation is "invested with no such proprietorship" in anything which comes under that head.*

Chief Joseph and his band consented to move. Chief Joseph says: "I said in my heart that, rather than have war, I would give up my country. I would give up my father's grave. I would give up everything rather than have the blood of white men upon the hands of my people."

It was not easy for Joseph to bring his people to consent to move. The young men wished to fight. It has been told that, at this time, Chief Joseph rode one day through his village, with a revolver in each hand, saying he would shoot the first one of his warriors that resisted the Government. Finally, they gathered all the stock they could find, and began the move. A storm came, and raised the river so high that some of the cattle could not be taken across. Indian guards were put in charge of the cattle left behind. White men attacked these guards and took the cattle. After this Joseph could no longer restrain his men, and the warfare began, which lasted over two months. It was a masterly campaign on the part of the Indians. They were followed by General Howard; they had General Crook on their right, and General Miles in front, but they were not once hemmed in; and, at last, when they surrendered at Bear

* Annual Report of the Indian Commissioner for 1878, p. 60.

Paw Mountain, in the Montana Hills, it was not because they were beaten, but because, as Joseph says, "I could not bear to see my wounded men and women suffer any longer; we had lost enough already. * * * We could have escaped from Bear Paw Mountain if we had left our wounded, old women and children, behind. We were unwilling to do this. We had never heard of a wounded Indian recovering while in the hands of white men. * * * I believed General Miles, or I never would have surrendered. I have heard that he has been censured for making the promise to return us to Lapwai. He could not have made any other terms with me at that time. I could have held him in check until my friends came to my assistance, and then neither of the generals nor their soldiers would ever have left Bear Paw Mountain alive. On the fifth day I went to General Miles and gave up my gun, and said, 'From where the sun now stands, I will fight no more.' My people needed rest; we wanted peace."

The terms of this surrender were shamefully violated. Joseph and his band were taken first to Fort Leavenworth and then to the Indian Territory. At Leavenworth they were placed in the river bottom, with no water but the river water to drink.

"Many of my people sickened and died, and we buried them in this strange land," says Joseph. "I cannot tell how much my heart suffered for my people while at Leavenworth. The Great Spirit Chief who rules above seemed to be looking some other way, and did not see what was being done to my people."

Yet with a marvellous magnanimity, and a clear-headed sense of justice of which few men would be capable under the circumstances, Joseph says: "I believe General Miles would have kept his word if he could have done so. I do not blame him for what we have suffered since the surrender. I do not know who is to blame. We gave up all our horses, over eleven hundred, and all our saddles, over one hundred, and we have not heard from them since. Somebody has got our horses."

This narrative of Chief Joseph's is profoundly touching; a very Iliad of tragedy, of dignified and hopeless sorrow; and it stands supported by the official records of the Indian Bureau.

"After the arrival of Joseph and his band in Indian Territory, the bad effect of their location at Fort Leavenworth manifested itself in the prostration by sickness at one time of two hundred and sixty out of the four hundred and ten; and ' within a few months' in the death of ' more than one-quarter of the entire number.' "*

"It will be borne in mind that Joseph has never made a treaty with the United States, and that he has never surrendered to the Government the lands he claimed to own in Idaho. * * * Joseph and his followers have shown themselves to be brave men and skilful soldiers, who, with one exception, have observed the rules of civilized warfare. * * * These Indians were encroached upon by white settlers, on soil they believed to be their own, and when these encroachments became intolerable, they were compelled in their own estimation to take up arms."†

Chief Joseph and a remnant of his band are still in Indian Territory, waiting anxiously the result of the movement now being made by the Ponca chief, Standing Bear, and his friends and legal advisers, to obtain from the Supreme Court a decision which will extend the protection of the civil law to every Indian in the country.

Of the remainder of the Nez Percés (those who are on the Lapwai Reservation), the report of the Indian Bureau for 1879 is that they "support themselves entirely without subsistence from the Government; procure of their own accord, and at their own expense, wagons, harness, and other farming implements beyond the amount furnished by the Government under

---

* Annual Report of the Indian Commissioner for 1878, p. 33.
† Same Report, p. 34.

their treaty," and that "as many again as were taught were turned away from school for lack of room."

The Presbyterian Board of Foreign Missions has contributed during this year $1750 for missionary work among them, and the Indians themselves have raised $125.

Their reservation is thus described: "The majority of land comprising the reservation is a vast rolling prairie, affording luxuriant pasturage for thousands of their cattle and horses. The Clearwater River, flowing as it does directly through the reserve, branching out in the North, Middle, and South Forks, greatly benefits their locations that they have taken in the valleys lying between such river and the bluffs of the higher land, forming in one instance—at Kaimaih—one of the most picturesque locations to be found in the whole North-west. Situated in a valley on either side of the South Fork, in length about six miles, varying in width from one-half to two miles; in form like a vast amphitheatre, surrounded on all sides by nearly perpendicular bluffs rising two thousand feet in height, it forms one of the prettiest valleys one can imagine. A view from the bluff reveals a living panorama, as one sees the vast fields of waving grain surrounding well-built and tasty cottages adorned with porches, and many of the conveniences found among industrious whites. The sight would lead a stranger, not knowing of its inhabitance by Indians, to inquire what prosperous white settlement was located here. It is by far the most advanced in the ways of civilization and progress of any in the Territory, if not on the coast."

How long will the white men of Idaho permit Indians to occupy so fair a domain as this? The small cloud, no larger than a man's hand, already looms on their horizon. The closing paragraph of this (the last) report from the Nez Percés is:

"Some uneasiness is manifest about stories set afloat by renegade whites, in relation to their treatment at the expiration of their treaty next July, but I have talked the matter over, and they will wait patiently to see the action on the part of the Government. They are well civilized; but one mistake on the part of the Government at this time would destroy the effects of the past thirty years' teachings. Give them time and attention; they will astonish their most zealous friends in their progress toward civilization."

CHAPTER V.

THE word Sioux[6] is a contraction from the old French word "Nadouessioux," or "Enemies," the name given by the French traders to this most powerful and warlike of all the North-western tribes. They called themselves "Dakota," or "many in one," because so many bands under different names were joined together. At the time of Captain Carver's travels among the North American Indians there were twelve known bands of these "Nadouwessies." They entertained the captain most hospitably for seven months during the winter of 1766–'7 ; adopted him as one of their chiefs ; and when the time came for him to depart, three hundred of them accompanied him for a distance on his journey, and took leave with expressions of friendship for him, and good-will toward the Great Father, the English king, of whom he had told them. The chiefs wished him to say to the king "how much we desire that traders may be sent to abide among us with such things as we need, that the hearts of our young men, our wives, and children may be made glad. And may peace subsist between us so long as the sun, the moon, the earth, and the waters shall endure ;" and "acquaint the Great King how much the Nadouwessies wish to be counted among his good children."

Nothing in all the history of the earliest intercourse between the friendly tribes of North American Indians and the Europeans coming among them is more pathetic than the accounts of their simple hospitality, their unstinted invitations, and their

[6] A basic source on the Sioux is L. E. Textor, *Official Relations between the United States and the Sioux Indians* (Palo Alto, 1896). See also C. M. Oehler, *The Great Sioux Uprising* (New York, 1959) and Royal B. Hassrick, *The Sioux: Life and Customs of a Warrior Society* (Norman, Oklahoma, 1964).

guileless expressions of desire for a greater knowledge of the white men's ways.

When that saintly old bigot, Father Hennepin,[7] sailed up the Illinois River, in 1680, carrying his "portable chapel," chalice, and chasuble, and a few holy wafers "in a steel box, shut very close," going to teach the savages "the knowledge of the Captain of Heaven and Earth, and to use fire-arms, and several other things relating to their advantage," the Illinois were so terrified that, although they were several thousand strong, they took to flight "with horrid cries and howlings." On being reassured by signs and words of friendliness, they slowly returned—some, however, not until three or four days had passed. Then they listened to the good man's discourses with "great attention; afterward gave a great shout for joy," and "expressed a great gratitude;" and, the missionaries being footsore from long travel, the kindly creatures fell to rubbing their legs and feet "with oil of bears, and grease of wild oxen, which after much travel is an incomparable refreshment; and presented us some flesh to eat, putting the three first morsels into our mouths with great ceremonies."

It was a pity that Father Hennepin had no more tangible benefit than the doctrine of the "efficacy of the Sacraments" to communicate to the hospitable Illinois in return for their healing ointments. Naturally they did not appreciate this, and he proceeded on his way disheartened by their "brutish stupidity," but consoling himself, however, with the thought of the infants he had baptized. Hearing of the death of one of them, he says he is "glad it had pleased God to take this little Christian out of the world," and he attributed his own "preservation amidst the greatest dangers" afterward to "the care he took for its baptism." Those dangers were, indeed, by no means inconsiderable, as he and his party were taken prisoners by a roaming party of these Indians, called in the Father's quaint old book "Nadouwessians." He was forced to accompany

[7] A relatively modern edition of Father Louis Hennepin's work, reprinted from the second London printing of 1698, is *A New Discovery of a Vast Country* (Chicago, 1903).

them on their expeditions, and was in daily danger of being murdered by the more riotous and hostile members of the band. He found these savages on the whole "good-natured men, affable, civil, and obliging," and he was indebted for his life to the good-will of one of the chiefs, who protected him again and again at no inconsiderable danger to himself. The only evidence of religion among the Nadouwessies which he mentions is that they never began to smoke without first holding the pipe up to the sun, saying, "Smoke, sun!" They also offered to the sun the best part of every beast they killed, carrying it afterward to the cabin of their chief; from which Father Hennepin concluded that they had "a religious veneration for the sun."

The diplomatic relations between the United States Government and the Sioux began in the year 1815. In that year and the year following we made sixteen "treaties" of peace and friendship with different tribes of Indians—treaties demanding no cessions of land beyond the original grants which had been made by these tribes to the English, French, or Spanish governments, but confirming those to the United States; promising "perpetual peace," and declaring that "every injury or act of hostility committed by one or other of the contracting parties shall be mutually forgiven and forgot." Three of these treaties were made with bands of the Sioux—one of them with "the Sioux of the Leaf, the Sioux of the Broad Leaf, and the Sioux who shoot in the Pine-tops."

In 1825 four more treaties were made with separate Sioux bands. By one of those treaties—that of Prairie du Chien—boundaries were defined between the Chippewas and the Sioux, and it was hoped that their incessant feuds might be brought to an end. This hostility had continued unabated from the time of the earliest travellers in the country, and the Sioux had been slowly but steadily driven south and west by the victorious Chippewas. A treaty could not avail very much toward keeping peace between such ancient enemies as these. Fighting went on as before; and white traders, being exposed to the attacks of all war-parties, suffered almost more than the Indians themselves. The Government consoled itself for this spectacle of bloody war, which it was powerless to prevent, by the thought that the Indians would "probably fight on until some one or other of the tribes shall become too reduced and feeble to carry on the war, when it will be lost as a separate power" —an equivocal bit of philosophizing which was unequivocally stated in these precise words in one of the annual reports of the War Department.

In the third Article of the next treaty, also at Prairie du Chien, in 1830, began the trouble which has been from that day to this a source of never ending misunderstanding and of many fierce outbreaks on the part of the Sioux. Four of the bands by this article ceded and relinquished to the United States "forever" a certain tract of country between the Mississippi and the Des Moines River. In this, and in a still further cession, two other bands of Sioux, who were not fully represented at the council, must join; also, some four or five other tribes. Landed and "undivided" estate, owned in common by dozens of families, would be a very difficult thing to parcel out and transfer among white men to-day, with the best that fair intentions and legal skill combined could do; how much more so in those days of unsurveyed forests, unexplored rivers, owned and occupied in common by dozens of bands of wild and ignorant Indians, to be communicated with only by interpreters. Misconstructions and disputes about boundaries would have been inevitable, even if there had been all possible fairmindedness and good-will on both sides; but in this case there was only unfairmindedness on one side, and unwillingness on the other. All the early makers of treaties with the Indians congratulated themselves and the United States on the getting of acres of valuable land by the million for next to nothing, and, as years went on, openly lamented that "the Indians were beginning to find out what lands were worth;" while the Indians, anxious, alarmed, hostile at heart, seeing themselves harder and harder pressed on all sides, driven "to provide other sources for supplying their wants besides those of hunting, which must soon entirely fail them,"* yielded mile after mile with increasing sense of loss, which they were powerless to prevent, and of resentment which it would have been worse than impolitic for them to show.

The first annuities promised to the Sioux were promised by this treaty—$3000 annually for ten years to the Yankton and Santee bands; to the other four, $2000. The Yankton and Santee bands were to pay out of their annuity $100 yearly to the Otoes, because part of some land which was reserved for the half-breeds of the tribe had originally belonged to the Otoes. "A blacksmith, at the expense of the United States; also, instruments for agricultural purposes; and iron and steel to the amount of $700 annually for ten years to some of the bands, and to the amount of $400 to the others; also, $3000 a year 'for educational purposes,' and $3000 in presents distributed at the time," were promised them.

It was soon after these treaties that the artist Catlin[8] made his famous journeys among the North American Indians, and gave to the world an invaluable contribution to their history, perpetuating in his pictures the distinctive traits of their faces and their dress, and leaving on record many pages of unassailable testimony as to their characteristics in their native state. He spent several weeks among the Sioux, and says of them: "There is no tribe on the continent of finer looking men, and few tribes who are better and more comfortably clad and supplied with the necessaries of life. * * * I have travelled several years already among these people, and I have not had my scalp

---

* Treaty of Prairie du Chien.

[8] A modern, available edition of his work, appropriately illustrated, is George Catlin, *Episodes From Life Among the Indians and Last Rambles* (Norman, Oklahoma, 1959).

taken, nor a blow struck me, nor had occasion to raise my hand against an Indian; nor has my property been stolen as yet to my knowledge to the value of a shilling, and that in a country where no man is punishable by law for the crime of stealing. * * * That the Indians in their native state are drunken, is false, for they are the only temperance people, literally speaking, that ever I saw in my travels, or expect to see. If the civilized world are startled at this, it is the fact that they must battle with, not with me. These people manufacture no spirituous liquor themselves, and know nothing of it until it is brought into their country, and tendered to them by Christians.

"That these people are naked, is equally untrue, and as easily disproved with the paintings I have made, and with their beautiful costumes which I shall bring home. I shall be able to establish the fact that many of these people dress not only with clothes comfortable for any latitude, but that they dress also with some considerable taste and elegance. * * * Nor am I quite sure that they are entitled to the name of 'poor' who live in a country of boundless green fields, with good horses to ride; where they are all joint tenants of the soil together; where the Great Spirit has supplied them with an abundance of food to eat."

Catlin found six hundred families of the Sioux camped at one time around Fort Pierre, at the mouth of the Teton River, on the west bank of the Missouri. There were some twenty bands, each with their chief, over whom was one superior chief, called Ha-won-je-tah (the One Horn), whose portrait is one of the finest in Catlin's book. This chief took his name, "One Horn," from a little shell which he wore always on his neck. This shell had descended to him from his father, and he said "he valued it more than anything which he possessed: affording a striking instance of the living affection which these people often cherish for the dead, inasmuch as he chose to carry this name through life in preference to many others and more honorable ones he had a right to have taken from different battles and exploits of his extraordinary life." He was the fleetest man in the tribe; "could run down a buffalo, which he had often done on his own legs, and drive his arrow to the heart."

This chief came to his death, several years later, in a tragic way. He had been in some way the accidental cause of the death of his only son—a very fine youth—and so great was the anguish of his mind at times that he became insane. In one of these moods he mounted his favorite war-horse, with his bow and arrows in his hand, and dashed off at full speed upon the prairies, repeating the most solemn oath that he would slay the first living thing that fell in his way, be it man or beast, friend or foe. No one dared follow him, and after he had been absent an hour or two his horse came back to the village with two arrows in its body covered with blood. Fears of the most serious kind were now entertained for the fate of the chief, and a party of warriors immediately mounted their horses and retraced the animal's tracks to the place of the tragedy, where they found the body of their chief horribly mangled and gored by a buffalo-bull, whose carcass was stretched by the side of him.

A close examination of the ground was then made by the Indians, who ascertained by the tracks that their unfortunate chief, under his unlucky resolve, had met a buffalo-bull in the season when they are very stubborn, and unwilling to run from any one, and had incensed the animal by shooting a number of arrows into him, which had brought him into furious combat. The chief had then dismounted and turned his horse loose, having given it a couple of arrows from his bow, which sent it home at full speed, and then had thrown away his bow and quiver, encountering the infuriated animal with his knife alone, and the desperate battle had resulted in the death of both.

Many of the bones of the chief were broken, and his huge antagonist lay dead by his side, weltering in blood from a hundred wounds made by the chief's long and two-edged knife.

Had the provisions of these first treaties been fairly and promptly carried out, there would have been living to-day among the citizens of Minnesota thousands of Sioux families, good and prosperous farmers and mechanics, whose civilization would have dated back to the treaty of Prairie du Chien.

In looking through the records of the expenditures of the Indian Bureau for the six years following this treaty, we find no mention of any specific provisions for the Sioux in the matter of education. The $3000 annually which the treaty promised should be spent " on account of the children of the said tribes and bands," is set down as expended on the "Choctaw Academy," which was in Kentucky. A very well endowed institution that must have been, if we may trust to the fiscal reports of the Indian Bureau. In the year 1836 there were set down as expended on this academy: On account of the Miamis, $2000; the Pottawattomies, $5000; the Sacs, Foxes, and others, $3000; the Choctaws, $10,000; the Creeks, east, $3000; the Cherokees, west, $2000; the Florida Indians, $1000; the Quapaws, $1000; the Chickasaws, $3000; the Creeks, $1000: being a total of $31,000.

There were in this year one hundred and fifty-six pupils at the Choctaw Academy, sixteen of them being from the Sacs, Foxes, Sioux, and others represented in the Treaty of Prairie du Chien of 1830. For the education of these sixteen children, therefore, these tribes paid $3000 a year. The Miamis paid more in proportion, having but four youths at school, and $2000 a year charged to them. The Pottawattomies, on a treaty provision of $5000, educated twenty.

In 1836 Congress appropriated $2000 " for the purpose of extinguishing the Indian title between the State of Missouri and the Missouri River. The land owned here by the Indians was a long, narrow belt of country, separated from the rest of the Indian country by the Missouri River. The importance of it to the State of Missouri was evident—an "obvious convenience and necessity." The citizens of Missouri made representations to this effect; and though the President is said to have been "unwilling to assent, as it would be in disregard of the guarantee given to the Indians in the Treaty of Prairie du Chien, and might be considered by them as the first step in a series of efforts to obtain possession of their new country," he nevertheless consented that the question of such a cession should be submitted to them. Accordingly, negotiations were opened, and nearly all the Indians who had rights in these lands, "seeing that from their local position they could never be made available for Indian purposes," relinquished them.*

In 1837 the Government invited deputations of chiefs from many of the principal tribes to come to Washington. It was "believed to be important to exhibit" to them "the strength of the nation they would have to contend with" if they ventured to attack our borders, "and at the same time to impress upon them the advantages which flow from civilization." Among these chiefs came thirty chiefs and headmen of the Sioux; and, being duly "impressed," as was most natural, concluded treaties by which they ceded to the United States "all their land east of the Mississippi River, and all their islands in the same." These chiefs all belonged to the Medawakanton band, "community of the Mysterious Lakes."

The price of this cession was $300,000, to be invested for them, and the interest upon this sum, at five per cent., to be paid to them "annually forever;" $110,000 to be distributed among the persons of mixed blood in the tribe; $90,000 to be

* For this relinquishment the Government gave to the Lower Sioux presents to the amount of $400, and to the upper bands $530 in goods.

devoted to paying the just debts of the tribe; $8230 to be expended annually for twenty years in stock, implements, on physicians, farmers, blacksmiths, etc.; $10,000 worth of tools, cattle, etc., to be given to them immediately, "to enable them to break up and improve their lands;" $5300 to be expended annually for twenty years in food for them, "to be delivered at the expense of the United States;" $6000 worth of goods to be given to them on their arrival at St. Louis.

In 1838 the Indian Bureau reports that all the stipulations of this treaty have been complied with, "except those which appropriate $8230 to be expended annually in the purchase of medicines, agricultural implements, and stock; and for the support of a physician, farmers, and blacksmiths," and "bind the United States to supply these Sioux as soon as practicable with agricultural implements, tools, cattle, and such other articles as may be useful to them, to an amount not exceeding $10,000, to enable them to break up and improve their lands." The fulfilment or non-fulfilment of these stipulations has been left to the discretion of the agent; and the agent writes that it "must be obvious to any one that a general personal intercourse" on his part "is impracticable," and that "his interviews with many of the tribes must result from casualty and accident." This was undoubtedly true; but it did not, in all probability, occur to the Indians that it was a good and sufficient reason for their not receiving the $18,000 worth of goods promised.

Five thousand seven hundred and eighty-nine dollars were expended the next year under this provision of the treaty, and a few Indians, who "all labored with the hoe," raised their own crops without assistance. Six thousand bushels of corn in all were housed for the winter; but the experiment of turning hunters into farmers in one year was thought not to be, on the whole, an encouraging one. The "peculiar habits of indolence, and total disregard and want of knowledge of the value and uses of time and property," the agent says, "almost forbid hope." A more reasonable view of the situation would have seen in it very great hope. That out of five hundred warriors a few score should have been already found willing to work was most reassuring, and promised well for the future of the tribe.

For the next ten years affairs went on badly with the Sioux; they were continually attacked by the Chippewas, Ottawas, and others, and continually retaliated. The authorities took a sensible view of this state of things, as being the easiest way of securing the safety of the whites. "So long as they (the Indians) are at war with each other they will not feel a disposition to disturb the peace and safety of our exposed frontier settlements," wrote Governor Dodge, in 1840.

Whiskey traders flocked faster and faster into the neighborhood; fur traders, also, found it much more for their interest to trade with drunken Indians than with sober ones, and the Sioux grew rapidly demoralized. Their annuities were in arrears; yet this almost seemed less a misfortune than a blessing, since both money, goods, and provisions were so soon squandered for whiskey.

In 1842 several of the bands were reduced to a state of semi-starvation by the failure of corn crops, and also by the failure of the Senate to ratify a treaty they had made with Governor Doty in 1841.* Depending on the annuities promised in this treaty, they had neglected to make their usual provisions for the winter. Frosts, which came in June, and drought, which followed in July, combined to ruin their crops. For several years the water had been rapidly decreasing in all the lakes and streams north-west of Traverse de Sioux: the musk-rat ponds, from which the Indians used to derive considerable revenue, had dried up, and the musk-rats had gone, nobody knew where; the beaver, otter, and other furry creatures had

---

* Never ratified.

been hunted down till they were hard to find; the buffalo had long since been driven to new fields, far distant. Many of the Indians were too poor to own horses on which to hunt. They were two hundred miles from the nearest place where corn could be obtained, even if they had money to pay for it. Except for some assistance from the Government, they would have died by hundreds in the winter of this year.

In 1849 the "needs" of the white settlers on the east side of the Mississippi made it imperative that the Sioux should be again removed from their lands. "The desirable portions of Minnesota east of the Mississippi were already so occupied by a white population as to seem to render it absolutely necessary to obtain without delay a cession from the Indians on the west side of the river, for the accommodation of our citizens emigrating to that quarter, a large portion of whom would probably be compelled to precipitate themselves on that side of the Mississippi."

Commissioners were accordingly sent to treat with the Indians owning these desired lands. In the instructions given to these commissioners there are some notable sentences: "Though the proposed purchase is estimated to contain some twenty millions of acres, and some of it no doubt of excellent quality," there are "sound reasons why it is comparatively valueless to the Indians, and a large price should not be paid for it." Alive to the apparent absurdity of the statement that lands which are "absolutely necessary" for white farmers are "comparatively valueless" to Indians whom the Government is theoretically making every effort to train into farmers, and who have for the last ten years made appreciable progress in that direction, the commissioner adds, "With respect to its being valuable to the United States, it is more so for the purpose of making room for our emigrating citizens than for any other; and only a small part of it is now actually necessary for that object. * * * The extent of the proposed cession should be no

criterion of the amount that should be paid for it. On a full
consideration of the whole matter, it is the opinion of this office that from two to two and a half cents an acre would be an
ample equivalent for it." Some discretion is left to the commissioners as to giving more than this if the Indians are "not
satisfied;" but any such increase of price must be "based on
such evidence and information as shall fully satisfy the President and Senate."*

Reading farther on in these instructions, we come at last to
the real secret of this apparent niggardliness on the part of the
Government. It is not selfishness at all; it is the purest of
philanthropy. The Government has all along been suffering
in mind from two conflicting desires—"the desire to give these
Indians an equivalent for their possessions," and, on the other
hand, "the well-ascertained fact that no greater curse can be
inflicted on a tribe so little civilized as the Sioux than to have
large sums of money coming to them as annuities." * * * On
the whole, the commissioner says that we are called on, "as a
matter of humanity and duty toward this helpless race, to make
every exertion in our power not to place much money at their
discretion." The Government is beginning very well in this direction, it must be admitted, when it proposes to pay for Mississippi Valley lands in Minnesota only two and a half cents per
acre. "Humanity and duty" allied could hardly do more at
one stroke than that.

We cannot ascribe to the same philanthropy, however, the
withholding from 1837 to 1850 the $3000 a year which the
treaty of 1837 provided should be expended "annually" as the
President might direct, and which was not expended at all, because President after President directed that it should be ap-

---

* "Chrysostom was of opinion, and not without reason, that, in contracts,
as often as we strive earnestly to buy anything for less than it is worth,
or to have more than our just measure or weight, there was in that fact a
kind of theft."—GROTIUS on Contracts.

plied to educational purposes; and there being no evident and
easy way of expending it in that manner, it was allowed to
accumulate, until in 1850 it amounted, according to the report
of Governor Ramsey, of Minnesota, to $50,000. The governor
also thinks better than the United States Government does of
the country to be relinquished this year by the Sioux. He
says that it will be "settled with great rapidity, possessing as
it does from its situation considerable prospective commercial
as well as agricultural advantages." It was evidently very
cheap at two and a half cents an acre.

In this same code of instructions by the Indian Bureau there
is a record of another instance of the Government's disregard
of treaty stipulations. At the time of the treaty of Prairie du
Chien, in 1850, the Sioux chiefs had requested that a certain
tract be set apart and bestowed upon the half-breeds of their
nation. This was provided for in the ninth Article of that
treaty; but the Government refused to give to the half-breeds
any title to this land, except "in the same manner as other Indian titles are held." It was agreed, however, that the President might "assign to any of said half-breeds, to be held by
him or them in fee-simple, any portion of said tract not exceeding a section of six hundred and forty acres to an individual."
This tract of land was known as the "Half-breed Reservation
on Lake Tepin."

The half-breeds had made almost unintermitting efforts to
have these assignments made, but the Government had as constantly refused to do it. The Indian Bureau now assigns two
reasons why this treaty stipulation was never fulfilled: 1st,
that "the half-breeds, or most of them, would be speculated
upon by designing persons, and cheated out of their reservations;" 2d, that, "on account of the quality of the lands, some
would necessarily have much better reservations than others,
which would engender dissatisfaction and heart-burning among
themselves as well as against the United States." The Bureau

felicitates itself that "the only title they now have to this land, therefore, is that by which other Indians hold their lands, viz., the occupant or usufruct right, and this they enjoy by the permission of the United States." Such being the case, and as the Government would probably never find it expedient and advisable to make the assignment referred to, this tract, whatever may be the character of the land, must be and would continue comparatively worthless to them.

Nevertheless, it appears that in 1841 one of the three treaties made with the Sioux, but not ratified, was with these very half-breeds for this same "valueless" tract of 384,000 acres of land; that they were to be paid $200,000 for it, and also to be paid for all the improvements they had made on it; and that the treaty commissioners are still instructed "to allow them for it now whatever sum the commissioners deem it to be" fairly worth; "under no circumstances," however, "to exceed the sum stipulated in 1841." Putting this all into plain English, it simply means that in 1830 the Government promised to let a band of men take out tracts of land in fee-simple, and settle down like other men on their homesteads; that for ten years the men begged to do so, and were refused; that at the end of ten years, thinking there was no hope of anything better, they agreed to sell the whole tract back to the Government for $200,000; that this bargain, also, the Government did not fulfil (the treaties never being ratified), and nine years later was found congratulating itself on the fact that, by reason of all these unfulfilled agreements, the land was still "held only in the same manner as other Indian titles are held"—*i. e.*, not "held" at all—only used on sufferance of the Government, and could be taken possession of at any time at the Government's pleasure. (This matter was supposed to be finally settled in 1854 by a law of Congress; but in 1856 the thing appears to have been still unsettled. A commission had been sent out to investigate it, and the report was that "the subject has been one of some difficulty and intricacy; but the final report of the commissioners has just been received, and steps will be taken at once to cause the scrip to issue to the parties entitled thereto.")

A little farther on in this same notable document is a mention of another tract, of which it is now "desirable to extinguish the title." This was set apart by the tenth Article of that same old treaty for the half-breeds of the Omahas, Otoes, Iowas, and Yankton and Santee Sioux. This contains about 143,000 acres, but is "supposed to be of much less value than that on Lake Tepin :" much less value than " valueless ;" but the "amount to be paid for it is left to the discretion" of the commissioners.

At this time the bands of the Medewakanton Sioux were occupying a tract of over two hundred miles along the west shore of the Mississippi, reaching also some twenty-five miles up the St. Peter's. The Yanktons, Santees, and other bands lived high up the St. Peter's, reaching over into the lands west of the Missouri, out of reach of ordinary facilities of intercourse. These bands were often in great distress for food, owing to the failure of the buffalo. They never lost an occasion to send imploring messages to the Great Father, urging him to help them. They particularly ask for hoes, that they may plant corn. In his report for 1850 the superintendent of the territory embracing these Indians says: "The views of most of those who have lived the longest among the Indians agree in one respect—that is, that no great or beneficial change can take place in their condition until the General Government has made them amenable to local laws—laws which will punish the evil-disposed, and secure the industrious in their property and individual rights."

Superintendents, agents, commissioners, secretaries, all reiteratedly recommending this one simple and necessary step toward civilization—the Indians themselves by hundreds imploring for titles to their farms, or at least " hoes "—why did the United States Government keep on and on in its obstinate way, feeding the Indian in gross and reckless improvidence with one hand, plundering him with the other, and holding him steadily down at the level of his own barbarism? Nay, forcing him below it by the newly added vices of gambling and drunkenness, and yet all the while boasting of its desire to enlighten, instruct, and civilize him. It is as inexplicable as it is infamous: a phenomenal thing in the history of the world.

In the summer of 1851 the desired treaties were made, the upper and lower bands of Sioux being treated with separately at Traverse de Sioux and at Mendota. The upper bands were soon disposed of, though "some few of them, having been taught to read," had become impressed with the idea that their country was of immense value, and at first demanded six million dollars for the lands to be ceded. The treaty with the lower bands—the Medawakantons and Wahpacootas—was "exceedingly difficult of attainment" on account of, firstly, "their proximity to the flourishing settlements on the east side of the Mississippi producing necessarily frequent contact with the whites, whose ideas of the great value of the country had been imparted to these Indians; secondly, their great experience in Indian diplomacy, being in the enjoyment already of liberal annuities under former stipulations"—all these things rendered them as "indifferent to the making of another treaty at present as the whites on their borders were anxious that their lands should he acquired." In consequence of this indomitable common-sense on the part of the Indians the sessions of the commissioners were tedious and long; not until a month had passed did they prevail on these Indians to sign away the coveted lands, "the garden-spot of the Mississippi Valley," and they were obliged to more than treble the number of cents per acre which they had been instructed to pay. For thirty-five millions of acres of land they agreed to pay nominally $3,075,000, which would be between eight and nine cents an acre. But as

$2,500,000 was to be held in trust, and only the interest at five per cent. to be paid to the Indians, and this only for the term of fifty years, at which time the principal was to revert to the Government, it will be easily reckoned that the Indians would receive, all told, only about six and one-quarter cents an acre. And taking into account the great value of the relinquished lands, and the price the Government would undoubtedly obtain for them, it will be readily conceded that Governor Ramsey was not too sanguine when he stated, in his report to the Interior Department, that the "actual cost to the Government of this magnificent purchase is only the sum paid in hand" ($575,000).

The governor says that it was "by no means the purpose" of the commission "to act other than justly and generously toward the Indians;" that "a continuation of the payment of large sums of interest annually would do them no further good" after fifty years had expired, and would be "inconsistent with sound governmental policy." He says that the Dakota nation, although warlike, is "friendly to the whites," and that it may be reasonably expected that, "by a judicious expenditure of the civilization and improvement funds provided for in these treaties," they will soon take the lead "in agriculture and other industrial pursuits."

One of the provisions of this treaty forbade the introduction of ardent spirits into the new reservation. This was put in in accordance with the "earnest desire" of the chiefs, who requested that "some stringent measures should be taken by the Government to exclude all kinds of liquors from their new home."

By this treaty the four great bands of Minnesota Sioux were all to be "consolidated together on one reservation in the upper part of the Mississippi Valley." This region was thought to be "sufficiently remote to guarantee" them against any pressure from the white population for many years to come. Farms were to be opened for them, mills and schools to be established,

and dwelling-houses erected.   They were to have now a chance
to own "that domestic country called home, with all the living
sympathies and all the future hopes and projects which people
it."   From this time "a new era was to be dated in the history of the Dakotas: an era full of brilliant promise."   The
tract of territory relinquished by them was "larger than the
State of New York, fertile and beautiful beyond description,"
far the best part of Minnesota.   It is "so far diversified in natural advantages that its productive powers may be considered
almost inexhaustible. * * * Probably no tract on the surface of
the globe is equally well watered. * * * A large part is rich
arable land; portions are of unsurpassed fertility, and eminent-
ly adapted to the production in incalculable quantities of the
cereal grains.   The boundless plains present inexhaustible fields
of pasturage, and the river bottoms are richer than the banks
of the Nile.   In the bowels of the earth there is every indication of extensive mineral fields."

It would seem that the assertion made only a few lines before this glowing paragraph—"to the Indians themselves the
broad regions which have been ceded are of inconsiderable
value"—could not be true.   It would seem that for eight thousand people, who, according to this same writer, "have outlived
in a great degree the means of subsistence of the hunter
state," and must very soon "resort to the pursuits of agriculture," nothing could have been more fortunate than to have
owned and occupied thirty-five millions of acres of just such
land as this.

They appear to be giving already some evidence of a disposition to turn this land to account.   The reports from the different farms and schools show progress in farming industry
and also in study.   The farming is carried on with difficulty,
because there are only a few carts and ploughs, which must be
used in turn by the different farmers, and therefore must come
to some quite too late to be of use, and there is much quarrel-

ling among them owing to this trouble. Nevertheless, these bands have raised over four thousand bushels of corn in the year. There is also a great opposition to the schools, because the Indians have been told that the accumulated fifty thousand dollars which is due to them would be paid to them in cash if it were not for the schools. Nevertheless, education is slowly progressing; in this year fifty copies of a little missionary paper called *The Dakota Friend* were subscribed for in the one mission station of Lac qui Parle, and sixty scholars were enrolled at the school. The blacksmith at St. Peter's reports that he has made during the year 2506 pieces of one sort and another for the Indians, and repaired 1430 more. Evidently a community keeping blacksmiths so busy as this are by no means wholly idle themselves.

It is worth while to dwell upon these seemingly trivial details at this point in the history of the Minnesota Sioux, because they are all significant to mark the point in civilization they had already reached, and the disposition they had already shown toward industry before they were obliged to submit to their first great removal. Their condition at the end of two years from the ratification of these treaties is curtly told in the official reports of the Indian Bureau:

"The present situation of that portion of the Sioux Indians parties to the treaties of July 23d and August 5th, 1851, is peculiar, unfortunate, and to them must prove extremely injurious. By these treaties they reluctantly parted with a very large extent of valuable country, which it was of the greatest importance to the Government to acquire. An insignificant portion of it near its western boundary, not deemed necessary or desirable for a white population for many years, if at all, was agreed to be reserved and assigned to them for their future residence. The Senate amended the treaties, striking out this provision, allowing ten cents an acre in lieu of the reservations, and requiring the President, with the assent of the Indians, if

they agreed to the amendments, to assign them such tracts of
country, beyond the limits of that ceded, as might be satisfactory for their future home.   To the amendments was appended
a proviso 'that the President may, by the consent of the Indians, vary the conditions aforesaid, if deemed expedient.'
The Indians were induced to agree to the amendments ; ' confiding in the justice, liberality, and humanity of the President
and the Congress of the United States, that such tracts of
country will be set apart for their future occupancy and home
as will be to them acceptable and satisfactory.'   Thus, not
only was the assent of the Indians made necessary to a country being assigned to them without the limits of that ceded,
but, by the authority given to the President to vary the conditions of the amendments to the treaties, he was empowered,
with the consent of the Indians, to place them upon the designated reservations, or upon any other portion of the ceded territory, ' if deemed expedient.'

    " To avoid collisions and difficulties between the Indians and
the white population which rapidly commenced pouring into
the ceded country, it became necessary that the former should
vacate at least a large portion of it without delay, while there
was neither the time nor the means to make the requisite
explorations to find a suitable location for them beyond the
limits of the cession.

    " Under these pressing and embarrassing circumstances the
late President determined to permit them to remain five years
on the designated reservations, if they were willing to accept
this alternative.   They assented, and many of them have been
already removed.   However unavoidable this arrangement, it
is a most unfortunate one.   The Indians are fully aware of its
temporary character, and of the uncertainty as to their future
position, and will consequently be disinclined and deterred
from any efforts to make themselves comfortable and improve
their condition.   The inevitable result must be that, at the end

of the time limited, they will be in a far worse condition than now, and the efforts and expenditures of years to infuse into them a spirit of improvement will all have been in vain.

"The large investments in mills, farms, mechanic shops, and other improvements required by the treaties to be made for their benefit, will be entirely wasted if the Indians are to remain on their reservations only during the prescribed five years. At the very period when they would begin to reap the full advantage of these beneficial provisions they would have to remove. Another unfortunate feature of this arrangement, if temporary, is that the Indians will have expended the considerable sums set apart in the treaties for the expenses of their removal to a permanent home, and for subsistence until they could otherwise provide it, leaving nothing for these important and necessary purposes in the event of another emigration. In view of these facts and considerations, no time should be lost in determining upon some final and permanent arrangement in regard to them."

The Governor of Minnesota also writes at this time: "The doubtful tenure by which this tribe hold their supposed reservation is well understood by their chiefs and headmen, and is beginning to give deep dissatisfaction, and throwing daily more and more obstacles in the way of their removal. This reservation will not be wanted for white men for many years.

"There is not wood, or timber, or coal sufficient for the purposes of civilization, except immediately on the St. Peter's and its tributaries. From near the vicinity of the new agency there commences a vast prairie of more than one hundred miles in extent, entirely destitute of timber, and I feel confident that we never shall be able to keep any very large number of them at their new agency, or near there.

"Already the fund set apart for the removal and subsistence the first year of the Sissetons and Wah-pa-tons has been expended, and all their provisions eaten up. Seventeen thousand dollars and upward have been expended by Governor Ramsey, and one year in advance of the time fixed by the treaty for their removal. This expenditure was made while he was getting them to sign the Senate amendments to the treaty of 1851, which they were very reluctant to do, and which not more than half the chiefs have signed. These Indians want the Government to confirm this reservation to them. I would recommend that this be done as the only means to satisfy them, and humanity demands it."

Here is a picture of a helpless people! Forced to give up the "garden-spot of the State," and accept in its stead an "insignificant tract, on the greater part of which there is not wood, or timber, or coal sufficient for civilization;" and then, before the ink of this treaty is dry, told that even from this insignificant tract they must promise to move at the end of five years. What words could characterize such a transaction between man and man? There is not a country, a people, a community in which it would be even attempted! Was it less base, or more, being between a strong government and a feeble race?

From the infamy of accomplishing this purpose the United States was saved. Remonstrances, and still more the resistance of the Indians, prevailed, and in 1854 we find the poor creatures expressing "much satisfaction" that the President has decreed that they are to remain permanently on their "insignificant tract."

The Upper Missouri Sioux are still suffering and destitute; a few of them cultivating little patches of ground, depending chiefly on the chase, and on roots and wild berries; when these resources fail there is nothing left for them but to starve, or to commit depredations on white settlers. Some of the bands, nevertheless, have scrupulously observed the stipulations of the Fort Laramie treaty in 1851, show a "strong desire for improvement," and are on the most friendly terms with the whites. These peaceable and friendly bands are much distressed, as well they may be, at the reckless course pursued by others of their tribe. They welcome the presence of the soldiers sent to chastise the offenders, and gladly render all the service to them they can, even against their relatives and friends.

In 1855 it is stated that "various causes have combined to prevent the Minnesota Sioux from deriving, heretofore, much substantial benefit from the very liberal provisions of the treaties of 1851. Until after the reservations were permanently assured to the Indians (1854) it would have been highly improper to have made the expenditures for permanent improvements, and since then the affairs of the agency have not been free from confusion."

"Large sums of money have been expended for these Sioux, but they have been indolent, extravagant, intemperate, and have wasted their means without improving, or seeming to desire to improve their condition."

Both these statements are made in grave good faith ; certainly without any consciousness of their bearing on each other. It is not stated, however, what specific means the Sioux could have employed "to improve their condition," had they "desired" to do so.

The summer of 1857 was one which will long be remembered by the citizens of Minnesota. It was opened by terrible massacres, which were all the work of a strolling outcast band of Sioux, not more than fifteen in number. They had been driven out of their tribe some sixteen years previous, and had been ever since then leading a wandering and marauding life. The beginning of the trouble was a trivial difficulty between one of the white settlers on Rock River and an Indian. The settler's dog bit the Indian, and the Indian shot the dog. For this the white settlers beat the Indian severely, and then went to the camp and by force took away all the guns of the band. This was at a season of the year when to be without guns meant simply to be without food, and the Indians were reduced at once to a condition of great suffering. By some means they either repossessed themselves of their guns or procured others, and, attacking the settlement, killed all the inhabitants except four women, whom they carried away with them, and treated with the utmost barbarity. The inevitable results of such horrors followed. The thousands of peaceable Indians in Minnesota, who did not even know of this outrage, were all held in one common terror and hatred by the general public; only the very great firmness and discretion of the military officers sent to deal with the outbreak saved Minnesota from a general uprising and attack from all the Sioux bands, who were already in a state of smouldering discontent by reason of the non-payment of their annuities. However, they obeyed the demands of the Government that they themselves should pursue this offending band, and either capture or exterminate it. They killed four, and took three prisoners, and then returned " much jaded and worn," and said they could do no more without the help of United States soldiers; and that they thought they had now done enough to show their loyalty, and to deserve the payment of their annuities. One of the chiefs said : " The man who killed white people did not belong to us, and we did not expect to be called to account for the people of another band. We have always tried to do as our Great Father tells us." Another said : " I am going to speak of the treaty. For fifty years we were to be paid $50,000 per annum. We were also promised $300,000 that we have not seen. I wish to say to my Great Father we were promised these things, but have not seen them yet. Why does not the Great Father do as he promised ?"

These hostilities were speedily brought to an end, yet the situation was by no means reassuring for the Indians. But one sentiment seemed to inspire the whole white population, and this was the desire to exterminate the entire Indian race.

"For the present," writes the superintendent, "it is equally important to protect the Indians from the whites as the whites from the Indians;" and this in spite of the fact that all the leading bands of the treaty Sioux had contributed warriors to go in pursuit of the murderers, had killed or captured all they could find, and stood ready to go again after the remaining eight, if the United States troops would go also and assist them. Spite of the exertions of one of the chiefs of the Lower Sioux, "Little Crow," who, the superintendent says, labored with him "night and day in organizing the party, riding continually between the lower and upper agencies," so that they " scarcely slept " till the war-party had set out on the track of the murderers; spite of the fact that the whole body of the Sioux, without exception, "received the intelligence with as much indignation and disapprobation as the whites themselves, and did their best to stand clear of any suspicion of or connection with the affair—spite of all this, they were in continual danger of being shot at sight by the terrified and unreasoning settlers. One band, under the chief Sleepy Eyes, were returning to their homes from a hunt; and while they were "wondering what the panic among the whites meant" (they having heard nothing of the massacre), were fired into by some of the militia volunteers.

The next day a white settler was found killed near that spot —presumably by some member of Sleepy Eyes' band. This excitement slowly abated, and for the next four years a steady improvement was visible in the Minnesota Sioux. Hundreds of them threw aside the blanket—the distinctive badge of their wild state; schools were well attended, and farms were well tilled. That there was great hostility to this civilization, on the part of the majority of the tribe, cannot be denied; but that was only natural—the inevitable protest of a high-spirited and proud race against abandoning all its race distinctions. When we see the men of Lorraine, or of Montenegro, ready to die for the sake merely of being called by the name of one power rather than by that of another, we find it heroic, and give them our sympathies; but when the North American Indian is ready to die rather than wear the clothes and follow the ways of the white man, we feel for him only unqualified contempt, and see in his instinct nothing more than a barbarian's incapacity to appreciate civilization.   Is this just?

In 1861 the Commissioner of Indian Affairs, visiting these Sioux, reports: " I was much surprised to find so many of the Sioux Indians wearing the garb of civilization, many of them living in frame or brick houses, some of them with stables or out-houses, and their fields indicating considerable knowledge of agriculture."   Their condition, he says, affords " abundant evidence of what may be accomplished among the Sioux Indians by steadily adhering to a uniform, undeviating policy.

" The number that live by agricultural pursuits is yet small compared with the whole; but their condition is so much better than that of the wild Indian, that they, too, are becoming convinced that it is the better way to live; and many are coming in, asking to have their hair cut, and for a suit of clothes, and to be located on a piece of land where they can build a house and fence in their fields."

Many more of them would have entered on the agricultural life had the Government provided ways and means for them to do so.   In this same report is a mention of one settlement of two thousand Indians at Big Stone Lake, who " have been hitherto almost entirely neglected.   These people complain that they have lived upon promises for the last ten years, and are really of opinion that white men never perform what they promise.   Many of them would go to work if they had any reasonable encouragement."

The annuities are still in arrears.   Every branch of the industries and improvements attempted suffers for want of the promised funds, and from delays in payments expected.   The worst result, however, of these delays in the fulfilment of treaty stipulations was the effect on the Indians. A sense of wrong in the past and distrust for the future was ever deepening in their minds, and preparing them to be suddenly thrown by any small provocation into an antagonism and hostility grossly disproportionate to the apparent cause. This was the condition of the Minnesota Sioux in the summer of 1862.

The record of the massacres of that summer is scarcely equalled in the history of Indian wars. Early in August some bands of the Upper Sioux, who had been waiting at their agency nearly two months for their annuity payments, and had been suffering greatly for food during that time—so much so that "they dug up roots to appease their hunger, and when corn was turned out to them they devoured it uncooked, like wild animals"—became desperate, broke into the Government warehouse, and took some of the provisions stored there. This was the real beginning of the outbreak, although the first massacre was not till the 18th. When that began, the friendly Indians were powerless to resist—in fact, they were threatened with their lives if they did not join. Nevertheless, some of them rescued whole families, and carried them to places of safety; others sheltered and fed women and children in their own lodges; many fled, leaving all their provisions behind—as much victims of the outbreak as the Minnesota people themselves. For three days the hostile bands, continually re-enforced, went from settlement to settlement, killing and plundering. A belt of country nearly two hundred miles in length and about fifty in width was entirely abandoned by the population, who flocked in panic to the towns and forts. Nearly a thousand were killed—men, women, and children—and nameless outrages were committed on many. Millions of dollars' worth of property were destroyed. The outbreak was quickly quelled by military force,

164

and a large number of Indians captured. Many voluntarily surrendered, bringing with them over two hundred whites that they had taken prisoners. A military commission tried these Indians, and sentenced over three hundred to be hung. All but thirty-nine were reprieved and put into prison. The remainder were moved to Dakota, to a barren desert, where for three years they endured sufferings far worse than death. The remainder escaped to the Upper Missouri region or to Canada.*

Minnesota, at a terrible cost to herself and to the United States Government, was at last free from the presence of Indians within her borders — Indians who were her enemies only because they had been treated with injustice and bad faith.

During this time the bands of Sioux in the Upper Missouri region had been more or less hostile, and military force in continual requisition to subdue them. Re-enforced by the Minnesota refugees, they became more hostile still, and in the summer of 1863 were in almost incessant conflict. In 1864 the Governor of Dakota Territory writes to the Department that the war is spreading into Nebraska and Kansas, and that if provision is not made for the loyal treaty Indians in that region before long, they also will join the hostiles. One band of the Sioux—the Yanktons—has been persistently loyal, and rendered great service through all the troubles. Fifty of these Yankton Sioux had been organized by General Sibley into a company of scouts, and had proved " more effective than twice the number of white soldiers." The only cost to the Government " of this service on the part of the Yanktons had been fifty suits of condemned artillery uniforms, arms, and rations in part to the scouts themselves."

In 1865 the Government, having spent about $40,000,000 on these campaigns, began to cast about for cheaper, if not

* All the Winnebagoes were removed from Minnesota at the same time.

more humane methods, and, partly at the instance of the Governor of Dakota, who knew very well that the Indians desired peace, sent out a commission to treat with them. There were now, all told, some 14,000 Sioux in this region, nearly 2000 being the refugees from Minnesota.

The report of this commission is full of significant statements. There seems to be no doubt that the great majority of the Indians are anxious for peace ; but they are afraid to meet the agents of the Government, lest they be in some way betrayed. Such bands as are represented, however, gladly assent to a treaty of peace and good-will. The commissioners speak with great feeling of the condition of the loyal Yanktons. "No improvements have been made on their lands, and the commissioners were obliged to issue provisions to them to keep them from starving. * * * No crops met the eye, nor is there the semblance of a school-house."

Yet by Article four of the treaty with the Yankton Sioux the United States Government had agreed to expend $10,000 in erecting a suitable building or buildings, and to establish and maintain one or more normal labor schools ; and it is to be read in the United States Statutes at Large that in each of the years 1860, 1861, 1862, and 1863, Congress appropriated $65,000, as per treaty, for the benefit of the Yankton Sioux.

"With the exception of a few miserable huts, a saw-mill, and a small amount of land enclosed, there are few vestiges of improvement. * * * They are reduced to the necessity of hunting for a living, and, unless soon reassured and encouraged, they will be driven to despair, and the great discontent existing among them will culminate in another formidable Indian war."

Nine treaties were concluded by this commission with as many different bands of Sioux, the Indians pledging themselves to abstain from all hostilities with each other and with the whites, and the Government agreeing to pay to the Indians fifteen dollars a head per annum, and to all who will settle down to farming twenty-five dollars a head.

In the winter following these treaties all these Indians faithfully kept their promises, in spite of terrible sufferings from cold and from lack of food. Some of them were at the old Crow Creek Reservation in Dakota, where they were "kept from absolute starvation only by the issue to them of such scanty supplies as could be spared from the stores at Fort Sully, and from the agency." It is much to the credit of these Indians that, in spite of their manifold sufferings, scarcely a case of stealing occurred among them, they being determined to keep their faith to the Government.

"They will run like chickens to gather the offal from the slop buckets that are carried from the garrison kitchens; while they pass a pile of corn and hundreds of loose cattle without touching a thing, except when told they may gather up the grains of corn from the ground where the rats in their depredations have let it fall from the sacks," says the report of one of the commissioners.

In the summer of 1865 still further treaties were concluded with the Indians of the plains, and all the Sioux, with the exception of those in the British possessions, were now pledged to peace. This summer also saw the first recognition on the part of the Government of its flagrant injustice toward the friendly Minnesota Sioux who were moved to Crow Creek, Dakota, at the time of the massacre. There were nearly one thousand of these—mostly old men, women, and children—many of them the widows and children of those who had been hung or were in prison at Davenport. For three years they had been "quiet and patient in their sufferings."

The two hundred prisoners in Davenport had also shown "an excellent disposition and entire submission," although many of them were known and proved to have been "absolutely guiltless of any acts of hostility; and not only this, but deserving of reward for the rescue of white captives." Certificates, petitions, and letters showing these facts were forwarded from Iowa to the Department, but the commissioner says, in his report for 1866, that "they have been mislaid in their passage through the various departments, and cannot be found!"

There was still another class of these Indians deserving of help from the Government — some two hundred and fifty friendly farmer Indians, who were living in 1862 quietly on their farms, "who have acted as scouts for the Government; who never committed any acts of hostility, nor fled with those who did commit them," and have still remained friendly through these four years, "while compelled to a vagabond life by the indiscriminate confiscation of all their land and property."

"The crops belonging to these farmer Indians were valued at $125,000, and they had large herds of stock of all kinds, fine farms, and improvements. The United States troops engaged in suppressing the massacre, also the prisoners taken by them—in all, some 3500 men—lived for fifty days on this property."

Strong efforts were made by Bishop Whipple and others to obtain from the Government some aid for these friendly Indians, and the sum of $7500 was appropriated by Congress for that purpose. The letter of Bishop Whipple, who was requested to report on the division of this sum, is so eloquent a summing up of the case of these Indians, that it ought to be placed on permanent record in the history of our country. He writes:

"There is positive injustice in the appropriation of so miserable a pittance. * * * A much larger sum would not pay the amount which we honestly owe these men. The Government was the trustee of the Upper and Lower Sioux. It held several millions of dollars for their benefit—the joint property of the tribes. These friendly Sioux had abandoned their wild life, and adopted the dress, habits, and customs of civilization ; and in doing this, which placed them in open opposition to the traditions of their tribes, they were pledged the protection of the Government.   By a mistaken policy, by positive neglect to provide a government, by the perversion of funds due them for the sale of one-half their reservations, by withholding their annuities until two months after they were due (which was caused by the use of a part of these funds for claims), by permitting other causes of dissatisfaction to go on unheeded, we provoked the hostility of the wild Indians, and it went on until it ripened in massacre.   These farmer Indians had been pledged a patent for their farms : unless we violated our solemn pledge, these lands were theirs by a title as valid as any title could be.   They had large crops, sufficient to support General Sibley's army for a number of weeks.   They lost all they had —crops, stock, clothing, furniture.   In addition to this, they were deprived of their share in these annuities, and for four years have lived in very great suffering.   You can judge whether $5000 shall be deemed a just reward* for the bravery and fidelity of men who, at the risk of their own lives, were instrumental in saving white captives, and maintained their friendship to the whites.

"I submit to you, sir, and through you hope to reach all who fear God and love justice, whether the very least we can do for all the friendly Sioux is not to fulfil the pledges we made years ago, and give to each of them a patent of eighty acres of land, build them a house, and provide them cattle, seeds, and implements of husbandry ?"

In 1866 all these Sioux were removed, and, in spite of the

---

* Two thousand five hundred of the seven thousand five hundred dollars had been especially set aside by the Government (unjust in its rewards as in its punishments) for Chief Other Day, who was really less deserving than many others.

protestations of the Nebraska citizens, settled on reservations on the Niobrara River, in Northern Nebraska. It soon became evident that this place was undesirable for a reservation, both on account of its previous occupancy by the whites and scarcity of timber.

In the fall they removed again to the mouth of Bazile Creek. Temporary buildings were again erected, and here they spent the winters of 1866 and 1867. In February they were cheered by the invitation sent their chiefs and headmen to visit Washington. They went, feeling sure that they should get a home for themselves and people. "All they got was a promise that a commission should be sent out to visit them the next year." They were told, however, to move to Breckenridge, on the west bank of the Missouri, plant crops there, and were promised that, if they liked the place, they should have it "secured to them as a permanent home." Accordingly, the "agency buildings" were once more removed, and two hundred acres of land were planted. Before the crops were harvested the commission arrived, and urged the Indians to move farther up the Missouri. The Indians being averse to this, however, they were allowed to remain, and told that if they would cultivate the soil like white men—take lands in severalty—the Government would assist them. The Indians gladly consented to this, and signed a treaty to that effect. But in 1868 their agent writes: "That treaty is not yet ratified, and, instead of assistance to open farms, their appropriation has been cut down one half. After paying for supplies purchased on credit last year, it is entirely insufficient for clothing and subsistence, and leaves nothing for opening farms, procuring cattle," etc. These Indians, only five years previous, had been living on good farms, and had $125,000 worth of stock, implements, etc. No wonder their agent writes: "Leave them without a home a few years longer, and you offer strong inducements for them to become idle and worthless."

It is an intricate and perplexing task to attempt now to
follow the history of the different bands of the Sioux tribe
through all their changes of location and affiliation—some in
Dakota, some in Nebraska, and some on the Upper Arkansas
with the hostile Cheyennes and Arapahoes—signing treaties one
summer, and on the war-path the next—promised a home in
spring, and ordered off it before harvest—all the time more
and more hemmed in by white settlers, and more and more
driven out of their buffalo ranges by emigrations—liable at any
time to have bodies of United States soldiers swoop down on
them and punish whole bands for depredations committed by
a handful of men, perhaps of a totally distinct band—the wonder is not that some of them were hostile and vindictive, but
that any of them remained peaceable and friendly. Bandied
about from civil authorities to military—the War Department
recommending " that all Indians not on fixed reservations be
considered at war," and proceeded against accordingly, and the
Interior Department neglecting to provide them with "fixed
reservations," or to define or enforce the boundaries of even
their temporary reservations—tricked, cheated on all sides—
starving half the time—there is not a tribe of all the persecuted tribes of Indians that has a more piteous record than the
Sioux.   Nevertheless, we find many of the bands, in 1870, advancing in civilization.   In the Yankton band nearly one hundred children are in school, and eight hundred acres of land
are under cultivation.   The Lower Yanktons are peaceful and
quiet, although they are near the Brulés, who are always roving and hostile.   The Sissetons and Wahpetons, who were by
a treaty of 1867 placed on reservations in Dakota, are "industrious, and fast advancing in agricultural pursuits."   Four
schools are in operation among them.   The Yanktons are
" anxious to farm, and state that the Government has promised
to assist and teach them to farm ; that they are and have been
ready for some time, but as yet the agent has not received any

instructions or funds to permit of their accomplishing their desire."

Two events, important in the history of the Sioux tribe, happened in 1869 and 1870. One was the visit of a delegation of chiefs and headmen from several of the bands, under the leadership of the chief Red Cloud,[9] to Washington, Philadelphia, and New York. They had thus an opportunity of relating all their grievances, and of receiving the Government's declarations of good intentions toward them. Red Cloud, after his return home, became an ardent and determined advocate of peace and loyalty. The other was the withdrawal of a portion of the Santee Sioux from their band, for the purpose of taking up farms under the Homestead Act, and becoming independent citizens. The story of this experiment, and the manner in which it was met by the United States Government, is best told in the words of Dr. Williamson, a missionary, who had lived thirty-five years among them, and who pleaded thus warmly for them in a letter addressed to the Department in the summer of 1870: "Several considerations have influenced the Dakotas in going to the Big Sioux River: 1st. The soil and climate are more similar to that to which they have been accustomed in Minnesota, their former home, than is that of their reservation on the Missouri; 2d. Feeling that they were men capable of sustaining themselves if a fair opportunity is afforded them, they felt that it was degrading to live as sinecures and pensioners dependent on Government for food and clothing; 3d. And chiefly a desire to make homes for their families where they could be subjected to, and protected by, the laws of the United States, the same as all other men are. This they thought could not be the case on their reservation.

"These Sioux were parties to the treaties made in 1851, by which they and other bands ceded to the United States all the best settled parts of Minnesota west of the Mississippi for less than one-hundredth part of its present value, and much less

[9] George E. Hyde, *Red Cloud's Folk, A History of the Oglala Sioux Indians* (Norman, Oklahoma, 1937) and, by the same author, *A Sioux Chronicle* (Norman, Oklahoma, 1956), a continuation of the former book.

than the lands were worth to them as hunting-grounds. And while as hunters they needed no protection of the law, they knew that as agriculturists they could not live without it; and they positively refused to sell their hunting-grounds till the Commissioner of the United States promised that they should be protected in their persons and property the same as white men. Government never accorded to them this protection, which, in the view of the Indians, was a very important consideration in selling the lands. This neglect on the part of the Government led to yearly complaints, and the massacres of 1862. * * * These Sioux were most of them previous to the war living in comfortable homes, with well-cultivated farms and teams," and were receiving by annuity provisions, either in money or the equivalent, about $50 a head annually, from interest on their money invested in the bonds of the Government. These Indians, in taking up their new homesteads, were required by the Department to renounce, on oath, all claims on the United States for annuities. Without doubt, citizenship of the United States, the protection of our laws, is worth a great sum; but is it wise or right in our Government to require these natives of the country to purchase, at a price of several thousands of dollars, that which is given without money or price to every immigrant from Asia, Europe, or Africa that asks for it?

"Besides their annuities, there is due them from the Government the proceeds of the sale of their old reservation on the Minnesota River, which is more than forty miles long and ten wide; which, after paying expenses of survey and sale, are, according to a law of the United States, to be expended in assisting them to make homes elsewhere; and as these lands were valued at $1 25 an acre and upward, and are rapidly selling, the portion which will be due each of the Indians cannot be less than $200 or $300—or $1000 for each family. The oath required of them is supposed to bar them from any claim to this also. Now, I cannot see how this decision of the Indian Department is consistent either with justice or good policy, and it is certainly inconsistent with both the spirit and letter of Articles six and ten of a treaty between the United States of America and different bands of Sioux Indians, concluded in 1868, and ratified and proclaimed February, 1869. * * * What I ask for them is that our Government restore to them a part of what we took from them, and give them the same chance to live and thrive which we give to all the other inhabitants of our country, whether white or black. * * * That some aid is very necessary must be obvious to you, who know how difficult it is for even white men, trained to work, and with several hundred dollars in property, to open a new farm in this Western wilderness. Their number is probably greater than you are aware of. When I administered the Lord's Supper there on the first Sabbath of this month, there were present seventy-seven communicants of our church, besides quite a number of other persons. * * * It is owing to the Santee Sioux—partly to those on the Big Sioux River, chiefly to those near Fort Wadsworth—that in the last five years not a single white inhabitant of Minnesota or Iowa has been murdered by the wild Indians, while many have been cut off in every frontier State and Territory south-west of the Missouri. So long as the Christian Sioux can be kept on the frontier, the white settlements are safe. * * * In conclusion, I wish again to call your attention to the fact that these Indians on the Big Sioux purchase citizenship at a very great sum, and to entreat you to do all in your power to secure for them that protection of person or property for which they bargain, and without which nothing our Government can do will make them prosperous or happy."

No attention was paid to this appeal; and the next year the indefatigable missionary sent a still stronger one, setting forth that this colony now numbered fifty families; had been under the instruction of the American Board of Commissioners for Foreign Missions for many years ; had a church of one hundred members ; a native preacher, partly supported by them ; had built log-cabins on their claims, and planted farms, " many of them digging up the ground with hoes and spades."

Dr. Williamson reiterates the treaty provisions under which he claims that these Indians are entitled to aid. The sixth Article of the treaty of 1868 closes as follows : " Any Indian or Indians receiving a patent for land under the foregoing provisions, shall thereby and henceforth become and be a citizen of the United States, and be entitled to all the privileges and immunities of such citizenship, and shall at the same time retain all his rights and benefits accruing to Indians under this treaty."

This treaty goes on to provide most liberally for all Indians adopting the civilized mode of life. Article eighth specially provides for supplying them with seed and agricultural implements, and this is what they most of all need.

The encouragement held forth in this treaty was one great motive in leading these people to break tribal influences, so deleterious to improvement, and adopt our democratic civilization. Is it not base tyranny to disappoint them ? They are the first Sioux, if not the first Indians in the United States to adopt the spirit and life of our American civilization. They have of their own accord done just what the Government has been for generations trying to get the Indians to do. And now will the Government refuse this helping hand ? To our shame, it has for two years refused. And why ? Because the Indians said, " If we become civilized, it is necessary for us to break up tribal relations, and settle down like white men."

In 1873 the Government at last yielded to this request, and sent out oxen, wagons, ploughs, etc., enough to stock thirty farms. In 1874, Dr. Williamson, having been appointed a special agent for them, reports their progress : " They all live in log-houses and wear citizens' dress. * * * One hundred and nineteen can read their own language fluently. They all go to

church regularly. They have broken one hundred and sev
enty-seven acres of new prairie. Twenty new houses have been
built. * * * They have cut and hauled two hundred cords of
wood, hauling some of it forty miles to market. * * * They have
done considerable freighting with their teams, going sometimes
a hundred miles away. They have earned thirty-five hundred
dollars, catching small furs. * * * One Indian has the contract
for carrying the mail through Flandreau, for which he receives
one thousand dollars a year. * * * It is but a few miles from
Flandreau to the far-famed pipe-stone quarry, and these Indians make many little sums by selling pipes, rings, ink-glasses,
etc., made of this beautiful red stone. * * * They are anxious
to be taught how to make baskets, mats, cloth; and the young
men ask to be taught the blacksmith and carpenter trades."

This is a community that only five years before had pushed
out into an unbroken wilderness without a dollar of money,
without a plough, to open farms. "Without ploughs, they
had to dig the sod with their hoes, and at the same time make
their living by hunting. They suffered severe hardships, and
a number of their best men perished in snow-storms. Believing they were carrying out the wishes of the Great Father, as
expressed in the treaty of 1868, to which they were parties,
they were disappointed when for three years no notice was
taken of them." There is something pathetic in the gratitude
they are said now to feel for the niggardly gift of a few oxen,
wagons, and ploughs. They have apparently given over all
hope of ever obtaining any of the money due them on account
of their lands sold in Minnesota. No further allusion is made
to it by Dr. Williamson.

From the Yankton Sioux this year comes a remarkable report: "We have no jail, no law except the treaty and the
agent's word, yet we have no quarrels, no fighting, and, with
one or two exceptions, not a single case of drunkenness during
the year. This I consider remarkable, when we take into con-

sideration the fact that the reservation is surrounded by ranches where liquors of all kinds can be obtained." Is there another .village of two thousand inhabitants in the United States of which this can be said?

In this year a commission was sent to treat with some of the wilder bands of Sioux for the relinquishment of their right to hunt and roam over a large part of their unneeded territory in Kansas and Nebraska. Some of the chiefs consented. Red Cloud's band refused at first; " but on being told that the right would soon be taken from them," after a delay of two days they " agreed to accept," merely stipulating that their share of the twenty-five thousand dollars promised should be paid in horses and guns. They insisted, however, on this proviso: " That we do not surrender any right of occupation of the country situated in Nebraska north of the divide, which is south of and near to the Niobrara River and west of the one hundredth meridian."

It was a significant fact that, when these Sioux gave up this hunting privilege, " they requested that nearly all the $25,000 they received in compensation for this relinquishment should be expended in cows, horses, harness, and wagons," says the Commissioner of Indian Affairs in 1875.

There are still some thousand or more of hostile Sioux roaming about under the famous chief Sitting Bull[10] living by the chase when they can, and by depredations when they must; occasionally, also, appearing at agencies, and drawing rations among the other Indians unsuspected. The remainder of the bands are steadily working their way on toward civilization. The Santees are a Christian community; they have their industrial-schools, Sabbath-schools, and night-schools; they publish a monthly paper in the Dakota tongue, which prints twelve hundred copies. The Yanktons have learned to weave, and have made cloth enough to give every Indian woman in the tribe one good dress. The Flandreau citizen Sioux have a

[10] Regarding Sitting Bull see Stanley Vestal, *Sitting Bull: Champion of the Sioux* (Boston, 1932), written from the Indian viewpoint.

Presbyterian church of one hundred and thirty-five members, and pay half the salary of the native preacher. On the occasion of an anniversary meeting of the Dakota missionaries there, these people raised one hundred dollars to pay for their entertainment. These three bands are far the most advanced, but all the others are making steady progress.

In 1876 the news from the Sioux on the agencies is that, owing to the failure of appropriations, the Indian Bureau had been unable to send the regular supplies, and the Indians, being in "almost a starving condition," had been induced, by the "apparent purpose of the Government to abandon them to starvation," to go north in large numbers, and join the hostile camps of Sitting Bull. This was in the spring; again in mid-summer the same thing happened, and many of the Indians, growing still more anxious and suspicious, left their agencies to join in the war.

Congress would probably have paid little attention at this time to the reading of this extract from "Kent's Commentaries:" "Treaties of peace, when made by the competent power, are obligatory on the whole nation. If the treaty requires the payment of money to carry it into effect, and the money cannot be raised but by an act of the legislature, the treaty is morally obligatory upon the legislature to pass the law; and to repeal it would be a breach of the public faith."

A disturbed and unsettled condition of things prevailed at all the Sioux agencies, consequent on this state of things. Companies of troops were stationed at all of them to guard against outbreaks. Owing to lack of funds, the Yanktons were obliged to give up their weaving and basket-making. At the Standing Rock Agency, after the Indians had planted eight hundred and seventy-two dollars' worth of seeds—of corn, potatoes, and other vegetables—the grasshoppers came and devoured them. "Many of these Indians, with their whole families, stood all day in their fields fighting these enemies, and in several places succeeded so far as to save a considerable part of their crops." The Santees were made very anxious and unhappy by fresh rumors of their probable removal. Public sentiment at the East, knowing no difference between different tribes of Sioux, regarded it as maudlin sentimentalism to claim for the Santees any more rights than for the hostiles that had murdered General Custer. One of the agents in Dakota writes:

" The recent troubles in the Indian country, and the existing uncertainty as to the future intentions of the Government toward the Indians, occasion considerable uneasiness among them. * * * Reports are circulated that no further assistance will be rendered by the Government, as the Great Council in Washington refuses to furnish money unless the Indians are turned over to the War Department. Every inducement. is held out to encourage secession from the agencies, and strengthen the forces of the hostile camp. It is not surprising that, in view of the non-arrival of supplies, and the recent order of the War Department to arrest parties leaving and arriving, that people less credulous than Indians would feel undecided and uneasy. * * * It must be remembered that the whole Sioux nation is related, and that there is hardly a man, woman, or child in the hostile camp who has not blood relations at one or the other of the agencies."

Contrast the condition into which all these friendly Indians are suddenly plunged now, with their condition only two years previous : martial law now in force on all their reservations; themselves in danger of starvation, and constantly exposed to the influence of emissaries from their friends and relations, urging them to join in fighting this treacherous government that had kept faith with nobody—neither with friend nor with foe; that made no discriminations in its warfare between friends and foes; burning villages occupied only by women and children; butchering bands of Indians living peacefully under protection of its flag, as at Sand Creek, in Colorado — no wonder that one of the military commander's official reports says, "The hostile body was largely re-enforced by accessions from the various agencies, where the malcontents were, doubtless, in many cases, driven to desperation by starvation and the heartless frauds perpetrated on them;" and that the Interior Department is obliged to confess that, "Such desertions were largely due to the uneasiness which the Indians had long felt on account of the infraction of treaty stipulations by the white invasion of the Black Hills, seriously aggravated at the most critical period by irregular and insufficient issues of rations, necessitated by inadequate and delayed appropriations."

It was at this time that Sitting Bull made his famous reply: "Tell them at Washington if they have one man who speaks the truth to send him to me, and I will listen to what he has to say."

The story of the military campaign against these hostile Sioux in 1876 and 1877 is to be read in the official records of the War Department, so far as statistics can tell it. Another history, which can never be read, is written in the hearts of widowed women in the Sioux nation and in the nation of the United States.

Before midsummer the Sioux war was over. The indomitable Sitting Bull had escaped to Canada—that sanctuary of refuge for the Indian as well as for the slave. Here he was visited in the autumn by a commission from the United States, empowered by the President to invite him with his people to return, and be " assigned to agencies," and treated "in as friendly a spirit as other Indians had been who had surrendered." It was explained to him that every one of the Indians who had surrendered had "been treated in the same manner as those of your nation who, during all the past troubles, remained peaceably at their agencies." As a great part of those who had fled from these same agencies to join Sitting Bull had done so because they were starving, and the Government knew this (had printed the record of the fact in the reports of two of its Departments), this was certainly a strange phraseology of invitation for it to address to Sitting Bull. His replies and those of his chiefs were full of scathing sarcasm. Secure on British soil, they had for once safe freedom of speech as well as of action, and they gave the United States Commissioners very conclusive reasons why they chose to remain in Canada, where they could "trade with the traders and make a living," and where their women had "time to raise their children."

The commissioners returned from their bootless errand, and the Interior Department simply entered on its records the statement that "Sitting Bull and his adherents are no longer considered wards of the Government." It also enters on the same record the statement that "in the months of September and October, 1876, the various Sioux agencies were visited by a commission appointed under the Act of Congress, August 15th of that year, to negotiate with the Sioux for an agreement to surrender that portion of the Sioux Reservation which included the Black Hills, and certain hunting privileges outside that reserve, guaranteed by the treaty of 1868; to grant a right of way across their reserve; and to provide for the removal of the Red Cloud and Spotted Tail bands to new agencies on the Missouri River. The commission were also authorized to take steps to gain the consent of the Sioux to their removal to the Indian Territory. * * * The commission were successful in all the negotiations with which they were charged, and the Indians made every concession that was desired by the Government, although we were engaged at that very time in fighting their relatives and friends." The only comment needed on this last paragraph is to suggest that a proper list of errata for that page should contain: "For 'although' read 'because!'" "On behalf of the United States the agreement thus entered into provided for subsisting the Sioux on a stated ration until they should become self-supporting; for furnishing schools, and all necessary aid and instruction in agriculture and the mechanical arts, and for the allotment of lands in severalty."

In accordance with this act, a commission was sent to select a location on the Missouri River for the two new Sioux agencies (the Red Cloud and Spotted Tail).

"For the former the site chosen is the junction of Yellow Medicine and Missouri rivers, and at that point agency buildings have just been erected," says the Report of the Indian Bureau for 1877. "For the latter the old Ponca Reserve was decided on, where the agency buildings, storehouses, one hundred and fifty Indian homes, and five hundred acres of cultivated fields, left vacant by the Poncas, offer special advantages for present quarters."

The commissioner says: "The removal of fourteen thousand Sioux Indians at this season of the year, a distance of three hundred miles from their old agencies in Nebraska to their new quarters near the Missouri River, is not a pleasant matter to contemplate. Neither the present Secretary of the Interior nor the present Commissioner of Indian Affairs is responsible for the movement, but they have carried out the law faithfully though reluctantly. The removal is being made in accordance with the Act of August 15th, 1876. It is proper to say here that I cannot but look on the necessity thus imposed by law on the executive branch of the Government as an unfortunate one, and the consequences ought to be remedied as speedily as possible.

"Let us for a moment consider that the Spotted Tail Agency was in 1871 on the west bank of the Missouri River, where the whites became exceedingly troublesome, and the river afforded abundant facilities for the introduction of intoxicating liquors. In 1874 the Red Cloud and Spotted Tail agencies were removed to what a subsequent survey proved to be the State of Nebraska—the former agency one hundred and sixty-five miles from Cheyenne, and the latter one hundred and eight miles from Sidney, the nearest points on the Union Pacific Railroad. Here the usual ill-fortune attending the removal of these Indians was again exemplified in placing the agencies on absolutely barren land, where there was no possibility of cultivating the soil, no hope of their being enabled to become self-supporting, and where they have of necessity been kept in the hopeless condition of paupers."

In the hope of placing these Indians upon arable land, where they might become civilized and self-supporting, the determination was hastily taken to remove them back to the Missouri River. This step was taken without a proper examination of other points on their reservation, where it is stated that " a sufficient quantity of excellent wheat lands can be found on either bank of the White River, and where there is also timber sufficient in quantity and quality for all practical purposes. * * * The Indian chiefs, in their interview with the President in September last, begged that they might not be sent to the Missouri River, as whiskey-drinking and other demoralization would be the consequence. This was the judgment of the best men of the tribe; but the necessity was one that the President could not control. The provisions and supplies for the ensuing winter had been placed, according to law, on the Missouri, and, owing to the lateness of the season, it was impossible to remove them to the old agencies. Accordingly, the necessities of the case compelled the removal of these Indians in the midst of the snows and storms of early winter, which have already set in."

If there were absolutely no other record written of the management of Indian affairs by the Interior Department than this one page of the history of these two bands of the Sioux tribe, this alone would be enough to show the urgent need of an entirely new system. So many and such hasty, ill-considered, uninformed, capricious, and cruel decisions of arbitrary power could hardly be found in a seven years' record of any known tyrant; and there is no tyrant whose throne would not have been rocked, if not upset, by the revolutions which would have followed on such oppressions.

There is a sequel to this story of the removal of the Red Cloud and Spotted Tail bands—a sequel not recorded in the official reports of the Department, but familiar to many men in the Western country. Accounts of it—some humorous, some severe—were for some time floating about in Western newspapers.

The Red Cloud and Spotted Tail bands of Sioux consented to go to the old Ponca Reserve only after being told that all their supplies had been sent to a certain point on the Missouri River with a view to this move; and it being too late to take all this freight northward again, they would starve if they stayed where they were. Being assured that they would be allowed to go back in the spring, and having a written pledge from General Crook (in whose word they had implicit faith) that the Government would fulfil this promise, they at last very reluctantly consented to go to the Ponca Reserve for the winter. In the spring no orders came for the removal. March passed, April passed—no orders. The chiefs sent word to their friend, General Crook, who replied to them with messages sent by a swift runner, begging them not to break away, but to wait a little longer. Finally, in May, the Commissioner of Indian Affairs went himself to hold a council with them. When he rose to speak, the chief Spotted Tail sprung up, walked toward him, waving in his hand the paper containing the promise of the Government to return them to White Clay Creek, and exclaimed, "All the men who come from Washington are liars, and the bald-headed ones are the worst of all! I don't want to hear one word from you—you are a bald-headed old liar! You have but one thing to do here, and that is to give an order for us to return to White Clay Creek. Here are your written words;

and if you don't give this order, and everything here is not on wheels inside of ten days, I'll order my young men to tear down and burn everything in this part of the country! I don't want to hear anything more from you, and I've got nothing more to say to you:" and he turned his back on the commissioner and walked away.   Such language as this would not have been borne from unarmed and helpless Indians; but when it came from a chief with four thousand armed warriors at his back, it was another affair altogether.   The order was written. In less than ten days everything was "on wheels," and the whole body of these Sioux on the move to the country they had indicated; and the Secretary of the Interior says, naïvely, in his Report for 1868, "The Indians were found to be quite determined to move westward, and the promise of the Government in that respect was faithfully kept."

The reports from all the bands of Sioux for the past two years have been full of indications of their rapid and encouraging improvement.   "The most decided advance in civilization has been made by the Ogallalla and Brulé Sioux," says the Report of the Indian Bureau for 1879.   "Their progress during the last year and a half has been simply marvellous."

And yet this one band of Ogallalla Sioux has been moved, since 1863, eight times.   Is it not a wonder that they have any heart to work, any hope of anything in the future?

"It is no longer a question," says this same report, "whether Indians will work.   They are steadily asking for opportunities to do so, and the Indians who to-day are willing and anxious to engage in civilized labor are largely in the majority; * * * there is an almost universal call for lands in severalty; * * * there is a growing desire to live in houses; the demand for agricultural implements and appliances, and for wagons and harness for farming and freighting purposes, is constantly increasing."

That all this should be true of these wild, warlike Sioux,

after so many years of hardships and forced wanderings and removals, is incontrovertible proof that there is in them a native strength of character, power of endurance, and indomitable courage, which will make of them ultimately a noble and superior race of people, if civilization will only give them time to become civilized, and Christians will leave them time and peace to learn Christianity.

CHAPTER VI.

THE PONCAS.[11]

In 1803 Captain Lewis and Lieutenant Clarke, of the First United States Infantry, were commissioned by Congress to explore the river Missouri from its mouth to its source, to "seek the best water communication from thence to the Pacific Ocean," and to enter into conference with all the Indian tribes on their route, with a view to the establishment of commerce with them. They report the "Poncars" as "the remnant of a nation once respectable in point of numbers; they formerly resided on a branch of the Red River of Lake Winnipeg; being oppressed by Sioux, they removed to the west side of the Missouri, on Poncar River, where they built and fortified a village, and remained some years; but, being pursued by their ancient enemies, the Sioux, and reduced by continual wars, they have joined and now live with the Mahas (Omahas), whose language they speak." Their numbers are estimated by Lewis and Clarke as being only about two hundred, all told; but this small estimate is probably to be explained by the fact that at this time the tribe was away on its annual buffalo-hunt, and their village had been so long empty and quiet that a buffalo was found grazing there. A few years later the tribe is reckoned at four hundred: in a census of the Indian tribes, taken by General Porter in 1829, they are set down at six hundred. The artist Catlin, who visited them a few years later, rated them a little less. He gives an interesting account of the chief of the tribe, named Shoo-de-ga-cha (Smoke), and his young and pretty wife, Hee-la'h-dee (the Pure Fountain), whose portraits he painted.

[11] Regarding the Poncas see George A. Dorsey, *The Ponca Sun Dance* (Chicago, 1905), Thomas Tibbles, *The Ponca Chiefs* (Boston, 1880), and Earl W. Hayter, ''The Ponca Removal,'' *North Dakota Historical Quarterly*, VI (1931–1932), pp. 262–275.

He says: "The chief, who was wrapped in a buffalo-robe, is a noble specimen of native dignity and philosophy. I conversed much with him, and from his dignified manners, as well as from the soundness of his reasoning, I became fully convinced that he deserved to be the sachem of a more numerous and prosperous tribe. He related to me with great coolness and frankness the poverty and distress of his nation—and with the method of a philosopher predicted the certain and rapid extinction of his tribe, which he had not the power to avert. Poor, noble chief, who was equal to and worthy of a greater empire! He sat on the deck of the steamer, overlooking the little cluster of his wigwams mingled among the trees, and, like Caius Marius weeping over the ruins of Carthage, shed tears as he was descanting on the poverty of his ill-fated little community, which he told me had 'once been powerful and happy; that the buffaloes which the Great Spirit had given them for food, and which formerly spread all over their green prairies, had all been killed or driven out by the approach of white men, who wanted their skins; that their country was now entirely destitute of game, and even of roots for food, as it was one continuous prairie; and that his young men, penetrating the countries of their enemies for buffaloes, which they were obliged to do, were cut to pieces and destroyed in great numbers. That his people had foolishly become fond of fire-water, and had given away everything in their country for it; that it had destroyed many of his warriors, and would soon destroy the rest; that his tribe was too small and his warriors too few to go to war with the tribes around them; that they were met and killed by the Sioux on the north, by the Pawnees on the west, by the Osages and Konzas on the south, and still more alarmed from the constant advance of the pale faces—their enemies from the east—with whiskey and small-pox, which already had destroyed four-fifths of his tribe, and would soon impoverish and at last destroy the remainder of them.' In this way did this shrewd philosopher lament over the unlucky destiny of his tribe, and I pitied him with all my heart."

The day before Catlin arrived at this village this old chief's son—the young Hongs-kay-de—had created a great sensation in the community by accomplishing a most startling amount of bigamy in a single day. Being the chief's son, and having just been presented by his father with a handsome wigwam and nine horses, he had no difficulty whatever in ingratiating himself with the fathers of marriageable daughters, and had, with ingenious slyness, offered himself to and been accepted by four successive fathers-in-law, promising to each of them two horses—enjoining on them profound secrecy until a certain hour, when he would announce to the whole tribe that he was to be married. At the time appointed he appeared, followed by some of his young friends leading eight horses. Addressing the prospective father - in - law who stood nearest him, with his daughter by his side, he said, "You promised me your daughter: here are the two horses." A great hubbub immediately arose; the three others all springing forward, angry and perplexed, claiming his promises made to them. The triumphant young Turk exclaimed, "You have all now acknowledged your engagements to me, and must fulfil them. Here are your horses." There was nothing more to be said. The horses were delivered, and Hongs-kay-de, leading two brides in each hand, walked off with great dignity to his wigwam.

This was an affair totally unprecedented in the annals of the tribe, and produced an impression as profound as it could have done in a civilized community, though of a different character —redounding to the young prince's credit rather than to his shame—marking him out as one daring and original enough to be a "Big Medicine." Mr. Catlin says that he visited the bridal wigwam soon afterward, and saw the "four modest little wives seated around the fire, seeming to harmonize very well." Of the prettiest one—"Mong-shong-shaw" (the Bending Willow)—he took a portrait, and a very sweet-faced young woman she is too, wrapped in a beautifully ornamented fur robe, much handsomer and more graceful than the fur-lined circulars worn by civilized women.

The United States' first treaty with this handful of gentle and peaceable Indians was made in 1817. It was simply a treaty of peace and friendship.

In 1825 another was made, in which the Poncas admit that "they reside within the territorial limits of the United States, acknowledge their supremacy, and claim their protection." They also admit "the right of the United States to regulate all trade and intercourse with them." The United States, on their part, "agree to receive the Poncar tribe of Indians into their friendship and under their protection, and to extend to them from time to time such benefits and acts of kindness as may be convenient, and seem just and proper to the President of the United States."

After this there is little mention, in the official records of the Government, of the Poncas for some thirty years. Other tribes in the Upper Missouri region were so troublesome and aggressive that the peaceable Poncas were left to shift for themselves as they best could amidst all the warring and warring interests by which they were surrounded. In 1856 the agent of the Upper Platte mentions incidentally that their lands were being fast intruded upon by squatters; and in 1857 another agent reports having met on the banks of the Missouri a large band of Poncas, who made complaint that all the Indians on the river were receiving presents and they were overlooked; that the men from the steamboats cut their trees down, and that white settlers were taking away all their land. In 1858 the Commissioner for Indian Affairs writes: "Treaties were entered into in March and April last with the Poncas and Yankton Sioux, who reside west of Iowa, for the purpose of extinguishing their title to all the lands occupied and claimed by them, except small portions on which to colonize and domesticate them. This proceeding was deemed necessary in order to obtain such control over these Indians as to prevent their interference with our settlements, which are rapidly extending in that direction. These treaties were duly laid before the Senate at its last regular session, but were not, it is understood, finally acted on by that body.

"Relying on the ratification of their treaty, and the adoption of timely measures to carry out its provisions in their favor, the Poncas proceeded in good faith to comply with its stipulations by abandoning their settlements and hunting-grounds, and withdrawing to the small tract reserved for their future home. Being without a crop to rely upon, and having been unsuccessful in their usual summer hunt, they were reduced to a state of desperation and destitution. As nothing had been done for them under the treaty, they concluded it was void, and threatened to fall back upon their former settlements, some of the most important of which had, in the mean time, been taken possession of by numerous white persons."

The Poncas never heard of Grotius or Vattel; but, in assuming that the treaty was void because it was not fulfilled, they only acted on the natural principles of the law of nations and of treaties, as laid down by all authorities. Thucydides said: "They are not the first breakers of a league who, being deserted, seek for aid to others, but they that perform not by their deeds what they have promised to do upon their oaths."

In consequence of this delay to fulfil the treaty provisions, the Government was forced to step in at the last moment and "incur a heavy expense" in furnishing the Poncas with food enough to keep them from starving; and in 1859, under this pressure, the Senate ratified the treaty. By it the Poncas ceded and relinquished to the United States all the lands they had ever owned or claimed, "wherever situate," except a small tract between the Ponca and Niobrara rivers. In consideration of this cession, the United States Government agreed "to protect the Poncas in the possession of this tract of land, and their persons and property thereon, during good behavior on their part; to pay them annuities annually for thirty years—$12,000 for the first five years, then $10,000 for ten years, then $8000 for fifteen years; to expend $20,000 for their subsistence during the first year, for building houses, etc.; to establish schools, and to build mills, mechanics' shops, etc.; to give $20,000 for the payment of the existing obligations of the tribe."

Two years later the agent newly appointed to take charge of the Poncas reports to the Department the amount of improvements made on the reservation: "One saw and grist-mill; two agency houses—story and a half houses—without inside lining or plastering, 16 by 26 and 18 by 32 feet in size; six small round log-houses (three with a small shed for a stable), a light log-corral for cattle, and a canvas shed for storing under; and about sixty acres of ground, broken, comprised all the improvements."

Evidently a very small part of the $20,000 had been spent as yet. He did not find an Indian on the reservation. From fear of the Sioux (who in 1860 had stolen from them more than half the horses they owned) they had moved down the Niobrara River, some twenty miles nearer the Missouri. It was with the greatest difficulty that the agent induced them to return; and after they did so, they huddled their tents close about the agency buildings, and could not be induced to go half a mile away unless accompanied by some of the white employés.

As the agent had no food to feed them with, and no money to buy any (spite of the appropriation of $20,000 for subsistence and house-building), he induced them to go off on a hunt; but in less than a month they came straggling back, "begging for provisions for their women and children, whom they had

left on the plains half-starved, having been unable to find any
game, or any food except wild-turnips. Some of them went
to visit the Omahas, others the Pawnees, where they remained
until the little corn they had planted produced roasting-ears.
In the mean time those who were here subsisted mainly on
wild-cherries and plums and the wild-turnip, and traded away
most of their blankets and annuity goods for provisions."

In 1863 the reports are still more pitiful. "They started
on their summer hunt toward the last of May, immediately after the first hoeing of their corn. At first they were successful and found buffaloes; but afterward, the ground being occupied by the Yanktons, who were sent south of the Niobrara
by the general commanding the district, and who were about
double the number, and with four times as many horses, they
soon consumed what meat they had cured, and were compelled
to abandon the chase. They commenced to return in the latter part of July. They went away with very high hopes, and
reasonably so, of a large crop, but returned to see it all withered and dried up. In the mean time the plains had been burnt
over, so that they could not discover the roots they are in the
habit of digging. Even the wild-plums, which grow on bushes
down in ravines and gullies, are withered and dried on the
limbs. The building I occupy was constantly surrounded by a
hungry crowd begging for food. * * * I am warned by military
authority to keep the Poncas within the limits of the reservation; but this is an impossibility. There is nothing within its
limits, nor can anything be obtained in sufficient quantity, or
brought here soon enough to keep them from starving. * * *
The Poncas have behaved well—quite as well, if not better
than, under like circumstances, the same number of whites would
have done. I have known whole families to live for days together on nothing but half-dried corn-stalks, and this when
there were cattle and sheep in their sight."

At this time martial law was in force on many of the Indian

reservations, owing to the presence of roving bands of hostile Sioux, driven from Minnesota after their outbreak there.

The Poncas through all these troubles remained loyal and peaceable, and were " unwavering in their fidelity to their treaty," says the Indian Commissioner.

In December of this year what the governmental reports call " a very unfortunate occurrence " took place in Nebraska. A party of Poncas, consisting of four men, six women, three boys, and two girls, returning from a visit to the Omahas, had camped for the night about twelve miles from their own reservation. In the night a party of soldiers from a military post on the Niobrara River came to their camp, and began to insult the squaws, " offering money with one hand, and presenting a revolver with the other." The Indians, alarmed, pulled up their lodge, and escaped to a copse of willows near by. The soldiers fired at them as they ran away, and then proceeded to destroy all their effects. They cut the lodge covers to pieces, burnt the saddles and blankets, cut open sacks of beans, corn, and dried pumpkin, and strewed their contents on the ground, and went away, taking with them a skin lodge-covering, beaver-skins, buffalo-robes, blankets, guns, and all the small articles. The Indians' ponies were hid in the willows. Early in the morning they returned with these, picked up all the corn which had not been destroyed, and such other articles as they could find, packed their ponies as best they might, and set off barefooted for home. After they had gone a few miles they stopped and built a fire to parch some corn to eat. Some of the women and children went to look for wild-beans, leaving three women and a child at the camp. Here the soldiers came on them again. As soon as the Indians saw them coming they fled. The soldiers fired on them, wounding one woman by a ball through her thigh; another, with a child on her back, by two balls through the child's thighs, one of which passed through the mother's side. These women were fired on as they were crossing the river on the ice. The soldiers then took possession of the six ponies and all the articles at the camp, and left. The squaws and children who were looking for beans were half a mile below; a little dog belonging to them barked and revealed their hiding-place in the willows. The soldiers immediately turned on them, dismounted, and, making up to them, deliberately shot them dead as they huddled helplessly together—three women and a little girl!

One of the boys, a youth, ran for the river, pursued by the soldiers. On reaching the river he dived into the water through a hole in the ice; as often as he lifted his head they fired at him. After they went away he crawled out and escaped to the agency. One of the murdered women, the mother of this boy, had three balls in her head and cheek, her throat cut, and her head half-severed by a sabre-thrust; another, the youngest woman, had her cloth skirt taken off and carried away, and all her other clothes torn from her body, leaving it naked!

The men who did this deed belonged to Company B of the Seventh Iowa Cavalry.

The outrage was promptly reported to the Department, and the general commanding the Nebraska District detailed an officer to examine into it. There was some correspondence between the military authorities relative to it, but with no result; and in the report of the next year the Indian Commissioner says: "Attention was called last year to the fact that the murderers of several of this loyal and friendly tribe had not been discovered and punished. I trust that, as there seems to be no probability that this will be done, a special appropriation may be made for presents to the relatives of the deceased."

In 1865 a supplementary treaty was made with the Poncas, extending their reservation down the Niobrara to the Missouri River; and the Government agreed to pay them $15,000, for the purpose of indemnifying them for the loss they had sustained in this outrage and in others. For the ratification of this treaty also they waited two years; and in 1867 the Superintendent of the Dakota Territory says: "Schools would have been in operation at the Ponca Agency before this time but for the long delay in ratifying the supplementary treaty of 1865; and now that this measure has fortunately been accomplished, there can be no further necessity for delay, and it is confidently believed another year will witness the foundation and rapid progress of an English school at this agency."

This superintendent, having been in office only one year, was probably not familiar with the provisions of the treaty of 1859 with the Poncas, in which, by Article three, the United States Government had promised "to establish and maintain for ten years, at an annual expense not to exceed $5000, one or more manual labor schools for the education and training of the Ponca youth in letters, agriculture, mechanics, and housewifery."

This educational annuity has but one more year to run; whatever may have been done with it up to this time, it really is now being spent on schools, and it seems a great pity that it should soon cease. The Governor of Dakota, in 1868, evidently thinks so too, for he writes to the Department, in the autumn of 1868: "A school has been in successful operation at this agency (the Ponca) for the past nine months, with an average attendance of about fifty scholars, and with every evidence of advancement in the primary department of an English education. But just at this interesting period of its existence we are notified by the agent that with this fiscal year all funds for school as well as for agricultural purposes cease, agreeably to the terms and conditions of their original treaty. This will be a serious and irreparable calamity if not remedied by the most generous action of the Government. If funds for this purpose cannot be otherwise procured, the Poncas are willing and anxious to transfer their old reservation to the Government for a moderate extension of these important and indispensable benefits."

The governor also says that in the past year the Poncas have paid out of their annuity money for all the improvements which had been made on lands occupied by certain white settlers, who were ejected from their new reservation by the terms of the last treaty.

In the report for 1869 we read that the Ponca school has been "discontinued for want of funds." The Department earnestly recommends an appropriation of $25,000 to put it in operation again. The new Governor of Dakota seconds the recommendation, and regrets to say that, "for the enlightenment of the 35,000 Indians embraced in the Dakota Superintendency, there is not one school in operation."

In 1870 an appropriation of $5000 was made by the Department from a general educational fund, for the purpose of resuming this school. The condition of the Poncas now is, on the whole, encouraging; they are "not only willing, but extremely anxious to learn the arts by which they may become self-supporting, and conform to the usages of white men. With the comparatively small advantages that have been afforded them, their advancement has been very great."

In the summer of 1869 they built for themselves sixteen very comfortable log-houses; in the summer of 1870 they built forty-four more; with their annuity money they bought cook-stoves, cows, and useful implements of labor. They worked most assiduously in putting in their crops, but lost them all by drought, and are in real danger of starvation if the Government does not assist them. All this while they see herds of cattle driven across their reservation to feed the lately hostile Sioux—flour, coffee, sugar, tobacco, by the wagon-load, distributed to them—while their own always peaceable, always loyal, long-suffering tribe is digging wild roots to eat, and in actual danger of starvation. Nevertheless they are not discouraged, knowing that but for the drought they would have had ample food from their farms, and they make no attempts to retaliate on the Sioux for raiding off their horses and stock, because they hope "that the Government will keep its faith with them," and that suitable remuneration for these losses will be made them, according to the treaty stipulations.

For the next two years they worked industriously and well; three schools were established; a chapel was built by the Episcopal mission; the village began to assume the appearance of permanence and thrift; but misfortune had not yet parted company with the Poncas. In the summer of 1873 the Missouri River suddenly overflowed, washed away its banks hundreds of yards back, and entirely ruined the Ponca village. By working night and day for two weeks the Indians saved most of the buildings, carrying them half a mile inland to be sure of safety. The site of their village became the bed of the main channel of the river; their cornfields were ruined, and the lands for miles in every direction washed and torn up by the floods.

"For nearly two weeks," the agent writes, "the work of salvage from the ever-threatening destruction occupied our whole available force night and day. We succeeded in carrying from the river bank to near half a mile inland the whole of the agency buildings, mechanics' houses, stabling, and sheds —more than twenty houses—nearly every panel of fencing. The Poncas worked well and long, often through the night; and the fact that the disaster did not cost us ten dollars of actual loss is to be attributed to their labor, continuous and persevering—working sometimes over the swiftly-flowing waters, terrible and turbid, on the edge of the newly-formed current but a few inches below them, and into which a fall would have been certain death, even for an Indian."

In one year after this disaster they had recovered themselves marvellously; built twenty new houses; owned over a hundred head of cattle and fifty wagons, and put three hundred acres of land under cultivation (about three acres to each male in the tribe). But this year was not to close without a disaster. First came a drought; then three visitations of locusts, one after the other, which so completely stripped the fields that "nothing was left but a few prematurely dry stalks and straw." One hundred young trees which had been set out—box-elder, soft maple, and others—withered and died.

In 1875 the locusts came again, destroyed the corn and oats, but left the wheat. Much of this crop, however, was lost, as there was only one reaping-machine on the agency, and it could not do all of the work. Many of the Indians saved a part of their crop by cutting it with large butcher-knives; but this was slow, and much of the wheat dried up and perished before it could be harvested by this tedious process.

This year was also marked by a flagrant instance of the helplessness of Indians in the courts. Two Poncas were waylaid by a party of Santees, one of the Poncas murdered, and the other seriously wounded. This occurred at the Yankton Agency, where both parties were visiting. When the case was brought up before the courts, a motion was made to quash the indictment for want of jurisdiction, and the judge was obliged to sustain the motion, there being under the present laws no jurisdiction whatever "over crimes committed by one Indian on the person or property of another Indian in the Indian country."

In 1876 the project of consolidating all the Indians in the United States upon a few reservations began to be discussed and urged. If this plan were carried out, it would be the destiny of the Poncas to go to the Indian Territory. It was very gratuitously assumed that, as they had been anxious to be allowed to remove to Nebraska and join the Omahas, they would be equally ready to remove to Indian Territory—a process of reasoning whose absurdity would be very plainly seen if it were attempted to apply it in the case of white men.

After a series of negotiations, protestations, delays, and bewilderments, the tribe at last gave what the United States Government chose to call a "consent" to the removal. The story of the influences, deceits, coercions brought to bear on these unfortunate creatures before this was brought about, is one of the most harrowing among the harrowing records of our dealings with the Indians. A party of chiefs were induced, in the first place, to go, in company with a United States inspector— Kemble by name—to the Indian Territory, to see whether the country would suit them. It was distinctly promised to them that, if it did not suit them, they should then be permitted to go to Washington and consult with the President as to some further plan for their establishment.

The story of this journey and of its results is best told in the words of one of the Ponca chiefs, Standing Bear. No official document, no other man's narrative—no, not if a second Homer should arise to sing it—could tell the story so well as he tells it :

"We lived on our land as long as we can remember. No one knows how long ago we came there. The land was owned by our tribe as far back as memory of men goes.

"We were living quietly on our farms. All of a sudden one white man came. We had no idea what for. This was the inspector. He came to our tribe with Rev. Mr. Hinman. These two, with the agent, James Lawrence, they made our trouble.

"They said the President told us to pack up—that we must move to the Indian Territory.

"The inspector said to us : 'The President says you must sell this land. He will buy it and pay you the money, and give you new land in the Indian Territory.'

"We said to him : 'We do not know your authority. You have no right to move us till we have had council with the President.'

"We said to him : 'When two persons wish to make a bargain, they can talk together and find out what each wants, and then make their agreement.'

" We said to him : ' We do not wish to go. When a man owns anything, he does not let it go till he has received payment for it.'

" We said to him : ' We will see the President first.'

" He said to us : 'I will take you to see the new land. If you like it, then you can see the President, and tell him so. If not, then you can see him and tell him so.' And he took all ten of our chiefs down. I went, and Bright Eyes' uncle went. He took us to look at three different pieces of land. He said we must take one of the three pieces, so the President said. After he took us down there he said : ' No pay for the land you left.'

" We said to him : ' You have forgotten what you said before we started. You said we should have pay for our land. Now you say not. You told us then you were speaking truth.' All these three men took us down there. The man got very angry. He tried to compel us to take one of the three pieces of land. He told us to be brave. He said to us : ' If you do not accept these, I will leave you here alone. You are one thousand miles from home. You have no money. You have no interpreter, and you cannot speak the language.' And he went out and slammed the door. The man talked to us from long before sundown till it was nine o'clock at night.

" We said to him : ' We do not like this land. We could not support ourselves. The water is bad. Now send us to Washington, to tell the President, as you promised.'

" He said to us : ' The President did not tell me to take you to Washington ; neither did he tell me to take you home.'

" We said to him : ' You have the Indian money you took to bring us down here. That money belongs to us. We would like to have some of it. People do not give away food for nothing. We must have money to buy food on the road.'

"He said to us: 'I will not give you a cent.

"We said to him: 'We are in a strange country. We cannot find our way home. Give us a pass, that people may show us our way.'

"He said: 'I will not give you any.'

"We said to him: 'This interpreter is ours. We pay him. Let him go with us.'

"He said: 'You shall not have the interpreter. He is mine, and not yours.'

"We said to him: 'Take us at least to the railroad; show us the way to that.'

"And he would not. He left us right there. It was winter. We started for home on foot. At night we slept in hay-stacks. We barely lived till morning, it was so cold. We had nothing but our blankets. We took the ears of corn that had dried in the fields; we ate it raw. The soles of our moccasins wore out. We were barefoot in the snow. We were nearly dead when we reached the Otoe Reserve. It had been fifty days. We stayed there ten days to strengthen up, and the Otoes gave each of us a pony. The agent of the Otoes told us he had received a telegram from the inspector, saying that the Indian chiefs had run away; not to give us food or shelter, or help in any way. The agent said: 'I would like to understand. Tell me all that has happened. Tell me the truth.'"

(This Otoe agent afterward said that when the chiefs entered his room they left the prints of their feet in blood on the floor as they came in.)

"Then we told our story to the agent and to the Otoe chiefs —how we had been left down there to find our way.

"The agent said: 'I can hardly believe it possible that any one could have treated you so. That inspector was a poor man to have done this. If I had taken chiefs in this way, I would have brought them home; I could not have left them there.'

"In seven days we reached the Omaha Reservation. Then

we sent a telegram to the President: asked him if he had authorized this thing. We waited three days for the answer. No answer came.

"In four days we reached our own home. We found the inspector there. While we were gone, he had come to our people and told them to move.

"Our people said: 'Where are our chiefs? What have you done with them? Why have you not brought them back? We will not move till our chiefs come back.'

"Then the inspector told them: 'To-morrow you must be ready to move. If you are not ready you will be shot.' Then the soldiers came to the doors with their bayonets, and ten families were frightened. The soldiers brought wagons; they put their things in and were carried away. The rest of the tribe would not move.

"When we got there, we asked the inspector why he had done this thing, and he got very angry.

"Then we said to him: 'We did not think we would see your face again, after what has passed. We thought never to see your face any more. But here you are.'

"We said to him: 'This land is ours. It belongs to us. You have no right to take it from us. The land is crowded with people, and only this is left to us.'

"We said to him: 'Let us alone. Go away from us. If you want money, take all the money which the President is to pay us for twelve years to come. You may have it all, if you will go and leave us our lands.'

"Then, when he found that we would not go, he wrote for more soldiers to come.

"Then the soldiers came, and we locked our doors, and the women and children hid in the woods. Then the soldiers drove all the people the other side of the river, all but my brother Big Snake and I. We did not go; and the soldiers took us and carried us away to a fort and put us in jail.

There were eight officers who held council with us after we got there. The commanding officer said : ' I have received four messages telling me to send my soldiers after you. Now, what have you done ?'

" Then we told him the whole story. Then the officer said : ' You have done no wrong. The land is yours ; they had no right to take it from you. Your title is good. I am here to protect the weak, and I have no right to take you ; but I am a soldier, and I have to obey orders.'

" He said : ' I will telegraph to the President, and ask him what I shall do. We do not think these three men had any authority to treat you as they have done. When we own a piece of land, it belongs to us till we sell it and pocket the money.'

" Then he brought a telegram, and said he had received answer from the President. The President said he knew nothing about it.

" They kept us in jail ten days. Then they carried us back to our home. The soldiers collected all the women and children together ; then they called all the chiefs together in council ; and then they took wagons and went round and broke open the houses. When we came back from the council we found the women and children surrounded by a guard of soldiers.

" They took our reapers, mowers, hay-rakes, spades, ploughs, bedsteads, stoves, cupboards, everything we had on our farms, and put them in one large building. Then they put into the wagons such things as they could carry. We told them that we would rather die than leave our lands ; but we could not help ourselves. They took us down. Many died on the road. Two of my children died. After we reached the new land, all my horses died. The water was very bad. All our cattle died ; not one was left. I stayed till one hundred and fifty-eight of my people had died. Then I ran away with thirty of my people, men and women and children. Some of the children were orphans. We were three months on the road. We were weak and sick and starved. When we reached the Omaha Reserve the Omahas gave us a piece of land, and we were in a hurry to plough it and put in wheat. While we were working the soldiers came and arrested us. Half of us were sick. We would rather have died than have been carried back; but we could not help ourselves."

Nevertheless they were helped. The news of their arrest, and the intention of the Government to take them back by force to Indian Territory, roused excitement in Omaha. An Omaha editor and two Omaha lawyers determined to test the question whether the Government had a legal right to do it. It seemed a bold thing, almost a hopeless thing, to undertake. It has passed into a proverb that Providence is on the side of the heaviest battalions : the oppressed and enslaved in all ages have felt this. But there are times when a simple writ of ha- beas corpus is stronger than cannon or blood-hounds ; and this was one of these times. Brought into the District Court of the United States for the District of Nebraska, these Poncas were set free by the judge of that court. Will not the name of Judge Dundy stand side by side with that of Abraham Lin- coln in the matter of Emancipation Acts?

The Government attorney, the Hon. G. M. Lambertson, made an argument five hours long, said to have been both "ingenious and eloquent," to prove that an Indian was not entitled to the protection of the writ of habeas corpus, "*not* being a person or citizen under the law."

Judge Dundy took several days to consider the case, and gave a decision which strikes straight to the root of the whole matter—a decision which, when it is enforced throughout our land, will take the ground out from under the feet of the horde of unscrupulous thieves who have been robbing, oppressing, and maddening the Indians for so long, that to try to unmask and expose their processes, or to make clean their methods, is a task before which hundreds of good men—nay, whole denominations of good men—disheartened, baffled, and worn-out, have given up.

When Standing Bear found that by the decision of Judge Dundy he was really a free man, and could go where he pleased, he made a speech which should never be forgotten or left out in the history of the dealings of the United States Government with the Indians.

After a touching expression of gratitude to the lawyers who had pleaded his cause, he said: " Hitherto, when we have been wronged, we went to war to assert our rights and avenge our wrongs. We took the tomahawk. We had no law to punish those who did wrong, so we took our tomahawks and went to kill. If they had guns and could kill us first, it was the fate of war. But you have found a better way. You have gone into the court for us, and I find that our wrongs can be righted there. Now I have no more use for the tomahawk. I want to lay it down forever."

Uttering these words with eloquent impressiveness, the old chief, stooping down, placed the tomahawk on the floor at his feet; then, standing erect, he folded his arms with native dignity, and continued: " I lay it down. I have no more use for it. I have found a better way."

Stooping again and taking up the weapon, he placed it in Mr. Webster's hands, and said: " I present it to you as a token of my gratitude. I want you to keep it in remembrance of this great victory which you have gained. I have no further use for it. I can now seek the ways of peace."

The first use that Standing Bear made of his freedom was to endeavor to procure the freedom of his tribe, and establish their legal right to their old home in Dakota. Accompanied by a young and well-educated Omaha girl and her brother as interpreters, and by Mr. Tibbles, the champion and friend to

whom he owed his freedom, he went to the Eastern States, and
told the story of the sufferings and wrongs of his tribe to large
audiences in many of the larger cities and towns.   Money was
generously subscribed everywhere for the purpose of bringing
suits to test the question of the Poncas' legal right to the lands
which the United States Government had by treaty ceded to
them in specified "townships," thus giving to them the same
sort of title which would be given to any corporation or individual.

Very soon this movement of Standing Bear and his companions began to produce on the community a strong effect,
shown by the interest in their public meetings, and by expressions of strong feeling in the newspapers.   This attracted the
attention of the authorities at Washington.   Letters were published contradicting many of Standing Bear's assertions; statements were circulated injurious to the reputation of all members of the party.   A careful observer of the whole course of
the Department of the Interior in this matter could not fail to
come to the conclusion that for some mysterious, unexplained,
and unexplainable reason the Department did not wish — in
fact, was unwilling—that the Ponca tribe should be reinstated
on its lands.   Discussions on the matter grew warm.   The inspector who had been concerned in their removal published
long letters reflecting equally on the veracity of Standing Bear
and of the Secretary of the Interior.   Standing Bear replied
in a few pithy words, which were conclusive in their proving
of the falsity of some of the inspector's statements.   The Secretary, also, did not think it beneath his dignity to reply in
successive newspaper articles to the inspector's reflections upon
him ; but the only thing that was made clear by this means was
that either the Secretary or the inspector, or both, said what
was not true.

In Boston the interest in the Ponca case reached such a
height that a committee was appointed to represent the case in

Washington, and to secure legislation upon it. Standing Bear and his party went to Washington, and, in spite of the secret hostility of the Interior Department, produced a powerful impression upon Congress. Senator Dawes, of Massachusetts, and Senator Morgan, of Alabama, both became warm advocates of their cause. The subject once started, case after case came up for investigation; and the Congressional committees called for evidence in regard to several of the more striking instances of injustice to Indians.

White Eagle, one of the Ponca chiefs, who had lost his wife and four children, and who was himself fast sinking under disease developed by the malarial Indian Territory, came to Washington and gave eloquent testimony in behalf of his tribe. The physicians there predicted that he had not three months to live. A bill was introduced into Congress for restoring to the Poncas their old reservation in Dakota, and putting their houses, farms, etc., in the same good condition they were at the time of their removal.

The story of that removal was written out in full at the time by the agent who superintended it. That he should forward this report to the Department of the Interior was natural; but that the Department of the Interior should have been willing to publish it to the country, to have it on the official record of its management of Indian affairs for the year 1877, is strange. It will make a fitting conclusion to this sketch of the history of the Ponca tribe. The name of this agent was E. A. Howard. He calls the report "Journal of the March."

"*May 21st.* Broke camp at seven o'clock and marched to Crayton, a distance of thirteen miles. Roads very heavy. The child that died yesterday was here buried by the Indians, they preferring to bury it than to have it buried by the white people.

"*May 22d.* Broke camp at seven o'clock and marched to

Neligh, a distance of about twenty-five miles. The day was cool, and, the road being high and comparatively good, the travel was made without much inconvenience.

"*May 23d.* The morning opened with light rain; but at eight o'clock a terrific thunder-storm occurred of two hours' duration, which was followed by steady rain throughout the day, in consequence of which we remained in camp. During the day a child died, and several women and children were reported sick, and medical attendance and medicine were procured for them.

"*May 24th.* Buried the child that died yesterday in the cemetery at Neligh, giving it a Christian burial. Broke camp at ten o'clock and marched about eight miles, crossing the Elkhorn River about two miles below Oakdale Village. Were unable to cross at Neligh, the road being about two feet under water and the bridges being washed away. The road was fearfully bad, and much time and labor were expended in making the road and bridges at all passable over the Elk-horn flats, where the crossing was effected.

"*May 25th.* Broke camp at six o'clock and marched twenty miles, to a point on Shell Creek. No wood at this place, and none to be had except what little had been picked up and brought in by the trains. Weather cold, damp, and dreary. The Indians during the day behaved well, and marched splendidly.

"*May 26th.* The morning opened with a heavy continuous rain, which prevailed until ten o'clock Broke camp at eleven o'clock and marched eight miles farther down Shell Creek, when it again commenced raining, and we went into camp. The evening set in cold and rainy, and no wood to be had except what was purchased of a settler.

"*May 27th.* The morning opened cold, with a misty rain. Rain ceased at half-past seven o'clock, and we broke camp at eight and marched eight miles farther down Shell Creek, when, a heavy thunder-storm coming on, we again went into camp. Several of the Indians were here found to be quite sick, and having no physician, and none being attainable, they gave us much anxiety and no little trouble. The daughter of Standing Bear, one of the chiefs, was very low of consumption, and moving her with any degree of comfort was almost impossible, and the same trouble existed in transporting all the sick.

"*May 28th*. Last evening I gave orders to break camp at five o'clock this morning, intending, if practicable, to reach Columbus before night; but a heavy thunder-storm prevailed at that time. Broke camp at seven o'clock. Marched seven miles, when we came to a slough confluent to Shell Creek, which was only made passable after two hours of active work in cutting willow-brush and bringing a large quantity of wheat straw from a distance of thirty rods, with which we covered the road thickly. After crossing the slough we marched to a point on Shell Creek and camped, having made about fourteen miles during the day.

"*May 29th*. Broke camp at seven o'clock and crossed Shell Creek. For about five miles the road led over a divide, and was quite good; but in coming down on the flats, which extended for five miles between the Bluffs and Columbus, we found the roads for the entire distance almost impassable, owing to the many deep, miry sloughs which cross the road, and the generally flooded and yielding condition of the soil aside from the sloughs. Teams had to be frequently doubled, in order to get the wagons through. The difficulties were finally overcome, and the train marched into Columbus at two o'clock, and went into camp at Soap Fork, having made a march of about ten miles, the march of five miles across the flats occupying about seven hours. Major Walker, who had accompanied us from the Niobrara River to this place with twenty-five soldiers, under orders from the War Department, took leave of us, and returned to Dakota."

It was asserted again and again by the Secretary of the Interior, and by the inspector, E. C. Kemble, that these Indians were not removed by force—that they consented to go.

In another part of this same report this agent says:

"On the 15th" (six days before the "march" began) "I held another council, which was largely attended by the chiefs, headmen, and soldiers of the tribe, and which was of more than four hours' duration. At this council the Indians maintained that the Government had no right to move them from the reservation, and demanded, as an inducement or equivalent for them to give up the reservation and move to the Indian Territory—first, the payment to them by the Government of the sum of $3,000,000 ; and, second, that, before starting, I should show to them the sum of $40,000 which they had been told had been appropriated by the Government for their removal. To all of which I replied positively in the negative, telling them that I would not accede to nor consider any demands that they might make; but that I would take under my consideration reasonable requests that they might submit touching their removal, and, as their agent, do what I could for them in promoting their welfare; that I demanded that they should at all times listen to my words; that they should go with me to their new home; and that *they should without delay give me their final answer whether they would go peaceably or by force.* The Indians refused to give answer at this time; the council closed without definite results; and the Indians dispersed with a sullen look and determined expression."

This evidently was not the "consent" of which we have heard. We come to it presently.

"On the following morning, however, May 16th, they sent word to me, at an early hour, that they had considered my words, and had concluded to go with me, and that they wanted assistance in getting the old and infirm, together with their property, over the Niobrara River, which was much swollen by the rains and at a low temperature."

What a night must these helpless creatures have passed before this "consent" was given! Seven hundred people, *more than half of them women and children ;* a farming people, not armed with rifles, as the Ogallalla Sioux were, when, one year later, on this same ground, the Chief Spotted Tail told Commissioner Hayt that, if he did not give an order to have his tribe on the way back to White Clay Creek in ten days, his young men would go on the war-path at once; and the much-terrified commissioner wrote the order then and there, and the Sioux were allowed to go where they had chosen to go. Behold the difference between the way our Government treats the powerful and treats the weak! What could these Ponca farmers do? They must, "without delay," give their "final answer whether they would go peaceably or *by force.*" What did "*by force*" mean? It was "*by force*" that the Government undertook to compel the Cheyennes to go to Indian Territory; and in that Cheyenne massacre the Cheyenne men, women, children, and babies were all shot down together!

What could these Ponca farmers do? What would any father, brother, husband have done under the circumstances? He would have "consented" to go.

The agent, as was wise, took them at their word, quickly, and that very day, "at five o'clock P.M., had the entire tribe, with their effects, across the river, off the reservation, and in camp in Nebraska."

The agent should have said, "with part of their effects," for it was only a part, and a very small part, that this helpless *consenting* party were allowed to take with them. All their agricultural implements and most of their furniture were left behind.

"It was a hard day's work," the getting the tribe and their "effects" across the river, the agent says; "the river being about forty rods wide, and the current so swift that it was found impossible to move the goods across in any other way

than by packing them on the shoulders of the men, the quick-
sand bottom rendering it unsafe to trust them on the backs
of animals; even the wagons having to be drawn across by
hand."

Let us dwell for a moment on this picture. Seven hundred
helpless, heart-broken people beginning their sad journey by
having to ford this icy stream with quicksands at bottom.
The infirm, the sick, the old, the infants, all carried " by packing them on the shoulders of the men !" What a scene ! The
Honorable Secretary of the Interior said, in one of the letters
in his newspaper controversy with the inspector in regard to
the accounts of this removal, that "the highly-colored stories
which are told about the brutal military force employed in
compelling their [the Poncas'] removal from Dakota to the
Indian Territory are sensational fabrications; at least, the official record, which is very full, and goes into minute details,
does not in the least bear them out."

There was never any accusation brought against the " military force" of " brutality " in this removal. The brutality
was on the part of the Government. The simple presence
of the "military force" was brutal. It meant but one thing.
The Indians understood it, and the Government[12] intended that
they should understand it; and when the agent of the Government said to these Indians that they must give him their " final
answer whether they would go peaceably or by force," he
intended that they should understand it. Has anybody any
doubt what were the orders under which that "military force"
was there ? any doubt what it would have been the military
duty of Major Walker to have done in case the Poncas had refused to "consent" to go?

And now let us return to the " Official Record," which is,
indeed, as the Honorable Secretary of the Interior says, " very
full," and "goes into minute details," and let us see in how
much it will "bear us out;" and when we have done with this

[12] Forever distrustful of government, Mrs. Jackson wrote to an
editor that a society which "deluges a country once in four years
with such a flood of corruption and malignity as we are forced to
wade and wallow in every election year, is a bad one." A.l.s.,
Helen Hunt Jackson to William Hayes Ward, Nov. 1, 1876,
Huntington Library, San Marino, Calif.

"Official Record," let us ask ourselves if any imagination could have invented so "highly-colored" a "story" as it tells.

"*June 2d.* Broke camp at seven o'clock and marched seventeen miles, going into camp near Ulysses. Roads in bad condition.

"*June 3d.* Had some trouble in getting started. Broke camp at eleven o'clock and marched eight miles. Went into camp on Blue River. Many people sick, one of whom was reported in a dying condition. Had bad roads. Rained during afternoon.

"*June 4th.* Broke camp at six o'clock. Marched fifteen miles, and went into camp on Lincoln Creek, near Seward.

"*June 5th.* Broke camp at seven o'clock. Marched fourteen miles, and went into camp near Milford. Daughter of Standing Bear, Ponca chief, died at two o'clock, of consumption.

"*June 6th.* Remained in camp all day, for the purpose of obtaining supplies. Prairie Flower, wife of Shines White and daughter of Standing Bear, who died yesterday, was here given Christian burial, her remains being deposited in the cemetery at Milford, Nebraska, a small village on Blue River.

"In this connection I wish to take official knowledge and recognition of the noble action performed by the ladies of Milford, in preparing and decorating the body of the deceased Indian woman for burial in a style becoming the highest civilization. In this act of Christian kindness they did more to ameliorate the grief of the husband and father than they could have done by adopting the usual course of this untutored people and presenting to each a dozen ponies. It was here that, looking on the form of his dead daughter thus arrayed for the tomb, Standing Bear was led to forget the burial-service of his tribe, and say to those around him that he was desirous of leaving off the ways of the Indian and adopting those of the white men.

"*June 7th.* Quite a heavy rain during the afternoon. The storm, most disastrous of any that occurred during the removal of the Poncas under my charge, came suddenly upon us while in camp on the evening of this day.   It was a storm such as I never before experienced, and of which I am unable to give an adequate description.   The wind blew a fearful tornado, demolishing every tent in camp, and rending many of them into shreds, overturning wagons, and hurling wagon-boxes, camp-equipages, etc., through the air in every direction like straws. Some of the people were taken up by the wind and carried as much as three hundred yards.   Several of the Indians were quite seriously hurt, and one child died the next day from injuries received, and was given Christian burial.   The storm caused a delay until the 8th for repairs, and for medical attendance upon the injured.

"*June 8th.* Broke camp at Milford and marched seven miles.   Roads very bad.   Child died during the day.

"*June 9th.* Put the child that died yesterday in the coffin and sent it back to Milford, to be buried in the same grave with its aunt, Prairie Flower.   Broke camp at seven o'clock and marched to within three miles of Crete.

"*June 10th.* Broke camp at seven o'clock and marched one mile beyond De Witt, where I employed a physician to visit camp and prescribe for the sick.   A woman had a thumb accidentally cut off, which caused further commotion in the camp.

"*June 12th.* Broke camp at seven o'clock and marched to within two miles of Otoe Agency.   Crossed Wolf Creek with a part of the train, the crossing being very difficult; but the Indians worked splendidly."

"The Indians worked splendidly!"   Is not this a well-nigh incredible record of patience and long-suffering?   These poor creatures, marching from ten to twenty-five miles a day, for twenty-two days, through muddy sloughs, swollen rivers, in tempests and floods and dreary cold, leaving their wives and their children dead by the way—dead of the sufferings of the march—are yet docile, obedient, and " work splendidly !"

"*June* 13*th*. After considerable time we succeeded in building a bridge over Wolf Creek out of drift-timber, and succeeded in crossing the balance of the train. Broke camp and marched three miles, and went into camp again near Otoe Agency.

"*June* 14*th*. Water-bound, and had to remain in camp all day waiting for creek to run down. The Otoe Indians came out to see the Poncas, and gave them ten ponies.

"*June* 15*th*. Still water-bound. Remained in camp all day.

"*June* 16*th*. Broke camp at seven o'clock and reached Marysville, Kansas, where we went into camp. During the march a wagon tipped over, injuring a woman quite severely. Indians out of rations, and feeling hostile."

What wonder that the Indians felt hostile ? Hunger added to all the rest of their direful misery !

"*June* 18*th*. Broke camp at seven o'clock. Marched nine miles and went into camp at Elm Creek. Little Cottonwood died. Four families determined to return to Dakota. I was obliged to ride nine miles on horseback to overtake them, to restore harmony, and settle difficulty in camp. Had coffin made for dead Indian, which was brought to camp at twelve o'clock at night from Blue Rapids. A fearful thunder-storm during the night, flooding the camp-equipage."

This is a "highly-colored" story, indeed ! The darkness; the camp flooded by the driving rain ; thunder and lightning; a messenger arriving at midnight with a coffin ; the four families of desperate fugitives setting out to flee back to their homes ! What "sensational fabrication" could compete with this ?

"*June* 19*th*. The storm of last night left the roads in an impassable condition, and, in consequence, was obliged to remain in camp all day. Buried Little Cottonwood in a cemetery about five miles from camp. * * *

"*June* 25*th*. Broke camp at six o'clock. Marched to a point about fifteen miles farther up Deep Creek. Two old women died during the day. * * *

"*June* 30*th*. Broke camp at six o'clock. Passed through Hartford, and camped about six miles above Burlington. A child of Buffalo Chief died during the day. * * *

"*July* 2*d*. Broke camp at six o'clock. Made a long march of fifteen miles for Noon Camp, for reason that no water could be got nearer. An Indian became hostile, and made a desperate attempt to kill White Eagle, head chief of the tribe. For a time every male in camp was on the war-path, and for about two hours the most intense excitement prevailed, heightened by continued loud crying by all the women and children."

This Indian, who is reported here as having "become hostile," no doubt, tried to kill White Eagle for having allowed the tribe to be brought into all this trouble. It is the general feeling among the less intelligent members of a tribe that their chiefs are bound, under all circumstances, to see that they come to no harm.

"*July* 9*th*. Broke camp at six o'clock, passing through Baxter Springs at about one o'clock. Just after passing Baxter Springs a terrible thunder-storm struck us. The wind blew a heavy gale and the rain fell in torrents, so that it was impossible to see more than four or five rods distant, thoroughly drenching every person and every article in the train, making a fitting end to a journey commenced by wading a river and thereafter encountering innumerable storms.

"During the last few days of the journey the weather was exceedingly hot, and the teams terribly annoyed and bitten by green-head flies, which attacked them in great numbers. Many of the teams were nearly exhausted, and, had the distance been but little farther, they must have given out. The people were all nearly worn out from the fatigue of the march, and were heartily glad that the long, tedious journey was at an end, that

they might take that rest so much required for the recuperation of their physical natures." Now let us see what provision
the Government had made for that "rest" and "recuperation,"
surely "much required" and fairly earned. Not one dollar had
been appropriated for establishing them in their new home; not
one building had been put up. This people was set down in a
wilderness without one provision of any kind for their shelter.

"It is a matter of astonishment to me," says Agent Howard
(p. 100 of this "Report"), "that the Government should have
ordered the removal of the Ponca Indians from Dakota to the
Indian Territory without having first made some provision for
their settlement and comfort. Before their removal was carried
into effect an appropriation should have been made by Congress sufficient to have located them in their new home, by
building a comfortable home for the occupancy of every family
of the tribe. As the case now is, no appropriation has been
made by Congress except of a sum little more than sufficient
to remove them; and the result is that these people have been
placed on an uncultivated reservation, to live in their tents as
best they may, and await further legislative action."

This journal of Mr. Howard's is the best record that can ever
be written of the sufferings of the Poncas in their removal
from their homes. It is "highly colored;" but no one, however
much it may be for his interest to do so, can call it "a sensational fabrication," or can discredit it in the smallest particular,
for it is an "official record," authorized and endorsed by being
published in the "Annual Report" of the Secretary of the Interior.

The remainder of the Ponca tribe is still in Indian Territory,
awaiting anxiously the result of the efforts to restore to them
their old homes, and to establish the fact of their indisputable
legal right to them.

CHAPTER VII.

THE WINNEBAGOES.

THE Winnebagoes[13] belonged to the Dakota family, but, so far as can be known, were naturally a peace-loving people, and had no sympathy with the more warlike tribes of their race. The Algonquins gave them the name of Winnebagoes, or "people of the salt-water;" and as the Algonquin word for salt-water and stinking-water was the same, the French called them "Les Puants," or "Stinkards." The Sioux gave them a more melodious and pleasing name, "O-ton-kah," which signified "The large, strong people."

Bancroft, in his account of the North American tribes, says: "One little community of the Dakota (Sioux) family had penetrated the territories of the Algonquins: the Winnebagoes dwelling between Green Bay and the lake that bears their name preferred to be environed by Algonquins than to stay in the dangerous vicinity of their own kindred."

One of the earliest mentions that is found of this tribe, in the diplomatic history of our country, is in the reports given of a council held in July, 1815, at "Portage des Sioux," in Missouri, after the treaty of Ghent. To this council the Winnebagoes refused to send delegates; and their refusal was evidently considered a matter of some moment. The commissioners "appointed to treat with the North-western Indians" at this time reported that they found "the Indians much divided among themselves in regard to peace with the United States." Some of them "spoke without disguise of their opposition to military establishments on the Mississippi," and

[13] There is little scholarship on the Winnebagoes. See, however, Joseph Schafer, *The Winnebago-Horicon Basin* (Madison, Wisconsin, 1937) and Bruce E. Mahan, "Winnebago and Pottawattamie," *Palimpsest* IX (1928), pp. 53–55.

many of them, "among whom were the Winnebagoes, utterly refused to send deputies to the council." This disaffection was thought by the commissioners to be largely due to the influence of British traders, who plied the Indians with gifts, and assured them that war would soon break out again between the United States and Great Britain. It is probable, however, that the Winnebagoes held themselves aloof from these negotiations more from a general distrust of white men than from any partisan or selfish leaning to the side of Great Britain; for when Dr. Jedediah Morse visited them, only seven years later, he wrote: "There is no other tribe which seems to possess so much jealousy of the whites, and such reluctance to have intercourse with them, as this."

Spite of this reluctance they made, in 1816, a treaty "of peace and friendship with the United States," agreeing "to remain distinct and separate from the rest of their nation or tribe, giving them no assistance whatever until peace shall be concluded between the United States and their tribe or nation." They agreed also to confirm and observe all the lines of British, French, or Spanish cessions of land to the United States.

In 1825 the United States Government, unable to endure the spectacle of Indians warring among themselves, and massacring each other, appears in the North-western country as an unselfish pacificator, and compels the Sacs, Foxes, Chippewas, and Sioux, including the Winnebagoes, to make a treaty of peace and friendship with each other and with the United States. The negotiations for this treaty occupied one month; which does not seem a long time when one considers that the boundaries of all the lands to be occupied by these respective tribes were to be defined, and that in those days and regions definitions of distance were stated in such phrases as "a half day's march," "a long day's march," "about a day's paddle in a canoe," "to a point where the woods come out into the meadows," "to a point on Buffalo River, half way between its source and its mouth." These were surely precarious terms for peace to rest upon, especially as it was understood by all parties that " no tribe shall hunt within the actual limits of any other without their consent."

At the close of this treaty there occurred a curious incident, which Schoolcraft calls " an experiment on the moral sense of the Indians with regard to intoxicating liquors." " It had been said by the tribes that the true reason for the Commissioners of the United States speaking against the use of ardent spirits by the Indians, and refusing to give them, was the fear of expense, and not a sense of its bad effects. To show them that the Government was above such a petty motive, the commissioners had a long row of tin camp-kettles, holding several gallons each, placed on the grass; and then, after some suitable remarks, each kettle was spilled out in their presence. The thing was ill-relished by the Indians, who loved the whiskey better than the joke."

At this time the lands of the Winnebagoes lay between the Rock and the Wisconsin rivers, along the shore of Winnebago Lake, and the Indians claimed that the whole lake belonged to them. It was here that President Morse had found them living in 1822. He gives the following graphic picture of their pleasant home: "They have five villages on the Lake, and fourteen on Rock River. The country has abundance of springs, small lakes, ponds, and rivers; a rich soil, producing corn and all sorts of grain. The lakes abound with fine-flavored, firm fish." Of the Indians themselves, he says: "They are industrious, frugal, and temperate. They cultivate corn, potatoes, pumpkins, squashes, and beans, and are remarkably provident. They numbered five hundred and eighty souls."

In 1827 a third treaty was signed by the Winnebagoes, Chippewas, and Menomonies with the United States and with each other. This treaty completed the system of boundaries of their lands, which had been only partially defined by the two

previous treaties. Of these three treaties Schoolcraft says:
"These three conferences embody a new course and policy for
keeping the tribes in peace, and are founded on the most enlarged consideration of the aboriginal right of fee-simple to
the soil. They have been held exclusively at the charge and
expense of the United States, and contain no cession of territory."

They were the last treaties of their kind. In 1828 the people of Northern Illinois were beginning to covet and trespass
on some of the Indian lands, and commissioners were sent to
treat with the Indians for the surrender of such lands. The
Indians demurred, and the treaty was deferred; the United
States in the mean time agreeing to pay to the four tribes
$20,000, "in full compensation for all the injuries and dam-
ages sustained by them in consequence of the occupation of
any part of the mining country."

In 1829 a benevolent scheme for the rescue of these hard-
pressed tribes of the North-western territory was proposed by
Mr. J. D. Stevens, a missionary at Mackinaw. He suggested
the formation of a colony of them in the Lake Superior region.
He says—and his words are as true to-day, in 1879, as they
were fifty years ago: "The Indian is in every view entitled to
sympathy. The misfortune of the race is that, seated on the
skirts of the domain of a popular government, they have no
vote to give. They are politically a nonentity. * * * The whole
Indian race is not worth one white man's vote. If the Indian
were raised to the right of giving his suffrage, a plenty of politicians on the frontiers would enter into plans to better him;
whereas now the subject drags along like an incubus in Congress."

It did, indeed. Appropriations were sadly behindhand. The
promises made to the Indians could not be fulfilled, simply
because there was no money to fulfil them with. In 1829 a
Washington correspondent writes to Mr. Schoolcraft: "There

is a screw loose in the public machinery somewhere.   In 1827
we were promised $48,000 for the Indian service, and got
$30,000; in 1828 $40,000, and got $25,000."   A little later
the Secretary of War himself writes: "Our annual appropriation has not yet passed; and when it will, I am sure I cannot
tell."

In 1830 the all-engrossing topic of Congress is said to be
"the removal of the Indians. It occupies the public mind
throughout the Union, and petitions and remonstrances are
pouring in without number."

Meantime the Indians were warring among themselves, and
also retaliating on the white settlers who encroached upon their
lands.   The inevitable conflict had begun in earnest, and in
September of 1832 the Winnebagoes were compelled to make
their first great cession of territory to the United States.   In
exchange for it they accepted a tract west of the Mississippi,
and before the 1st of June, 1833, most of those who were living on the ceded lands had crossed the river to their new
homes.   Their title to this new country was not so good as
they probably supposed, for the treaty expressly stated that it
was granted to them "to be held as other Indian lands are
held."

Article three of this treaty said, "As the country hereby
ceded by the Winnebagoes is more extensive and valuable than
that given by the United States in exchange," the United States
would pay to the Winnebagoes $10,000 annually in specie for
twenty-seven years.   The Government also promised to put up
buildings for them, send teachers, make various allowances for
stock, implements, tobacco, etc., and to furnish them with a
doctor.

The Winnebagoes agreed to deliver up some of their number who had murdered white settlers.   Lands were granted by
patent to four Winnebagoes by name—two men and two
women; for what reason, does not appear in the treaty.

Five years later the Winnebagoes ceded to the United States all their lands east of the Mississippi, and also relinquished the right to occupy, "except for hunting," a portion of that which they owned on the west side. For this cession and relinquishment they were to receive $200,000; part of this sum to be expended in paying their debts, the expense of their removal and establishment in their new homes, and the rest to be invested by the United States Government for their benefit.

In 1846 the Winnebagoes were forced to make another treaty, by which they finally ceded and sold to the United States "all right, title, interest, claim, and privilege to all lands heretofore occupied by them;" and accepted as their home, "to be held as other Indian lands are held," a tract of 800,000 acres north of St. Peter's, and west of the Mississippi. For this third removal they were to be paid $190,000 — $150,000 for the lands they gave up, and $40,000 for relinquishing the hunting privilege on lands adjacent to their own. Part of this was to be expended in removing them, and the balance was to be "left in trust" with the Government at five per cent. interest.

This reservation proved unsuited to them. The tribe were restless and discontented; large numbers of them were continually roaming back to their old homes in Iowa and Wisconsin, and in 1855 they gladly made another treaty with the Government, by which they ceded back to the United States all the land which the treaty of 1846 had given them, and took in exchange for it a tract eighteen miles square on the Blue Earth River. The improved lands on which they had been living, their mills and other buildings, were to be appraised and sold to the highest bidder, and the amount expended in removing them, subsisting them, and making them comfortable in their new home. This reservation, the treaty said, should be their "permanent home;" and as this phrase had never before been used in any of their treaties, it is to be presumed that the

Winnebagoes took heart at hearing it. They are said to have "settled down quietly and contentedly," and have gone to work immediately, "ploughing, planting, and building."

The citizens of Minnesota did not take kindly to their new neighbors. "An indignation meeting was held; a petition to the President signed; and movements made, the object of all which was to oust these Indians from their dearly-purchased homes," says the Report of the Indian Commissioner for 1855.

Such movements, and such a public sentiment on the part of the population surrounding them, certainly did not tend to encourage the Winnebagoes to industry, or to give them any very sanguine hopes of being long permitted to remain in their "permanent home." Nevertheless they worked on, doing better and better every year, keeping good faith with the whites and with the Government, and trusting in the Government's purpose and power to keep faith with them. The only serious faults with which they could be charged were drunkenness and gambling, and both of these they had learned of the white settlers. In the latter they had proved to be apt scholars, often beating professional gamblers at their own game.

They showed the bad effects of their repeated removals, also, in being disposed to wander back to their old homes. Sometimes several hundred of them would be roaming about in Wisconsin. But the tribe, as a whole, were industrious, quiet, always peaceable and loyal, and steadily improving. They took hold in earnest of the hard work of farming; some of them who could not get either horses or ploughs actually breaking up new land with hoes, and getting fair crops out of it. Very soon they began to entreat to have their farms settled on them individually, and guaranteed to them for their own; and the Government, taking advantage of this desire on their part, made a treaty with them in 1859, by which part of their lands were to be "allotted" to individuals in "severalty," as they had requested, and the rest were to be sold, the proceeds to be partly expended in improvements on their farms, and partly to be "left in trust" with the Government. This measure threw open hundreds of thousands of acres of land to white settlers, and drew the belt of greedy civilization much tighter around the Indians. Similar treaties to this had been already made with some of the Sioux tribes and with others. It was evident that "the surplus land occupied by the Indians was required for the use of the increasing white population," and that it was "necessary to reduce the reservations."

There is in this treaty of 1859 one extraordinary provision: "In order to render unnecessary any further treaty engagements or arrangements with the United States, it is hereby agreed and stipulated that the President, with the assent of Congress, shall have full power to modify or change any of the provisions of former treaties with the Winnebagoes, in such manner and to whatever extent he may judge to be necessary and expedient for their welfare and best interest."

It is impossible to avoid having a doubt whether the chiefs and headmen of the Winnebago tribe who signed this treaty ever heard that proviso. It is incredible that they could have been so simple and trustful as to have assented to it.

Prospects now brightened for the Winnebagoes. With their farms given to them for their own, and a sufficient sum of money realized by the sale of surplus lands to enable them to thoroughly improve the remainder, their way seemed open to prosperity and comfort. They "entered upon farming with a zeal and energy which gave promise of a prosperous and creditable future."

"Every family in the tribe has more or less ground under cultivation," says their agent. He reports, also, the minutes of a council held by the chiefs, which tell their own story:

"When we were at Washington last winter, we asked our Great Father to take $300,000 out of the $1,100,000, so that we could commence our next spring's work. We do not want all of the $1,100,000, only sufficient to carry on our improvements. This money we ask for we request only as a loan; and when our treaty is ratified, we want it replaced. We want to buy cattle, horses, ploughs, and wagons; and this money can be replaced when our lands are sold. We hope you will get this money: we want good farms and good houses. Many have already put on white man's clothes, and more of us will when our treaty is ratified.

"Father, we do not want to make you tired of talk, but hope you will make a strong paper, and urgent request of our Great Father in respect to our wishes."

In 1860 the Commissioner of Indian Affairs writes: "The Winnebagoes continue steadily on the march of improvement. * * * The progress of the Winnebagoes in agricultural growths is particularly marked with success. There have been raised by individuals as high as sixty acres of wheat on a single farm. * * * The agent's efforts have been directed to giving to each Indian his own allotment of land. * * * Wigwams are becoming as scarce as houses were two years ago. * * * All Indians who had horses ploughed and farmed their own lands. * * * The Indians were promised that new and comfortable houses should be built for them. The treaty not yet being ratified, I have no funds in my hands that could be made applicable to this purpose. * * * The greater part of the Indians have entreated me to carry out the meaning of the commissioner on his visit here, and the reasons for my not doing so do not seem comprehensible to them. * * * The school is in a flourishing condition."

In 1861 the commissioner writes that the allotment of lands in severalty to the Winnebagoes has been "substantially accomplished;" but that the sales of the remaining lands have not yet been made, owing to the unsettled condition of the country, and therefore the funds on which the Indians were depending for the improvements of their farms have not been paid to them. They complain bitterly that the provisions of the treaty of 1859 have not been fulfilled. "It has been two years and a half since this treaty was concluded," says the agent, "and the Indians have been told from one season to another that something would be done under it for their benefit, and as often disappointed, till the best of them begin to doubt whether anything will be done. * * * The Indians who have had their allotments made are 'clamoring for their certificates.'"

Drunkenness is becoming one of the serious vices of the tribe. They are surrounded on all sides by white men who traffic in whiskey, and who are, moreover, anxious to reduce the Indians to as degraded a state as possible. "There are some circumstances connected with the location of this tribe which make it more difficult to protect them from the ravages of liquor-selling than any other tribe. They are closely surrounded by a numerous white population, and these people feel very indignant because the Indians are settled in their midst, and are disposed to make it as uncomfortable for them to remain here as they can, hoping at some future time they may be able to cause their removal."

The time was not far distant. In 1862 we find the Winnebagoes in trouble indeed. A ferocious massacre of white settlers by the Sioux had so exasperated the citizens of Minnesota, that they demanded the removal of all Indians from the State. The people were so excited that not an Indian could step outside the limits of the reservation without the risk of being shot at sight. The Winnebagoes had utterly refused to join the Sioux in their attack on the whites, and had been threatened by them with extermination in consequence of this loyalty. Thus they were equally in danger from both whites and Indians: their position was truly pitiable.

In the Annual Report of the Interior Department for 1862 the condition of things is thus described: "While it may be

true that a few of the Winnebagoes were engaged in the atrocities of the Sioux, the tribe, as such, is no more justly responsible for their acts than our Government would be for a pirate
who happened to have been born on our territory.   Notwithstanding this, the exasperation of the people of Minnesota
appears to be nearly as great toward the Winnebagoes as toward the Sioux.   They demand that the Winnebagoes as well
as the Sioux shall be removed from the limits of the State.
The Winnebagoes are unwilling to move.   Yet the Minnesota
people are so excited that not a Winnebago can leave his reservation without risk of being shot; and as they have never
received their promised implements of agriculture, and the
game on their reservation is exhausted, and their arms have
been taken from them, they are starving."

Their agent writes: "These Indians have been remaining
here in a continuous state of suspense, waiting for the Government to cause the stipulations of the treaty of 1859 to be carried into operation: such has been their condition for three
years and a half, and they do not understand why it is so. * * *
The fact that a very few of the Winnebagoes were present
and witnessed, if they did not take part in, the massacre at the
Lower Sioux Agency, has caused the Winnebagoes themselves
to be universally suspected of disloyalty. * * * The hostile feelings of the white people are so intense, that I am necessitated
to use extra efforts to keep the Indians upon their own lands.
I have been notified by the whites that the Indians will be
massacred if they go out of their own country ; and it is but a
few days since an Indian was killed while crossing the Mississippi River, for no other reason than that he was an Indian,
and such is the state of public opinion that the murderer goes
unpunished."

As to the loyalty of the tribe, the agent says: "There is no
tribe of Indians more so."   There is "no doubt of their loyalty as a tribe. * * * In consequence of a threat made by the

Sioux, immediately upon their outbreak, that they (the Sioux) would exterminate the Winnebagoes unless they joined them in a raid against the white people, the Winnebagoes have lived in fear of an attack from the Sioux, and have almost daily implored me for protection. * * * To further assure them, I requested of the Governor of the State that two companies of United States infantry be stationed here in their midst, which has allayed their fears. * * * Notwithstanding the nearness of the belligerent Sioux, and the unfriendly feelings of the white people, and other unfortunate circumstances, I am confident that my Indians will remain loyal to the last. * * * They have been informed that, notwithstanding their fidelity to the Government and the people, the people of this State are memorializing Congress to remove them out of the State—which they consider very unjust under the circumstances, for they have become attached to this location and would not leave it willingly, and think their fidelity ought to entitle them to respect and kind treatment."

The "popular demand" of the people of Minnesota triumphed. In February, 1863, Congress passed an act authorizing the "peaceful and quiet removal of the Winnebago Indians from the State of Minnesota, and the settling of them on a new reserve." It was determined to locate them "on the Missouri River somewhere within a hundred miles of Fort Randall, where it is not doubted they will be secure from any danger of intrusion from whites." All their guns, rifles, and pistols were to be taken from them, "securely boxed up," labelled " with the names of their respective owners." The Department impressed it on the agent in charge of the removal that it was "absolutely necessary that no time should be lost in the emigrating of these Indians." The hostile Sioux were to be removed at the same time, and to a reservation adjoining the reservation of the Winnebagoes. The reports of the Indian Bureau for 1863 tell the story of this removal.

The commissioner says: "The case of the Winnebagoes is one of peculiar hardship. I am still of the opinion that this tribe was in no manner implicated in or responsible for the cruel and wanton outbreak on the part of the Sioux; but its consequences to the tribe have been as disastrous as unmerited. In obedience to the Act of Congress, and the popular demand of the people of Minnesota, they have been removed to a new location upon the Missouri River, adjoining that selected for the Sioux. Contrasting the happy homes, and the abundant supply for all their wants which they have left behind them, with the extreme desolation which prevails throughout the country, including their present location, and their almost defenceless state, as against the hostile savages in their vicinity, their present condition is truly pitiable; and it is not surprising that they have become to some extent discouraged, and are dissatisfied with their new homes. It cannot be disguised that their removal, although nominally peaceable and with their consent, was the result of the overwhelming pressure of the public sentiment of the community in which they resided; and it is to be feared that it will be many years before their confidence in the good faith of our Government, in its professed desire to ameliorate and improve their condition, will be restored. Their misfortunes and good conduct deserve our sympathy."

The Act of Congress above mentioned provides for the peaceable removal of the Indians. In its execution some of the members of the tribe were found unwilling to leave their homes; and as there was neither the disposition nor the power to compel them to accompany their brethren, they remained upon their old reservation. The most of them are represented as having entirely abandoned the Indian habits and customs, and as being fully qualified by good conduct and otherwise for civilized life. Many of them are enlisted in the military service, and all are desirous of retaining possession of the homes allotted to them under the provisions of their treaty.

"The trust lands belonging to the tribe have been placed in the market, and from the amount already sold has been realized $82,537 62. An appraisement has also been had of the lands of the diminished reserve, and the same will soon be placed in the market."

In the Report of the Superintendent of the North-west Territory for the same year is the following summing up of their case: "The case of these Winnebago Indians is one of peculiar hardship. Hurried from their comfortable homes in Minnesota, in 1863, almost without previous notice, huddled together on steamboats with poor accommodations, and transported to the Crow Creek Agency in Dakota Territory at an expense to themselves of more than $50,000, they were left, after a very imperfect and hasty preparation of their new agency for their reception, upon a sandy beach on the west bank of the Missouri River, in a country remarkable only for the rigors of its winter climate and the sterility of its soil, to subsist themselves where the most industrious and frugal white man would fail, five years out of six, to raise enough grain upon which to subsist a family. The stern alternative was presented to this unfortunate people, thus deprived of comfortable homes (on account of no crime or misdemeanor of their own), of abandoning this agency, or encountering death from cold or starvation. They wisely chose the former; and after encountering hardships and sufferings too terrible to relate, and the loss of several hundred of their tribe by starvation and freezing, they arrived at their present place of residence [the Omaha Agency] in a condition which excited the active sympathy of all who became acquainted with the story of their wrongs. There they have remained, trusting that the Government would redeem its solemn promise to place them in a position west of the Missouri which should be as comfortable as the one which they occupied in Minnesota.

"This tribe is characterized by frugality, thrift, and industry to an extent unequalled by any other tribe of Indians in the North-west. Loyal to the Government, and peaceable toward their neighbors, they are entitled to the fostering care of the General Government. The improvement of the homes which they have voluntarily selected for their future residence will place them in a short time beyond the reach of want, and take from the Government the burden of supplying their wants at an actual expense of $100,000."

It was in May, 1863, that the Winnebagoes gathered at Fort Snelling, ready for their journey. The chiefs are said to have "acquiesced in the move as a matter of necessity, for the protection of their people," but some of them "actually shed tears on taking leave." Colonel Mix, who was in charge of this removal, wrote to Washington, urgently entreating that tents at least might be provided for them on their arrival at their new homes in the wilderness. He also suggests that it is a question whether they ought to be settled so near the hostile Sioux, especially as just before leaving Minnesota some of the tribe had "scalped three Sioux Indians, thinking it would propitiate them in the kind regards of their Great Father at Washington, and, as a consequence, they would perhaps be permitted to remain in Minnesota."

The removal was accomplished in May and June. There were, all told, 1945 of the Winnebagoes. They arrived to find themselves in an almost barren wilderness—a dry, hard soil, "too strong for ploughs;" so much so, that it was "difficult to get a plough to run a whole day without breaking." A drought had parched the grass, so that in many places where the previous year several tons of good hay to an acre had been raised there was not now "pasturage for a horse." The cottonwood timber, all which could be procured, was "crooked, difficult to handle, full of wind-shakes, rots, etc." The channel of the Missouri River here was so "changeable," and the banks so low, that it was "dangerous to get too near." They were obliged therefore to settle half a mile away from the river. No wonder that on July 1st the Winnebagoes are reported as "not pleased with their location, and anxious to return to Minnesota, or to some other place among the whites." They gathered together in council, and requested Superintendent Thompson to write to their Great Father for permission "to move among the whites again. * * * They have lived so long among the whites that they are more afraid of wild Indians than the whites are." The superintendent hopes, however, they will be more contented as soon as he can get them comfortable buildings. But on July 16th we find Brigadier-general Sulley, commander of the North-western expedition against Indians, writing to the Department in behalf of these unfortunate creatures. General Sulley having been detained in camp near Crow Creek on account of the low water, the chiefs had gone to him with their tale of misery. "They stated that nothing would grow here. They dare not go out to hunt for fear of other tribes, and they would all starve to death. This I believe to be true, without the Government intends to ration them all the time. The land is sandy, dry, and parched up. * * * The land is poor; a low, sandy soil. I don't think you can depend on a crop of corn even once in five years, as it seldom rains here in the summer. * * * I find them hard at work making canoes, with the intention of quitting the agency and going to join the Omahas or some other tribe down the river. They said they had been promised to be settled on the Big Sioux River. * * * I told them they must stay here till they get permission from Washington to move; that, if they attempted it, they would be fired on by my troops stationed down the river."

This is a graphic picture of the condition of a band of two thousand human beings, for whose "benefit" $82,537 62 had just been realized from sale of their lands by the Government, to say nothing of the property they owned in lands yet unsold, and in annuity provisions of previous treaties to the amount of over $1,000,000 capital! Is not their long suffering, their patience, well-nigh incredible?

Spite of the dread of being fired on by the United States troops, they continued to make canoes and escape in them from this "new home" in the desert, and in October the Department of the Interior began to receive letters containing paragraphs like this: "I have also to report that small detachments of Winnebagoes are constantly arriving in canoes, locating on our reserve, and begging for food to keep them from starving."—*Agent for Omaha Agency.*

These are the men who only one year before had been living in comfortable homes, with several hundred acres of good ground under cultivation, and "clamoring for certificates" of their "allotted" farms—now shelterless, worse than homeless, escaping by canoe-loads, under fire of United States soldiers, from a barren desert, and "clamoring" for food at Indian agencies!

The Department of the Interior promptly reports to the Superintendent of Indian Affairs in Minnesota this "information," and calls it "astounding." The Department had "presumed that Agent Balcombe would adopt such measures as would induce the Winnebagoes to remain upon their reservation," and had "understood that ample arrangements had been made for their subsistence." It, however, ordered the Omaha agent to feed the starving refugees till spring, and it sent word to those still remaining on the reservation that they must not "undertake to remove without the consent of their Great Father, as it is his determination that a home that shall be healthy, pleasant, and fertile, shall be furnished to them at the earliest practicable moment."

This was in the autumn of 1863. In one year no less than 1222 of the destitute Winnebagoes had escaped and made their way to the Omaha Reservation in Nebraska. Here the

Superintendent of the Northern Superintendency held a council with them.

"They expressed," he says, "a strong desire to have some arrangement made by which they would be allowed to occupy a portion of that reservation. It was represented that the Omahas wished it also. * * * I found that I could not gain their consent to go back to their reservation, and I had no means within my reach of forcing them back, even if I had deemed it proper to do so." The superintendent recommended, therefore, that they be subsisted where they were "until some arrangement be made for their satisfaction, or some concert of action agreed upon between the War Department and the Interior Department by which they can be kept on their reservation after they shall have been moved there."

In September of this same year the agent for the Winnebago Reserve wrote that the absence of a protecting force had been one of the reasons of the Indians leaving in such numbers. "Both the Winnebagoes and Sioux who have stayed here have lived in fear and trembling close to the stockade, and have refused to separate and live upon separate tracts of land."

He gives some further details as to the soil and climate. "The region has been subject, as a general rule, to droughts, and the destructive visits of grasshoppers and other insects. The soil has a great quantity of alkali in it; it is an excessively dry climate; it very seldom rains, and dews are almost unknown here: almost destitute of timber. * * * It is generally supposed that game is plenty about here. This is an erroneous impression. There are but a very few small streams, an entire absence of lakes, and an almost entire destitution of timber—the whole country being one wilderness of dry prairie for hundreds of miles around; hence there is but a very little small game, fish, or wild fruit to be found. In former times the buffalo roamed over this country, but they have receded, and very seldom come here in any numbers. * * * The Indians must have horses to hunt them : horses they have not. The Winnebagoes had some when they first arrived, but they were soon stolen by the hostile Sioux."

Agent Balcombe must have led a hard life on this reservation. Exposed to all the inconveniences of a remote frontier, three hundred miles from any food-raising country ; receiving letters from the Interior Department expressing itself "astounded" that he does not "induce the Indians in his charge to remain on their reservation ;" and letters from citizens, and petitions from towns in Wisconsin, Minnesota, Iowa, and Nebraska, imploring him to "gather up" all the wandering Winnebagoes who have been left behind; unprovided with any proper military protection, and surrounded by hostile Indians — no wonder that he recommends to the Government "to remove and consolidate" the different tribes of Indians into "one territory" as soon as possible.

The effects of this sojourn in the wilderness upon the Winnebagoes were terrible. Not only were they rendered spiritless and desperate by sufferings, they were demoralized by being brought again into conflict with the wild Sioux. They had more than one skirmish with them, and, it is said, relapsed so far into the old methods of their barbaric life that at one of their dances they actually roasted and ate the heart of a Sioux prisoner! Yet in less than a year after they were gathered together once more on the Omaha Reservation, and began again to have hopes of a "permanent home," we find their chiefs and headmen sending the following petition to Washington :

"Our Great Father at Washington, all greeting,— From the chiefs, braves, and headmen of your dutiful children the Winnebagoes.

"Father, we cannot see you. You are far away from us. We cannot speak to you. We will write to you ; and, Father, we hope you will read our letter and answer us.

"Father: Some years ago, when we had our homes on Turkey River, we had a school for our children, where many of them learned to read and write and work like white people, and we were happy.

"Father: Many years have passed away since our school was broken up; we have no such schools among us, and our children are growing up in ignorance of those things that should render them industrious, prosperous, and happy, and we are sorry. Father: It is our earnest wish to be so situated no longer. It is our sincere desire to have again established among us such a school as we see in operation among your Omaha children. Father: As soon as you find a permanent home for us, will you not do this for us? And, Father, as we would like our children taught the Christian religion, as before, we would like our school placed under the care of the Presbyterian Board of Foreign Missions. And last, Father, to show you our sincerity, we desire to have set apart for its establishment, erection, and support, all of our school-funds and whatever more is necessary.

"Father: This is our prayer. Will not you open your ears and heart to us, and write to us?"

This letter was signed by thirty-eight of the chiefs and headmen of the Winnebagoes.

In March, 1865, a new treaty was made between the United States and this long-suffering tribe of Indians, by which, in consideration of their "ceding, selling, and conveying" to the United States all their right in the Dakota Reserve, the United States agreed "to set apart for the occupation and future home of the Winnebago Indians forever" a certain tract of 128,000 acres in Nebraska—a part of the Omaha Reservation which the Omahas were willing to sell. The United States also agreed to erect mills, break land, furnish certain amounts of seeds, tools, guns, and horses, oxen and wagons, and to subsist the tribe for one year, as some small reparation for the terrible losses and sufferings they had experienced. From this word "forever" the Winnebagoes perhaps took courage.

At the time of their removal from Minnesota, among the fugitives who fled back to Wisconsin was the chief De Carry. He died there, two years later, in great poverty. He was very old, but remarkably intelligent; he was the grandson of Ho-po-ko-e-kaw, or "Glory of the Morning," who was the queen of the Winnebagoes in 1776, when Captain Carver visited the tribe. There is nothing in Carver's quaint and fascinating old story more interesting than his account of the Winnebago country. He stayed with them four days, and was entertained by them "in a very distinguished manner." Indeed, if we may depend upon Captain Carver's story, all the North-western tribes were, in their own country, a gracious and hospitable people. He says: "I received from every tribe of them the most hospitable and courteous treatment, and am convinced that, till they are contaminated by the example and spirituous liquors of their more refined neighbors, they will retain this friendly and inoffensive conduct toward strangers."

He speaks with great gusto of the bread that the Winnebago women made from the wild maize. The soft young kernels, while full of milk, are kneaded into a paste, the cakes wrapped in bass-wood leaves, and baked in the ashes. "Better flavored bread I never ate in any country," says the honest captain.

He found the Winnebagoes' home truly delightful. The shores of the lake were wooded with hickory, oak, and hazel. Grapes, plums, and other fruits grew in abundance. The lake abounded in fish; and in the fall of the year with geese, ducks, and teal, the latter much better flavored than those found nearer the sea, as they "acquire their excessive fatness by feeding on the wild rice which grows so plentifully in these parts."

How can we bear to contrast the picture of this peace,

plenty, and gracious hospitality among the ancient Winnebagoes with the picture of their descendants—only two generations later—hunted, driven, starved? And how can we bear to contrast the picture of the drunken, gambling Winnebago of Minnesota with this picture which Captain Carver gives of a young Winnebago chief with whom he journeyed for a few days?

Captain Carver, after a four days' visit with the Winnebagoes, and "having made some presents to the good old queen, and received her blessing," went on his way. Two months later, as he was travelling to the Falls of St. Anthony, he encountered a young Winnebago chief going on an embassy to some of the bands of the "Nadouwessies" (Sioux). This young chief, finding that Captain Carver was about to visit the Falls, agreed to accompany him, "his curiosity having been often excited by the accounts he had received from some of his chiefs. He accordingly left his family (for the Indians never travel without their households) at this place under charge of my Mohawk servant, and we proceeded together by land, attended only by my Frenchman, to this celebrated place. We could distinctly hear the noise of the water full fifty miles before we reached the Falls; and I was greatly pleased and surprised when I approached this astonishing work of nature; but I was not long at liberty to indulge these emotions, my attention being called off by the behavior of my companion. The prince had no sooner gained the point that overlooks this wonderful cascade than he began with an audible voice to address the Great Spirit, one of whose places of residence he imagined this to be. He told him that he had come a long way to pay his adorations to him, and now would make him the best offerings in his power. He accordingly threw his pipe into the stream; then the roll that contained his tobacco; after these the bracelets he wore on his arms and wrists; next an ornament that encircled his neck, composed of beads and wires; and at last the ear-rings from his ears; in short, he presented to his god every part of his dress that was valuable. During this he frequently smote his breast with great violence, threw his arms about, and appeared to be much agitated. All this while he continued his adorations, and at length concluded them with fervent petitions that the Great Spirit would constantly afford us his protection on our travels, giving us a bright sun, a blue sky, and clear, untroubled waters; nor would he leave the place till we had smoked together with my pipe in honor of the Great Spirit.

"I was greatly surprised at beholding an instance of such elevated devotion in so young an Indian. * * * Indeed, the whole conduct of this young prince at once charmed and amazed me. During the few days we were together his attention seemed to be totally employed in yielding me every assistance in his power, and even in so short a time he gave me innumerable proofs of the most generous and disinterested friendship, so that on our return I parted from him with the greatest reluctance."

In 1866 the report from the Winnebagoes is that they are "improving;" manifest "a good degree of industry;" that the health of the tribe is generally poor, but "as good as can be expected when we remember their exposures and sufferings during the last three years." The tribe has "diminished some four or five hundred since they left Minnesota." One hundred soldiers have returned, "who have served with credit to themselves and to their tribe in the defence of their country." No school has yet been established on the agency, and this is said to be "their greatest want."

The superintendent writes: "The appropriations under the late treaty have all been made, and the work of fitting up the reservation is progressing. It affords me the highest personal satisfaction to assure the Department that this deeply-wronged and much-abused tribe will soon be in all respects comfortable and self-sustaining. They entered upon their new reservation late last May, and during the present year they have raised at least twenty thousand bushels of corn."

In 1867 the Commissioner of Indian Affairs says: "The Winnebagoes have a just claim against the Government on account of their removal from Minnesota, the expenses of which *were borne out of their own tribal funds.* The Government is clearly bound in all honor to refund to them moneys thus expended."

It would seem that there could have been no question in the beginning as to who should pay the costs of such a removal as that. It should not even have been a tax on the general Government, but on the State of Minnesota, which demanded it— especially as there was no shadow of doubt that the demand was made—not because the citizens of Minnesota had any real fear of the peaceable and kindly Winnebagoes (who were as much in terror of the Sioux as they were themselves), but because they "coveted the splendid country the Winnebagoes were occupying, and the Sioux difficulties furnished the pretext to get rid of them with the aid of Congressional legislation."

Some members of the tribe who remained in Minnesota still claimed their "allotted" lands; "their share of all moneys payable to the Winnebagoes under treaty stipulations, and that their share of the funds of the tribe be capitalized and paid to them in bulk; their peculiar relations as Indians be dissolved, and they left to merge themselves in the community where they have cast their lot." The commissioner urges upon the Government compliance with these requests.

In 1868 a school was opened on the Winnebago Agency, and had a daily attendance of one hundred and fifty scholars. The tribe adopted a code of laws for their government, and the year was one of peace and quietness, with the exception of some dissatisfaction on the part of the Indians in regard to three hundred cows, which, having been sent to the agency in fulfilment of one of the provisions of the treaty, were nevertheless ordered by the Indian Bureau to be "kept as Department stock." The Indians very naturally held that they had a right to these cows; nevertheless, they continued peaceable and contented, in the feeling that they had "at last found a home," where they might "hope to remain and cultivate the soil with the feeling that it is theirs, and that their children will not in a few days be driven from their well-tilled and productive lands." They are, however, "growing exceedingly anxious for the allotment of their lands in severalty."

In 1869 "preparations" were "being made for allotting the lands to heads of families."

In 1870 "the allotment of land in severalty to the Indians has been nearly completed, each head of a family receiving eighty acres. * * * The Indians anxiously look for the patents to these, as many have already commenced making improvements. * * * At least thirty have broken four acres of prairie apiece, and several have built houses. * * * Three schools are in operation, and four hundred acres of ground under cultivation."

In this year comes also an interesting report from the stray Winnebagoes left behind in Wisconsin. They and the stray Pottawottomies who are in the same neighborhood are "remarkably quiet and inoffensive, giving no cause of complaint; on the contrary, the towns and villages where they trade their berries, maple-sugar, etc., are deriving considerable benefit from them: a number have been employed in lumbering, harvesting, and hop-picking. A number of mill-owners and lumbermen have informed me that the Indians they have employed in their business have been steady, good hands. * * * There are nearly one thousand of these Winnebagoes. Some of them have bought land; others are renting it; and all express an anxiety that the 'Great Father' should give them a reservation in this region, and allow them to remain."

In 1871 the Nebraska Winnebagoes deposed their old chiefs,

and elected twelve new ones, to serve one year; these were mainly from the younger members of the tribe who were in favor of civilization and progress. This was an important step toward breaking up the old style of tribal relations.

In 1872 we hear again from the "strays" in Wisconsin. The whites having complained of them, Congress has appropriated funds to move them to their respective tribes "west of the Mississippi;" but the removal has not been undertaken "for various reasons," and the commissioner doubts "whether it can be accomplished without additional and severe legislation on the part of Congress, as the Indians are attached to the country, and express great repugnance to their contemplated removal from it."

The poor creatures are not wanted anywhere. Spite of their being "steady, good hands" for hired labor, and useful to towns and villages in furnishing fruits and fish, the Wisconsin people do not want them in their State. And the agent of the Winnebago Reservation writes, earnestly protesting against their being brought there. He thinks they are in moral tone far below the Indians under his charge. Moreover, he says "the prejudice in the surrounding country is such" that he believes it would be bad policy to remove any "more Indians" there. Nebraska does not like Indians any better than Wisconsin does, or Minnesota did. He adds also that his Indians "would be greatly stimulated to improve their claims if they could secure the titles for them. They have waited three years since the first allotments were made. It is difficult to make them believe that it requires so long a time to prepare the patents, and they are beginning to fear that they are not coming."

In 1873 the Winnebagoes are cited as a "striking example of what can be accomplished in a comparatively short time in the way of civilizing and Christianizing Indians. * * * Their beautiful tract of country is dotted over with substantially-built cottages; the farmers own their wagons, horses, harness, furniture of their houses — dress in civilized costume, raise crops—and several hundred Winnebago men assisted the farmers in adjoining counties during the late harvest in gathering their grain crop, and proved themselves efficient and satisfactory workmen."

In the winter of 1874 the Wisconsin "strays" were moved down to the Nebraska Reservation. They were discontented, fomented dissatisfaction in the tribe, and in less than a year more than half of them had wandered back to Wisconsin again; a striking instance of the differences in the Government's methods of handling different bands of Indians. The thirty Poncas who ran away from Indian Territory were pursued and arrested, as if they had been thieves escaping with stolen property; but more than five hundred Winnebagoes, in less than one year, stroll away from their reserve, make their way back to Wisconsin, and nothing is done about it.

In 1875 there are only two hundred and four of the Wisconsin "strays" left on the Nebraska Reservation. All the others are "back in their old haunts, where a few seem to be making a sincere effort to take care of themselves by taking land under the Homestead Act."

The Nebraska Winnebagoes are reported as being "nearly civilized;" all are engaged in civilized pursuits, "the men working with their own hands, and digging out of the ground three-fourths of their subsistence." They have raised in this year 20,000 bushels of corn, 5800 bushels of wheat, and 6000 bushels of oats and vegetables. They have broken 800 acres of new land, and have built 3000 rods of fencing. Nearly one-sixth of the entire tribe is in attendance at schools. The system of electing chiefs annually works well; the chiefs, in their turn, select twelve Indians to serve for the year as policemen, and they prove efficient in maintaining order.

What an advance in six years! Six years ago there were but twenty-three homes and only 300 acres of land under cultivation on the whole reservation; the people were huddled together in ravines and bottom-lands, and were dying of disease and exposure.

In 1876 the Winnebagoes are reported again as "fast emerging from a condition of dependence upon their annual appropriations. * * * Each head of a family has a patent for eighty acres of land. Many have fine farms, and are wholly supporting themselves and families by their own industry. * * * The issue of rations has been discontinued, except to the Wisconsin branch of the tribe and to the sick-list."

In what does this report differ from the report which would be rendered from any small farming village in the United States? The large majority "wholly supporting themselves and their families by their own industry;" a small minority of worthless or disabled people being fed by charity—*i. e.*, being fed on food bought, at least in part, by interest money due on capital made by sales of land in which they had a certain reckonable share of ownership. Every one of the United States has in nearly every county an almshouse, in which just such a class of worthless and disabled persons will be found; and so crowded are these almshouses, and so appreciable a burden is their support on the tax-payers of State and county, that there are perpetual disputes going on between the authorities of neighboring districts as to the ownership and responsibility of individual paupers: for the paupers in civilized almshouses are never persons who have had proceeds of land sales "invested" for their benefit, the interest to be paid to them "annually forever." It is for nobody's interest to keep them paupers, or to take care of them as such.

We now find the Winnebagoes once more quietly established in comfortable homes—as they were, in their own primitive fashion, in 1822, when Dr. Morse visited them on the shores of their beautiful lake; as they were, after our civilized fashion, in 1862, on the healthful and fertile up-lands of Minnesota. In their present home they seem to have reason, at last, to feel secure, to anticipate permanence, safety, and success. Their lands have been allotted to them in severalty : each head of a family has his patent for eighty acres. They are, in the main, self-supporting.

How does the United States Government welcome this success, this heroic triumph of a patient people over disheartening obstacles and sufferings?

In the Annual Report of the Secretary of the Interior for 1876 the Secretary says: "As a matter of economy, the greatest saving could be made by uniting all the Indians upon a few reservations; the fewer, the better." He says that there is land enough in the Indian Territory to give every Indian—man, woman, and child—in the country seventy-five acres apiece. He says, "The arguments are all in favor of the consolidation." He then goes on to enumerate those arguments: "Expensive agencies would be abolished; the Indians themselves can be more easily watched over and controlled; evil-designing men be the better kept away from them, and illicit trade and barter in arms and ammunition and whiskey prevented. Goods could be supplied at a greater saving; the military service relieved; the Indians better taught, and friendly rivalry established among them—those most civilized hastening the progress of those below them; and *most of the land now occupied as reserves reverting to the General Government, would be open to entry and sale.*"

Here are nine reasons given for removing all Indians to Indian Territory. Five of these reasons ostensibly point to benefits likely to accrue from this removal to the Indians. The other four point to benefits likely to accrue to the Government; the first three of these last are, simply, "saving;" the fourth is the significant one, "gain"—"most of the land reverting to the General Government would be open to entry and sale."

It was before this necessity of opening Indian lands "to entry and sale" that the Winnebagoes had been fleeing, from 1815 to 1863. It seems they are no safer now. There is evidently as much reason for moving them out of Nebraska as there was for moving them out of Wisconsin and Minnesota.

The Secretary goes on to say: "As soon as the Indian is taught to toil for his daily bread, and realize the sense of proprietorship in the results of his labor, it cannot but be further to his advantage to be able to appreciate that his labor is expended upon his individual possessions and for his personal benefit. * * * The Indian must be made to see the practical advantage to himself of his work, and feel that he reaps the full benefit of it. Everything should teach him that he has a home; * * * a hearth-stone of his own, around which he can gather his family, and in its possession be entirely secure and independent."

The logical relation of these paragraphs to the preceding one is striking, and the bearing of the two together on the case of the Winnebagoes is still more striking.

In the same report the Commissioner for Indian Affairs says: "If legislation were secured giving the President authority to remove any tribe or band, or any portion of a tribe or band, whenever in his judgment it was practicable, to any one of the reservations named, and if Congress would appropriate from year to year a sum sufficient to enable him to take advantage of every favorable opportunity to make such removals, I am confident that a few years' trial would conclusively demonstrate the entire feasibility of the plan. I believe that all the Indians in Kansas, Nebraska, and Dakota, and a part at least of those in Wyoming and Montana, could be induced to remove to the Indian Territory."

He adds "that the Indian sentiment is opposed to such removal is true," but he thinks that, "with a fair degree of persistence," the removal "can be secured." No doubt it can.

Later in the same report, under the head of "Allotments in

Severalty," he says : " It is doubtful whether any high degree of civilization is possible without individual ownership of land. The records of the past, and the experience of the present, testify that the soil should be made secure to the individual by all the guarantees which law can devise, and that nothing less will induce men to put forth their best exertions. It is essential that each individual should feel that his home is his own ; * * * that he has a direct personal interest in the soil on which he lives, and that that interest will be faithfully protected for him and for his children by the Government."

The commissioner and the secretary who wrote these clear statements of evident truths, and these eloquent pleas for the Indians' rights, both knew perfectly well that hundreds of Indians had had lands "allotted to them" in precisely this way, and had gone to work on the lands so allotted, trusting "that that interest would be faithfully protected by the Government ;" and that these "allotments," and the "certificates" of them, had proved to be good for nothing as soon as the citizens of a State united in a "demand" that the Indians should be moved. The commissioner and the secretary knew perfectly well, at the time they wrote these paragraphs, that in this one Winnebago tribe in Nebraska, for instance, "every head of a family owned eighty acres of land," and was hard at work on it—industrious, self-supporting, trying to establish that "hearthstone" around which, as the secretary says, he must "gather his family, and in its possession be entirely secure and independent." And yet the secretary and the commissioner advise the moving of this Winnebago tribe to Indian Territory with the rest : "all the Indians in Kansas, Nebraska, and Dakota" could probably be "induced to move," they say.

These quotations from this report of the Interior Department are but a fair specimen of the velvet glove of high-sounding phrase of philanthropic and humane care for the Indian, by which has been most effectually hid from the sight of the

American people the iron hand of injustice and cruelty which has held him for a hundred years helpless in its grasp.

In this same year an agent on one of the Nebraska agencies writes feelingly and sensibly:

"Nothing has tended to retard the progress of this tribe in the line of opening farms for themselves so much as the unsettlement occasioned by a continued agitation of the subject of selling their reservation and the removal of the tribe. * * * The improvement that has been made at this agency during the past three years in the direction of developing among the Indians the means of self-support, seems to have caused an uneasiness that has been prolific of a great deal of annoyance, inasmuch as it has alarmed this speculative element around us with the fear that the same (continued) will eventually plant the Indians on their present fertile land so firmly that they cannot be removed, and thus they be deprived of the benefits of manipulating the sale of their reservation."

Nevertheless, the Winnebagoes keep on in their work— building houses, school-buildings, many of them of brick made on the ground.

In this year (1876) they experienced a great injustice in the passing of an Act of Congress fixing the total amount to be expended for pay of employés at any one agency at not more than $10,000. This necessitated the closing of the fine building they had built at a cost of $20,000 for the purpose of an industrial boarding-school.

In this year's report their agent gives a resumé of the financial condition of the tribe: "By treaty proclaimed June 16th, 1838, the Winnebagoes ceded to the United States all their land east of the Mississippi, in consideration of which they were to receive $1,100,000. The balance of this, after making certain payments, was to be invested for their benefit, on which the United States guaranteed to pay them an annual interest of not less than five per cent.

"The Winnebagoes receive no support from the Government, other than from the interest appropriated annually on what remains of these funds. This in 1870 amounted to over $50,000. Since then the half-breeds, numbering one hundred and sixty persons, members of the tribe remaining in Minnesota at the time of the removal of the Indians from that State in 1863, have, in accordance with the provisions of the act making appropriations for the Indian service, approved March 3d, 1871, been paid their proportion of the principal of all Winnebago funds, as shown on the books of the Treasury at that time, including the proportion of $85,000, on which but five more instalments of interest were to be paid, per fourth Article treaty October 13th, 1846. In computing this proportion, the whole number of the tribe considered as being entitled to participate in the benefits of the tribal funds was 1531; which number included only those located on the Winnebago reservation in Nebraska at that time, in addition to the one hundred and sixty already spoken of. By this Act of Congress the Nebraska Winnebagoes, who comprise only that portion of the tribe which has complied with treaty stipulations, and quietly acquiesced in the demands of the Government, were deprived of nearly one-eighth part of their accustomed support.

"Other reductions were afterward made for the purchase of a reservation adjoining the old one in this State, and for removing to it the wandering bands of Winnebagoes in Wisconsin. These were supposed to have numbered in all nearly one thousand persons. They had not been in the habit of receiving any attention or acknowledgment from the Government since they, as a tribal organization, had declined to treat with it. Nearly all of them objected to removing from Wisconsin to their new reservation in Nebraska, and, as a natural consequence, soon returned after being compelled to do so. At the present time there are probably less than one hundred of the number remaining here. For the past three years the sum to which the

Wisconsin Winnebagoes would have been entitled had they remained on their reservation, amounting in all to $48,521 07, has been set apart, awaiting such act of Congress as will give relief in the premises; thus reducing the total amount received per annum by that portion of the tribe living on the reservation to but little more than one-half of what it was seven years ago. It seems needless to say that they are very much dissatisfied at this, and that when they refer to the subject I have some difficulty in satisfying them as to the justice of the governmental policy in setting apart funds (to be expended at some future time) for the benefit of certain individuals who persist in absenting themselves from their reservation, while others, who are absent but a few months, are deprived of all advantages from issues of supplies or payments that may have been made during their absence."

This case is a good illustration of the working of the trustee relation between the United States Government and its wards.

In 1877 we find the Secretary of the Interior still recommending that the Indians be "gradually gathered together on smaller reservations," to the end that "greater facilities be afforded for civilization." He reiterates that "the enjoyment and pride of individual ownership of property is one of the most effective civilizing agencies," and recommends that "allotments of small tracts of land should be made to the heads of families on all reservations, to be held in severalty under proper restrictions, so that they may have fixed homes."

The commissioner also recommends "a steady concentration of the smaller bands of Indians on the larger reservations." He calls attention again to the fact that there are 58,000 square miles in the Indian Territory "set apart for the use of Indians, and that there they can be fed and clothed at a greatly diminished expense; and, better than all, can be kept in obedience, and taught to become civilized and self-supporting."

In 1878 the Commissioner of Indian Affairs reports that a

bill has been drawn "providing for the removal and consolidation of certain Indians in the States of Oregon, Colorado, Iowa, Kansas, Nebraska, Wisconsin, and Minnesota, and the Territories of Washington and Dakota. * * * A reduction of twenty-five reservations and eleven agencies will thus be effected. * * * There will be restored to the public domain 17,642,455 acres of land." He says that "further consolidations of like character are not only possible, but expedient and advisable. * * * There is a vast area of land in the Indian Territory not yet occupied."

With the same ludicrous, complacent logic as before, he proceeds to give as the reason for uprooting all these Indians from the homes where they are beginning to thrive and take root, and moving them again—for the third, fourth, fifth, sixth, or seventh time, as it may be—the fact that, "among the most radical defects of the policy formerly pursued with the Indians, has been the frequent changes in their location which have been made. * * * Permanent homes, sufficient aid to enable them to build houses, cultivate the soil, and to subsist them until they have harvested their first crops, will wean them entirely from their old methods of life, and in the course of a few years enable them to become entirely self-supporting. * * * Among the more forcible arguments which can be presented in connection with this subject is the fact that the expenses attending the removal and consolidation of the Indians, as herein proposed, *will be more than met from the sale of lands vacated.* * * * Much of the land now owned by these Indians is valuable only for its timber, and may be sold at an appraised value for an amount far in excess of the price fixed by law, and yet leave a large margin of profit to the purchaser into whose hands the lands will fall. * * * I can see no reason why the Government should not avail itself of these facts, and in effecting the consolidation of the Indians, and the opening of the lands for settlement, sell the same for an amount sufficient

to support the Indians in their new locations, without any actual drain on the Treasury in the future. * * * The lands belong
to the Indians, and they are clearly entitled to receive the full
value of the same when sold."

In this sentence we reach the high-water mark of the sophistry and dishonesty of the Department's position. "The
lands belong to the Indians," but we will compel them to "restore to the public domain" (i. e., to give up to white settlers)
17,642,455 acres of them. The Indians "are clearly entitled
to receive the full value of the same when sold," but we will
compel them to expend that "full value" in removing to a
place where they do not want to go, opening new lands, building new houses, buying new utensils, implements, furniture and
stock, and generally establishing themselves, "without any actual drain on the Treasury" of the United States: and the
Department of the Interior "can see no reason why the Government should not avail itself of these facts."

All this is proposed with a view to the benefit of the Indians.
The report goes on to reiterate the same old story that the Indians must have "a perfect title to their lands;" that they have
come to feel that they are at any time liable to be moved,
"whenever the pressure of white settlers upon them may create
a demand for their lands," and that they "decline to make any
improvements on their lands, even after an allotment in severalty has been made, until they have received their patents for
the same," and that even "after the issue of patents the difficulties surrounding them do not cease." Evidently not, since,
as we have seen, it is now several years since every head of a
family among these Winnebagoes, whose "removal" the commissioner now recommends, secured his "patent" for eighty
acres of land.

Finally, the commissioner says: "Every means that human
ingenuity can devise, legal or illegal, has been resorted to for
the purpose of obtaining possession of Indian lands." Of this

there would seem to be left no doubt in the mind of any intelligent person, after reading the above quotations.

It is not to be wondered that when the news of such schemes as these reaches the Indians on their reservations great alarm and discontent are the result. We find in the reports from the Nebraska agencies for this year unmistakable indications of disheartenment and anxiety. The Winnebagoes are reported to be very anxious to be made citizens. A majority are in favor of it, "provided the Government will adopt certain measures which they consider necessary for the care and protection of their property."

They have had a striking illustration of the disadvantage of not being citizens, in an instance of the unpunished murder of one of their number by a white man. The story is related by the agent tersely and well, and is one of the notable incidents in the history of the relation between the United States Government and its wards.

"Henry Harris, a Winnebago in good standing, an industrious man and a successful farmer, was employed by Joseph Smith, a white man, to cut wood on his land in Dakota County, a short distance north of the reservation. While alone and thus engaged, on the 29th of last January, Harris was shot through the heart with a rifle-ball. I had his dead body taken before the coroner of the county, and at the inquest held before that officer it was shown, to the satisfaction of the jury that rendered a verdict in accordance therewith, that the Indian came to his death at the hands of one D. Balinska, who had been for many years leading a hermit's life on a tract of land that he owned adjoining the reservation, and who had threatened Harris's life a few months before, when they quarrelled about damages for corn destroyed by Balinska's horse. There being snow on the ground at the time of the murder, Balinska was tracked from his home to the place where, under cover, he did the shooting; and his shot-pouch, containing a moulded ball of the same weight as the one cut from the body of the Indian, was found near by and identified. Notwithstanding this direct evidence, which was laid before the Grand-jury of Dakota County, that honorable body was unwilling to find a ' true bill;' for the reason, as I understand, that it was only an Indian that was killed, and it would not be popular to incur the expense of bringing the case to trial. This is but another illustration of the difficulty of punishing a white man for a wrong committed against an Indian. I need hardly say that the Indians, when comparing this murder with that of a white man, committed eight years ago by five of their young men— who, upon less direct evidence, were sentenced to imprisonment in the State Penitentiary for life—are struck with the wonderful difference in the application of the same law to whites and Indians."

The report from the Winnebago Agency for 1879 tells the story of the sequel to this unpunished murder of Henry Harris. The agent says: " In my last report I referred to the murder of one of our best Indian farmers by a white man, who was afterward arrested and discharged without trial, though there was no question as to his guilt. As a sequel to this, one white man is known to have been killed last May by Holly Scott, a nephew of the murdered Indian; and another white man is supposed to have been killed by Eddy Priest and Thomas Walker, two young Indians who have left for Wisconsin. The murdered white men had temporarily stopped with the Indians. Their antecedents are unknown, and they are supposed to have belonged to the fraternity of tramps. Holly Scott was arrested by the Indian police, and turned over to the authorities of Dakota County for trial, the State Legislature having at its last session extended the jurisdiction of that county over this reservation, by what authority I am unable to say.

" The effect of these murders was to unsettle the Indians, nearly all industry being suspended for several weeks. They

feared that the white people would do as they did in Minnesota in 1862, after the Sioux massacre, when the Winnebagoes
were driven from their homes in Minnesota. * * * A number
of our most quiet and industrious men became alarmed, and
moved their families to Wisconsin, encouraged in so doing by
the hope of receiving from the Government a share of the
funds which have been set apart from the annual appropriations
during the past four years for the benefit of the Wisconsin
Winnebagoes, and which they suppose aggregate a large amount
which will soon be paid in cash."

This brings the story of the Winnebagoes down to the
present time. What its next chapter may be is saddening to
think. It is said by those familiar with the Nebraska Indians
that, civilized though they be, they will all make war to the
knife if the attempt is made by the Government to rob them
of their present lands on the plea again of offering them a
"permanent home." That specious pretence has done its last
duty in the United States service. No Indian is left now so
imbecile as to believe it once more.

Whether the Winnebagoes' "patents" in Nebraska would,
in such a case, prove any stronger than did their "certificates"
in Minnesota, and whether the Winnebagoes themselves, peaceable and civilized though they be, would side with the United
States Government, or with their wronged and desperate brethren, in such an uprising, it would be hard to predict.

CHAPTER VIII.

THE CHEROKEES.

THE Cherokees[14] were the Eastern Mountaineers of America. Their country lay along the Tennessee River, and in the highlands of Georgia, Carolina, and Alabama—the loveliest region east of the Mississippi River. Beautiful and grand, with lofty mountains and rich valleys fragrant with flowers, and forests of magnolia and pine filled with the singing of birds and the melody of streams, rich in fruits and nuts and wild grains, it was a country worth loving, worth fighting, worth dying for, as thousands of its lovers have fought and have died, white men as well as red, within the last hundred years.

When Oglethorpe came with his cargo of Madeira wine and respectable paupers from England in 1733, and lived in tents in midwinter on the shores of the Savannah River, one of the first conditions of safety for his colossal almshouse, in shape of a new colony, was that all the Indians in the region should become its friends and allies.

The reputation of his goodness and benevolence soon penetrated to the fastnesses of their homes, and tribe after tribe sent chiefs and headmen to greet him with gifts and welcome. When the Cherokee chief appeared, Oglethorpe said to him, "Fear nothing. Speak freely." "I always speak freely," answered the mountaineer. "Why should I fear? I am now among friends: I never feared, even among my enemies."

The principal intention of the English trustees who incorporated the Georgia colony was to provide a home for worthy persons in England who were "in decayed circumstances."

[14] Regarding the Cherokee, consult Morris L. Wardell, *A Political History of the Cherokee Nation* (Norman, Oklahoma, 1938), Henry Thompson Malone, *Cherokees of the Old South, A People in Transition* (Athens, Georgia, 1956) and Grace Steele Woodward, *The Cherokees,* (Norman, Oklahoma, 1963).

Among other great ends which they also avowed was "the civilization of the savages." In one of Oglethorpe's first reports to the trustees he says: "A little Indian nation—the only one within fifty miles—is not only in amity, but desirous to be subjects to his Majesty King George; to have lands given to them among us, and to breed their children at our schools. Their chief and his beloved man, who is the second man in the nation, desire to be instructed in the Christian religion."

The next year he returned to England, carrying with him eight Indian chiefs, to show them "so much of Great Britain and her institutions as might enable them to judge of her power and dignity. * * * Nothing was neglected," we are told, "that was likely to awaken their curiosity or impress them with a sense of the power and grandeur of the nation." They were received by the Archbishop of Canterbury, and by the Fellows of Eton, and for a space of four months were hospitably entertained, and shown all the great sights of London and its vicinity.

The tribes at home were much gratified by these attentions paid to their representatives, and sent out to the trustees a very curious missive, expressing their thanks and their attachment to General Oglethorpe. This letter was the production of a young Cherokee chief. It was written in black and red hieroglyphs on a dressed buffalo-skin. Before it was sent to England it was exhibited in Savannah, and the meaning of the hieroglyphs translated by an interpreter in a grand gathering of fifty Indian chiefs and all the principal people of Savannah. Afterward the curious document was framed and hung up in the Georgia Office in Westminster.

When the Wesleyan missionaries arrived in Georgia, two years later, some of the chiefs who had made this visit to England went to meet them, carrying large jars of honey and of milk as gifts, to "represent their inclinations;" and one of the chiefs said to Mr. Wesley, "I am glad you are come. When I was in England I desired that some one would speak the Great Word to me. I will go up and speak to the wise men of our nation, and I hope they will hear. But we would not be made Christians as the Spaniards make Christians; we would be taught before we are baptized."

In those early days Wesley was an intolerant and injudicious enthusiast. His missionary work in the Georgia Colony was anything but successful in the outset, either among the whites or the Indians, and there was ample justification for the reply which this same Indian chief made later when urged to embrace the doctrines of Christianity.

"Why, these are Christians at Savannah. Those are Christians at Frederica. Christians get drunk! Christians beat men! Christians tell lies! Me no Christian!" On another occasion Wesley asked him what he thought he was made for. "He that is above," answered the chief, "knows what he made us for. We know nothing; we are in the dark; but white men know much. And yet white men build great houses, as if they were to live forever. But white men cannot live forever. In a little time white men will be dust as well as I."

For twenty years Oglethorpe's colony struggled on under great difficulties and discouragements. Wars with France and with Spain; tiresome squabbles with and among Methodist missionaries, all combined to make Oglethorpe's position hard. Again and again England would have lost her colony except for the unswerving fidelity of the Indian allies; they gathered by hundreds to fight for Oglethorpe. In one expedition against the frontier, four hundred Creeks and six hundred Cherokees set out in one day, under an urgent call for help sent by Indian runners to their towns. His Indian friends were the only friends Oglethorpe had who stood by him past everything: nothing could shake their fidelity.

"He is poor; he can give you nothing," said the St. Augustine Spaniards to a Creek chief at this time; "it is foolish

for you to go to him:" and they showed to the Indian a fine
suit of scarlet clothes, and a sword, which they were about to
give to a chief of the Tennessees who had become their ally.

But the Creek answered, " We love him. It is true, he does
not give us silver; but he gives us everything we want that he
has. He has given me the coat off his back, and the blanket
from under him."

At last the trustees of the Georgia Colony lost patience:
very bitterly they had learned that paupers, however worthy,
are not good stuff to build new enterprises of. In eighteen
years the colony had not once furnished a sufficient supply of
subsistence for its own consumption: farms which had been
cultivated were going to ruin; and the country was rapidly de-
generating in every respect. Dishonest traders had tampered
with and exasperated the Indians, so that their friendliness
could no longer be implicitly trusted in. For everything that
went wrong the English Company was held responsible, and
probably there were no happier men in all England on the 20th
of June, 1752, than were the Georgia trustees, who on that
day formally resigned their charter, and washed their hands of
the colony forever.

The province was now formed into a royal government, and
very soon became the seat of frightful Indian wars. The new
authorities neither understood nor kept faith with the Indians:
their old friend Oglethorpe had left them forever, and the same
scenes of treachery and massacre which were being enacted at
the North began to be repeated with heart-sickening similarity
at the South. Indians fighting Indians—fighting as allies to-
day with the French, to-morrow with the English; treaties
made, and broken as soon as made; there was neither peace
nor safety anywhere.

At last, in 1763, a treaty was concluded with the chiefs and
headmen of five tribes, which seemed to promise better things.
The Cherokees and Creeks granted to the King of England a

large tract of land, cleared off their debts with the sum paid for it, and observed its stipulations faithfully for several years, until peace was again destroyed, this time by no fault of the Indians, in consequence of the revolt of the American Colonies against Great Britain. The English loyalists in Georgia now availed themselves of the Indians' old habit of allegiance to the Crown. One of their leading agents took a Cherokee woman as his mistress, placed her at the head of his table, gave her the richest dress and equipage that the country could afford, and distributed through her lavish gifts to all the Indians he could reach. When war actually broke out he retreated with her into the fastnesses of the Cherokee nation, where he swayed them at his will. Attempts to capture him were repelled by the Cherokees with ferocity. Prisoners taken by them at this time were tortured with great cruelty; one instance is recorded (in a journal kept by another prisoner, who escaped alive) of a boy about twelve years of age who was suspended by the arms between two posts, and raised about three feet from the ground. "The mode of inflicting the torture was by light-wood splints of about eighteen inches long, made sharp at one end and fractured at the other, so that the torch might not be extinguished by throwing it. After these weapons of death were prepared, and a fire made for the purpose of lighting them, the scene of horror commenced. It was deemed a mark of dexterity, and accompanied by shouts of applause, when an Indian threw one of these torches so as to make the sharp end stick into the body of the suffering youth without extinguishing the torch. This description of torture was continued for two hours before the innocent victim was relieved by death."

These are sickening details, and no doubt will be instinctively set down by most readers as proof of innate cruelty peculiar to the Indian race. Let us, therefore, set side by side with them the record that in this same war white men (British officers) confined white men ("rebels") in prison-ships, starved, and otherwise maltreated them till they died, five or six a day, then threw their dead bodies into the nearest marsh, and had them "*trodden down in the mud*—from whence they were soon exposed by the washing of the tides, and at low-water the prisoners beheld the carrion-crows picking the bones of their departed companions!" Also, that white men (British officers) were known at that time to have made thumb-screws out of musket-locks, to torture Georgia women, wives of "rebels," to force them to reveal the places where their husbands were in hiding. Innate cruelty is not exclusively an Indian trait.

The Cherokees had the worst of the fighting on the British side during the Revolution. Again and again their towns were burnt, their winter stores destroyed, and whole bands reduced to the verge of starvation. At one time, when hard pressed by the American forces, they sent to the Creeks for help; but the shrewd Creeks replied, "You have taken the thorns out of our feet; you are welcome to them." The Creeks, having given only limited aid to the British, had suffered much less severely. That any of the Indians should have joined the "rebel" cause seems wonderful, as they had evidently nothing to gain by the transfer of their allegiance to what must have appeared to them for a long time to be the losing side in the contest. For three years and a half Savannah was in the possession of the British, and again and again they had control of the entire State. And to show that they had no compunction about inciting the Indians to massacres they left many a written record —such, for instance, as this, which is in a letter written by General Gage from Boston, June, 1775: "We need not be tender of calling on the savages to attack the Americans."

The first diplomatic relations of the United States Government with the Cherokees were in the making of the treaty of Hopewell, in 1785. At the Hopewell council the United States commissioners said: "Congress is now the sovereign of all our country which we now point out to you on the map. They want none of your lands, nor anything else which belongs to you; and as an earnest of their regard for you, we propose to enter into articles of a treaty perfectly equal and conformable to what we now tell you. * * * This humane and generous act of the United States will no doubt be received by you with gladness, and held in grateful remembrance; and the more so, as many of your young men, and the greater number of your warriors, during the late war, were our enemies, and assisted the King of Great Britain in his endeavors to conquer our country."

The chiefs complained bitterly of the encroachments of white settlers upon lands which had been by old treaties distinctly reserved to the Cherokees. They demanded that some of these settlers should be removed; and when the commissioners said that the settlers were too numerous for the Government to remove, one of the chiefs asked, satirically, "Are Congress, who conquered the King of Great Britain, unable to remove those people?"

Finally, the chiefs agreed to accept payment for the lands which had been taken. New boundaries were established, and a general feeling of good-will and confidence was created. One notable feature in this council was the speech of an Indian woman, called the "war-woman of Chota." (Chota was the Cherokees' city of refuge. All murderers were safe so long as they lived in Chota. Even Englishmen had not disdained to take advantage of its shelter; one English trader who had killed an Indian, having fled, lived there for many months, his own house being but a short distance away. After a time he resolved to return home, but the headmen of the tribe assured him that, though he was entirely safe there, he would surely be killed if he left the town.) The chief who brought this "war-woman" to the council introduced her as "one of our beloved women who has borne and raised up warriors." She proceeded to say, " I am fond of hearing that there is a peace, and I hope you have now taken us by the hand in real friendship. I have a pipe and a little tobacco to give the commissioners to smoke in friendship. I look on you and the red people as my children. Your having determined on peace is most pleasing to me, for I have seen much trouble during the late war. I am old, but I hope yet to bear children who will grow up and people our nation, as we are now to be under the protection of Congress, and shall have no disturbance."

A brief summary of the events which followed on the negotiation of this treaty may be best given in the words of a report made by the Secretary of War to the President four years later. In July, 1789, General Knox writes as follows of the Cherokees : " This nation of Indians, consisting of separate towns or villages, are seated principally on the head-waters of the Tennessee, which runs into the Ohio. Their hunting-grounds extend from the Cumberland River along the frontiers of Virginia, North and South Carolina, and part of Georgia.

" The frequent wars they have had with the frontier people of the said States have greatly diminished their number. The commissioners estimated them in November, 1785, at 2000 warriors, but they were estimated in 1787 at 2650 ; yet it is probable they may be lessened since by the depredations committed on them.

" The United States concluded a treaty with the Cherokees at Hopewell, on the Keowee, the 28th of November, 1785, which is entered on the printed journals of Congress April 17th, 1786. The negotiations of the commissioners on the part of the United States are hereunto annexed, marked A. It will appear by the papers marked B. that the State of North Carolina, by their agent, protested against the said treaty as infringing and violating the legislative rights of that State.

" By a variety of evidence which has been submitted to the

last Congress, it has been proved that the said treaty has been entirely disregarded by the white people inhabiting the frontiers, styling themselves the State of Franklin. The proceedings of Congress on the 1st of September, 1788, and the proclamation they then issued on this subject, will show their sense of the many unprovoked outrages committed against the Cherokees.

"The information contained in the papers marked C., from Colonel Joseph Martin, the late agent to the Cherokees, and Richard Winn, Esq., will further evince the deplorable situation of the Cherokees, and the indispensable obligation of the United States to vindicate their faith, justice, and national dignity.

"The letter of Mr. Winn, the late superintendent, of the 1st of March, informs that a treaty will be held with the Cherokees on the third Monday of May, at the Upper War-ford on French Broad River. But it is to be observed that the time for which both he and Colonel Joseph Martin, the agent to the Cherokees and Chickasaws, were elected has expired, and therefore they are not authorized to act on the part of the Union. If the commissioners appointed by North Carolina, South Carolina, and Georgia, by virtue of the resolve of Congress of the 26th of October, 1787, should attend the said treaty, their proceedings thereon may soon be expected. But, as part of the Cherokees have taken refuge within the limits of the Creeks, it is highly probable they will be under the same direction; and, therefore, as the fact of the violation of the treaty cannot be disputed, and as the commissioners have not power to replace the Cherokees within the limits established in 1785, it is not probable, even if a treaty should be held, as stated by Mr. Winn, that the result would be satisfactory."

This is the summing up of the situation. The details of it are to be read in copious volumes of the early history of Tennessee, North and South Carolina, and Georgia—all under the head of "Indian Atrocities." To very few who read those

records does it occur that the Indians who committed these
" atrocities " were simply ejecting by force, and, in the con-
tests arising from this forcible ejectment, killing men who had
usurped and stolen their lands—lands ceded to them by the
United States Government in a solemn treaty, of which the
fifth Article was as follows :

" If any citizen of the United States or other person, not being an Indian, shall attempt to settle on any of the lands westward or southward of the said boundaries which are hereby
allotted to the Indians for their hunting-grounds, or having
already settled and will not remove from the same within six
months after the ratification of this treaty, such person shall
forfeit the protection of the United States, and the Indians
may punish him or not as they please."

It is evident that it is necessary to go back to the days of
the first treaties with our Indians to possess ourselves of the
first requisites for fair judgment of their conduct toward white
men.   What would a community of white men, situated precisely as these Cherokees were, have done ?   What did these
very Southern colonists themselves do to Spaniards who encroached on their lands ?   Fought them ; killed them ; burnt
their houses over their heads, and drove them into the sea !

In a later communication in the same year to the President,
the Secretary says : " The disgraceful violation of the treaty of
Hopewell with the Cherokees requires the serious consideration
of Congress.   If so direct and manifest contempt of the authority of the United States be suffered with impunity, it will
be in vain to attempt to extend the arm of the Government to
the frontiers.   The Indian tribes can have no faith in such imbecile promises, and the lawless whites will ridicule a government which shall on paper only make Indian treaties and regulate Indian boundaries."

The President, thus entreated, addressed himself to the Senate, and asked their advice.   He recapitulated the facts as set

forth by General Knox, "that upward of five hundred families are settled on the Cherokee lands," and asks,

"1st. Is it the judgment of the Senate that overtures shall be made to the Cherokees to arrange a new boundary, so as to embrace the settlements made by the white people since the treaty of Hopewell in November, 1785?

"2d. If so, shall compensation to the amount of $—— annu·ally, or of $—— in gross, be made to the Cherokees for the land they shall relinquish, holding the occupiers of the land accountable to the United States for its value?

"3d. Shall the United States stipulate solemnly to guarantee the new boundary which may be arranged?"

The Senate thereupon resolved that the President should, at his discretion, cause the Hopewell treaty to be carried out, or make a new one; but, in case a new one was made, the "Senate do advise and consent solemnly to guarantee the same."

Accordingly, in July, 1791, a new treaty—the treaty of Holston—was made with the Cherokees, new boundaries established, and $1000 a year promised to the tribe for the lands relinquished.

By the seventh Article of this treaty the United States "solemnly guarantee to the Cherokee nation all their lands not hereby ceded: the eighth Article reiterates the old permission that if any citizen of the United States or other person (not an Indian) shall settle on the Cherokees' lands, the Cherokees may punish him as they please. Article ninth says that no citizen or inhabitant of the United States shall hunt or destroy game on the Cherokee lands, or go into the Cherokee country without a passport from the governor or some other authorized person.

The next year the Cherokees sent an embassy to Philadelphia to ask for an increase of $500 in their annuity. One of the chiefs said that he had told Governor Blunt the year before that he would not consent to selling the lands for $1000 a year. "It would not buy a breech-clout for each of my nation ;" which was literally true.

To this additional annuity the Senate consented, and with this the chiefs said they were "perfectly satisfied." But they begged for the ploughs, hoes, cattle, etc., which had been promised in the treaty. They said, "Game is going fast away from among us. We must plant corn and raise cattle, and we want you to assist us."

In 1794 it was necessary to make another treaty, chiefly to declare that the Holston treaty was in "full force and binding." It had not been "fully carried into execution by reason of misunderstandings," it was said. This was very true ; white settlers had gone where they pleased, as if it did not exist ; Cherokees had murdered them, as they were, by their treaty, explicitly permitted to do. The whites had retaliated by unprovoked attacks on friendly Indians, and the Indians had retaliated again. The exasperated Indians implored Congress to protect them : the still more exasperated whites demanded of Congress to protect them. The Secretary of War writes despairingly, that "The desires of too many frontier white people to seize by force or fraud on the neighboring Indian lands continues to be an unceasing cause of jealousy and hatred on the part of the Indians ; and it would appear, upon a calm investigation, that until the Indians can be quieted on this point, and rely with confidence on the protection of their lands by the United States, no well-grounded hope of tranquillity can be entertained."

In this miserable manner, unjust equally to the white men and to the Indians, affairs went on for several years, until in 1801 it became absolutely necessary that in some way a definite understanding of boundaries, and an authoritative enforcement of rights on both sides, should be brought about; accordingly, commissioners were sent by the President "to obtain the con-

sent of the Cherokees" to new grants of land and establishment of boundaries. The instructions given to these commissioners are remarkable for their reiterated assertion of the Indians' unquestioned right to do as they please about ceding these
lands. Such phrases as these: "Should the Indians refuse to
cede to the United States any of the above-designated lands,"
and "you will endeavor to prevail upon them to cede," and
"you will endeavor to procure the consent of the Indians," are
proof of the fulness of the recognition the United States Government at that time gave of the Indians' "right of occupancy;" also of the realization on the part of the Government that
these Indian nations were powers whose good-will it was of importance to conciliate. "It is of importance," the instructions
say, "that the Indian nations generally should be convinced of
the certainty in which they may at all times rely upon the
friendship of the United States, and that the President will
never abandon them or their children;" and, "It will be in-
cumbent on you to introduce the desires of the Government in
such a manner as will permit you to drop them, as you may
find them illy received, without giving the Indians an opportunity to reply with a decided negative, or raising in them unfriendly and inimical dispositions. You will state none of them
in the tone of demands, but in the first instance merely mention
them as propositions which you are authorized to make, and
their assent to which the Government would consider as new
testimonials of their friendship."

Nevertheless, the Cherokees did reply with "a decided negative." They utterly refused to cede any more lands, or to give
their consent to the opening of any more roads through their
territory. But it only took four years to bring them to the
point where they were ready to acquiesce in the wishes of the
Government, and to make once more the effort to secure to
themselves an unmolested region, by giving up several large
tracts of land and a right of way on several roads. In 1805 they

concluded another treaty, ceding territory for which the United States thought it worth while to pay $15,000 immediately, and an annuity of $3000.

Ten years later (in 1816) they gave up all their lands in South Carolina, and the United States became surety that South Carolina should pay to them $5000 for the same. In the autumn of the same year they made still another cession of lands to the United States Government, for which they were to have an annuity of $6000 a year for ten years, and $5000 as compensation for the improvements they surrendered.

In 1817 an important treaty was concluded, making still further cessions of lands, and defining the position of a part of the Cherokee nation which had moved away, with the President's permission, to the Arkansas River in 1809. The eighth Article of this treaty promises that the United States will give to every head of an Indian family residing on the east side of the Mississippi, who may wish to become a citizen, "a reservation of six hundred and forty acres of land, in which they will have a life estate, with a reversion in fee-simple to their children."

What imagination could have foreseen that in less than twenty years the chiefs of this Cherokee nation would be found piteously pleading to be allowed to remain undisturbed on these véry lands? In the whole history of our Government's dealings with the Indian tribes, there is no record so black as the record of its perfidy to this nation. There will come a time in the remote future when, to the student of American history, it will seem well-nigh incredible. From the beginning of the century they had been steadily advancing in civilization. As far back as 1800 they had begun the manufacture of cotton cloth, and in 1820 there was scarcely a family in that part of the nation living east of the Mississippi but what understood the use of the card and spinning-wheel. Every family had its farm under cultivation. The territory was laid off into districts, with a council-house, a judge, and a marshal in each district. A national committee and council were the supreme authority in the nation. Schools were flourishing in all the villages. Printing-presses were at work.

Their territory was larger than the three States of Massachusetts, Rhode Island, and Connecticut combined. It embraced the North-western part of Georgia, the North-east of Alabama, a corner of Tennessee and of North Carolina. They were enthusiastic in their efforts to establish and perfect their own system of jurisprudence. Missions of several sects were established in their country, and a large number of them had professed Christianity, and were living exemplary lives.

There is no instance in all history of a race of people passing in so short a space of time from the barbarous stage to the agricultural and civilized. And it was such a community as this that the State of Georgia, by one high-handed outrage, made outlaws!—passing on the 19th of December, 1829, a law "to annul all laws and ordinances made by the Cherokee nation of Indians;" declaring " all laws, ordinances, orders, and regulations of any kind whatever, made, passed, or enacted by the Cherokee Indians, either in general council or in any other way whatever, or by any authority whatever, null and void, and of no effect, as if the same had never existed; also, that no Indian, or descendant of any Indian residing within the Creek or Cherokee nations of Indians, shall be deemed a competent witness in any court of this State to which a white man may be a party."

What had so changed the attitude of Georgia to the Indians within her borders? Simply the fact that the Indians, finding themselves hemmed in on all sides by fast thickening white settlements, had taken a firm stand that they would give up no more land. So long as they would cede and cede, and grant and grant tract after tract, and had millions of acres still left to cede and grant, the selfishness of white men took no alarm;

but once consolidated into an empire, with fixed and inalienable boundaries, powerful, recognized, and determined, the Cherokee nation would be a thorn in the flesh to her white neighbors.   The doom of the Cherokees was sealed on the day when
they declared, once for all, officially as a nation, that they would
not sell another foot of land.   This they did in an interesting
and pathetic message to the United States Senate in 1822.

Georgia, through her governor and her delegates to Congress,
had been persistently demanding to have the Cherokees compelled to give up their lands.   She insisted that the United
States Government should fulfil a provision, made in an old
compact of 1802, to extinguish the Indian titles within her
limits as soon as it could be peaceably done.   This she demanded should be done now, either peaceably or otherwise.

" We cannot but view the design of those letters," says this
message, " as an attempt bordering on a hostile disposition toward the Cherokee nation to wrest from them by arbitrary
means their just rights and liberties, the security of which is
solemnly guaranteed to them by these United States. * * * We
assert under the fullest authority that all the sentiments expressed in relation to the disposition and determination of the
nation never to cede another foot of land, are positively the
production and voice of the nation. * * * There is not a spot
out of the limits of any of the States or Territories thereof,
and within the limits of the United States, that they would
ever consent to inhabit; because they have unequivocally determined never again to pursue the chase as heretofore, or to
engage in wars, unless by the common call of the Government
to defend the common rights of the United States. * * * The
Cherokees have turned their attention to the pursuits of the
civilized man : agriculture, manufactures, and the mechanic arts
and education are all in successful operation in the nation at
this time ; and while the Cherokees are peacefully endeavoring
to enjoy the blessings of civilization and Christianity on the

soil of their rightful inheritance, and while the exertions and labors of various religious societies of these United States are successfully engaged in promulgating to them the words of truth and life from the sacred volume of Holy Writ, and under the patronage of the General Government, they are threatened with removal or extinction. * * * We appeal to the magnanimity of the American Congress for justice, and the protection of the rights and liberties and lives of the Cherokee people. We claim it from the United States by the strongest obligation which imposes it on them—by treaties: and we expect it from them under that memorable declaration, ' that all men are created equal; that they are endowed by their Creator with certain inalienable rights; that among these are life, liberty, and the pursuit of happiness.'"

The dignified and pathetic remonstrances of the Cherokee chiefs, their firm reiterations of their resolve not to part with their lands, was called by the angry Georgian governor "tricks of vulgar cunning," and "insults from the polluted lips of outcasts and vagabonds;" and he is not afraid, in an official letter to the Secretary of War, to openly threaten the President that, if he upholds the Indians in their rejection of the overtures for removal, the "consequences are inevitable," and that, in resisting the occupation of the Cherokee lands by the Georgians, he will be obliged to "make war upon, and shed the blood of brothers and friends."

To these Cherokees Mr. Jefferson had written, at one time during his administration, "I sincerely wish you may succeed in your laudable endeavors to save the remnant of your nation by adopting industrious occupations, and a government of regular law. In this you may always rely on the counsel and assistance of the United States."

In 1791 he had written to General Knox, defining the United States' position in the matter of Indian lands: "Government should firmly maintain this ground, that the Indians have a right to the occupation of their lands independent of the States within whose chartered lines they happen to be; that until they cede them by treaty, or other transaction equivalent to treaty, no act of a State can give a right to such lands. * * * The Government is determined to exert all its energy for the patronage and protection of the rights of the Indians."

And the year before General Washington had said to the Six Nations: "In future you cannot be defrauded of your lands. No State or person can purchase your lands unless at some public treaty held under the authority of the United States. The General Government will never consent to your being defrauded; but it will protect you in all your just rights. * * * You possess the right to sell, and the right of refusing to sell your lands. * * * The United States will be true and faithful to their engagements."

What could Cherokee men and women have thought when, only thirty years later, they found this United States Government upholding the State of Georgia in her monstrous pretensions of right to the whole of their country, and in her infamous cruelties of oppression toward them? when they found this United States Government sending its agents to seduce and bribe their chiefs to bargain away their country; even stooping to leave on the public records of official instructions to a commissioner such phrases as these: "Appeal to the chiefs and influential men—not together, but apart, at their own houses;" "make offers to them of extensive reservations in fee-simple, and other rewards, to obtain their acquiescence;" "the more careful you are to secure from even the chiefs the official character you bear, the better;" "enlarge on the advantage of their condition in the West: there the Government would protect them." This the Secretary of War called "moving on them in the line of their prejudices."

In a report submitted to the War Department in 1825 by Thomas L. McKenney is a glowing description of the Cherokee country and nation at that time: "The country is well watered; abundant springs of pure water are found in every part; a range of majestic and lofty mountains stretch themselves across it. The northern part is hilly and mountainous; in the southern and western parts there are extensive and fertile plains, covered partly with tall trees, through which beautiful streams of water glide. These plains furnish immense pasturage, and numberless herds of cattle are dispersed over them; horses are plenty; numerous flocks of sheep, goats, and swine cover the valleys and the hills. On Tennessee, Ustanula, and Canasagi rivers Cherokee commerce floats. The climate is delicious and healthy; the winters are mild; the spring clothes the ground with the richest scenery; flowers of exquisite beauty and variegated hues meet and fascinate the eye in every direction. In the plains and valleys the soil is generally rich, producing Indian-corn, cotton, tobacco, wheat, oats, indigo, and sweet and Irish potatoes. The natives carry on considerable trade with the adjoining States; some of them export cotton in boats down the Tennessee to the Mississippi, and down that river to New Orleans. Apple and peach orchards are quite common, and gardens are cultivated, and much attention paid to them. Butter and cheese are seen on Cherokee tables. There are many public roads in the nation, and houses of entertainment kept by natives. Numerous and flourishing villages are seen in every section of the country. Cotton and woollen cloths are manufactured: blankets of various dimensions, manufactured by Cherokee hands, are very common. Almost every family in the nation grows cotton for its own consumption. Industry and commercial enterprise are extending themselves in every part. Nearly all the merchants in the nation are native Cherokees. Agricultural pursuits engage the chief attention of the people. Different branches in mechanics are pursued. The population is rapidly increasing. * * * White men in the nation enjoy all the immunities and privileges of the Cherokee people, except that they are not eligible to public offices. * * * The Christian religion is the religion of the nation. Presbyterians, Methodists, Baptists, and Moravians are the most numerous sects. Some of the most influential characters are members of the Church, and live consistently with their professions. The whole nation is penetrated with gratitude for the aid it has received from the United States Government, and from different religious societies. Schools are increasing every year; learning is encouraged and rewarded; the young class acquire the English, and those of mature age the Cherokee system of learning. * * * Our relations with all nations are of the most friendly character. We are out of debt, and our public revenue is in a flourishing condition. Besides the amount arising from imports, perpetual annuity is due from the United States in consideration of lands ceded in former periods. Our system of government, founded on republican principles by which justice is equally distributed, secures the respect of the people. New Town, pleasantly situated in the centre of the nation, and at the junction of the Canasagi and Gusuwati, two beautiful streams, is the seat of government. The legislative power is vested in what is denominated in native dialect Tsalagi Tinilawige, consisting of a national committee and council. Members of both branches are chosen by and from the people for a limited period. In New Town a printing-press is soon to be established; also a national library and museum. An immense concourse of people frequent the seat of government when the Tsalagi Tinilawige is in session, which takes place once a year.

"The success which has attended the philological researches of one in the nation whose system of education has met with universal approbation among the Cherokees certainly entitles him to great consideration, and to rank with the benefactors of man. His name is Guess, and he is a native and unlettered Cherokee; but, like Cadmus, he has given to his people the

alphabet of their language.   It is composed of eighty-six characters, by which in a few days the older Indians, who had de-
spaired of deriving an education by means of the schools, and
who are not included in the existing school system, may read
and correspond."

Never did mountaineers cling more desperately to their
homes than did the Cherokees.   The State of Georgia put the
whole nation in duress, but still they chose to stay.   Year by
year high-handed oppressions increased and multiplied; military law reigned everywhere; Cherokee lands were surveyed,
and put up to be drawn by lottery; missionaries were arrested
and sent to prison for preaching to Cherokees; Cherokees were
sentenced to death by Georgia juries, and hung by Georgia
executioners.   Appeal after appeal to the President and to
Congress for protection produced only reiterated confessions
of the Government's inability to protect them—reiterated pro-
posals to them to accept a price for their country and move
away.   Nevertheless they clung to it.   A few hundreds went,
but the body of the nation still protested and entreated.   There
is nothing in history more touching than the cries of this people to the Government of the United States to fulfil its promises to them.   And their cause was not without eloquent advocates.   When the bill for their removal was before Congress,
Frelinghuysen, Sprague, Robbins, Storrs, Ellsworth, Evans,
Huntington, Johns, Bates, Crockett, Everett, Test—all spoke
warmly against it; and, to the credit of Congress be it said,
the bill passed the Senate by only one majority.

The Rev. Jeremiah Evarts published a series of papers in the
National Intelligencer under the signature of William Penn,
in which he gave a masterly analysis and summing up of the
case, recapitulated the sixteen treaties which the Government
had made with the Cherokees, all guaranteeing to them their

lands, and declared that the Government had "arrived at the bank of the Rubicon," where it must decide if it would or would not save the country from the charge of bad faith. Many of his eloquent sentences read in the light of the present time like prophecies. He says, "in a quarter of a century the pressure upon the Indians will be much greater from the boundless prairies, which must ultimately be subdued and inhabited, than it would ever have been from the borders of the present Cherokee country;" and asks, pertinently, "to what confidence would such an engagement be entitled, done at the very moment that treaties with Indians are declared not to be binding, and for the very reason that existing treaties are not strong enough to bind the United States." Remonstrances poured in upon Congress, petitions and memorials from religious societies, from little country villages, all imploring the Government to keep its faith to these people.

The Cherokees' own newspaper, *The Phœnix*, was filled at this time with the records of the nation's suffering and despair.

"The State of Georgia has taken a strong stand against us, and the United States must either defend us and our rights or leave us to our foe. In the latter case she will violate her promise of protection, and we cannot in future depend upon any guarantee to us, either here or beyond the Mississippi.

"If the United States shall withdraw their solemn pledges of protection, utterly disregard their plighted faith, deprive us of the right of self-government, and wrest from us our land, then, in the deep anguish of our misfortunes, we may justly say there is no place of security for us, no confidence left that the United States will be more just and faithful toward us in the barren prairies of the West than when we occupied the soil inherited from the Great Author of our existence."

As a last resort the Cherokees carried their case before the Supreme Court, and implored that body to restrain the State of Georgia from her unjust interference with their rights.

The reports of the case of the Cherokee Nation *vs.* the State of Georgia fill a volume by themselves, and are of vital importance to the history of Indian affairs. The majority of the judges decided that an Indian tribe could not be considered as a foreign nation, and therefore could not bring the suit. Judge Thompson and Judge Story dissented from this opinion, and held that the Cherokee tribe did constitute a foreign nation, and that the State of Georgia ought to be enjoined from execution of its unjust laws. The opinion of Chancellor Kent coincided with that of Judges Thompson and Story. Chancellor Kent gave it as his opinion that the cases in which the Supreme Court had jurisdiction would "reach and embrace every controversy that can arise between the Cherokees and the State of Georgia or its officers under the execution of the act of Georgia."

But all this did not help the Cherokees; neither did the fact of the manifest sympathy of the whole court with their wrongs. The technical legal decision had been rendered against them, and this delivered them over to the tender mercies of Georgia: no power in the land could help them. Fierce factions now began to be formed in the nation, one for and one against the surrender of their lands. Many were ready still to remain and suffer till death rather than give them up; but wiser counsels prevailed, and in the last days of the year 1835 a treaty was concluded with the United States by twenty of the Cherokee chiefs and headmen, who thereby, in behalf of their nation, relinquished all the lands claimed or possessed by them east of the Mississippi River.

The preamble of this treaty is full of pathos: "*Whereas,* The Cherokees are anxious to make some arrangement with the Government of the United States whereby the difficulties they have experienced by a residence within the settled parts of the United States under the jurisdiction and laws of the State governments may be terminated and adjusted; and with a view to reuniting their people in one body, and securing a perma-

nent home for themselves and their posterity in the country
selected by their forefathers without the territorial limits of
the State sovereignties, and where they can establish and enjoy
a government of their choice, and perpetuate such a state of
society as may be most consonant with their views, habits, and
condition, and as may tend to their individual comfort and
their advancement in civilization."

By this treaty the Cherokees gave up a country "larger than
the three States of Massachusetts, Rhode Island, and Connecticut combined, and received therefor five millions of dollars
and seven millions of acres of land west of the Mississippi."
This the United States "guaranteed, and secured to be conveyed in patent," and defined it by exact boundaries; and, "in addition to the seven millions of acres of land thus provided for
and bounded," the United States did "further guarantee to
the Cherokee nation a perpetual outlet west, and a free and unmolested use of all the country west of the western boundary
of said seven millions of acres, as far west as the sovereignty
of the United States and their rights of soil extend."

The fifth Article of this treaty is, "The United States hereby covenant and agree that the lands ceded to the Cherokee
nation in the foregoing article shall in no future time, without
their consent, be included within the territorial limits or jurisdiction of any State or Territory."

In the sixth Article is this promise: "The United States
agree to protect the Cherokee nation from domestic strife and
foreign enemies, and against intestine wars between the several tribes."

Even after this treaty was made a great part of the nation
refused to sanction it, saying that it did not represent their
wish; they would never carry it out; hundreds refused to receive any longer either money or supplies from the United
States agents, lest they should be considered to have thereby
committed themselves to the treaty.

In 1837 General Wool wrote from the Cherokee country that the people "uniformly declare that they never made the treaty in question. * * * So determined are they in their opposition that not one of all those who were present, and voted in the council held but a day or two since at this place, however poor or destitute, would receive either rations or clothing from the United States, lest they might compromise themselves in regard to the treaty. These same people, as well as those in the mountains of North Carolina, during the summer past preferred living on the roots and sap of trees rather than receive provisions from the United States. Thousands, I have been informed, had no other food for weeks."

For two years—to the very last moment allowed them by the treaty—they clung to their lands, and at last were removed only by military force. In May, 1838, General Scott was ordered to go with a sufficient military force to compel the removal. His proclamation "to the Cherokee people remaining in North Carolina, Georgia, Tennessee, and Alabama" opens thus:

"CHEROKEES,—The President of the United States has sent me with a powerful army to cause you, in obedience to the treaty of 1835, to join that part of your people who are already established on the other side of the Mississippi. Unhappily the two years which were allowed for the purpose you have suffered to pass away without following, and without making any preparation to follow; and now, or by the time that this solemn address shall reach your distant settlements, the emigration must be commenced in haste, but I hope without disorder. I have no power, by granting a further delay, to correct the error that you have committed. The full-moon of May is already on the wane, and before another shall have passed away every Cherokee man, woman, and child in those States must be in motion to join their brethren in the West."

The tone of this proclamation, at once firm and kindly, could not fail to profoundly impress the unfortunate people to whom

it was addressed. "My troops," said the humane and sympa-
thizing general, "already occupy many positions in the country
that you are to abandon, and thousands and thousands are approaching from every quarter, to render resistance and escape
alike hopeless. All those troops, regular and militia, are your
friends. Receive them and confide in them as such; obey
them when they tell you that you can remain no longer in this
country. Soldiers are as kind-hearted as brave, and the desire
of every one of us is to execute our painful duty in mercy. * * *

"Chiefs, headmen, and warriors, will you then, by resistance,
compel us to resort to arms? God forbid. Or will you by
flight seek to hide yourselves in mountains and forests, and
thus oblige us to hunt you down? Remember that in pursuit it may be impossible to avoid conflicts. The blood of the
white man or the blood of the red man may be spilt; and if
spilt, however accidentally, it may be impossible for the dis-
creet and humane among you or among us to prevent a general
war and carnage. Think of this, my Cherokee brethren! I
am an old warrior, and have been present at many a scene of
slaughter; but spare me, I beseech you, the horror of witness-
ing the destruction of the Cherokees. Do not even wait for
the close approach of the troops, but make such preparations
for emigration as you can, and hasten to this place, to Ross's
Landing, or to Guinter's Landing, where you will be received
in kindness by officers selected for the purpose. * * * This is
the address of a warrior to warriors. May its entreaties be
kindly received, and may the God of both prosper the Americans and Cherokees, and preserve them long in peace and
friendship with each other."

The reply of the council of the Cherokee nation to this proclamation is worthy to be put on record. They make no further protest against going; they simply ask the privilege of
undertaking the whole charge of the removal themselves. They
say: "The present condition of the Cherokee people is such

that all dispute as to the time of emigration is set at rest. Being already severed from their homes and their property, their persons being under the absolute control of the commanding general, and being altogether dependent on the benevolence and humanity of that high officer for the suspension of their transportation to the West at a season and under circumstances in which sickness and death were to be apprehended to an alarming extent, all inducements to prolong their stay in this country are taken away. And however strong their attachment to the homes of their fathers may be, their interests and their wishes are now to depart as early as may be consistent with their safety."

The council therefore submitted to General Scott several propositions: 1st. "That the Cherokee nation will undertake the whole business of removing their people to the west of the river Mississippi." Their estimates of cost, and arrangement as to time, intervals, etc., were wise and reasonable. To their estimate of $65,880 as the cost for every thousand persons transported General Scott objected, thinking it high. He said that he was "confident" that it would be found that out of every thousand there would be "at least five hundred strong men, women, boys, and girls not only capable of marching twelve or fifteen miles a day, but to whom the exercise would be beneficial; and another hundred able to go on foot half that distance daily." He also objected to the estimate of the ration at sixteen cents as too high.

The council replied that they believed the estimate reasonable, "having the comfortable removal of our people solely in view, and endeavoring to be governed, as far as that object will allow, by the rates of expenditure fixed by the officers of the Government. After the necessary bedding, cooking-utensils, and other indispensable articles of twenty persons—say, four or five families—are placed in a wagon, with subsistence for at least two days, the weight already will be enough to exclude, in our opinion, more than a very few persons being hauled. The great distance to be travelled, liability to sickness on the way of grown persons, and the desire of performing the trip in as short a time as possible, induce us still to think our estimate of that item not extravagant. * * * Whatever may be necessary in the emigration of our people to their comfort on the way, and as conducive to their health, we desire to be afforded them ; at the same time it is our anxious wish, in the management of this business, to be free at all times from the imputation of extravagance."   They added that the item of soap had been forgotten in their first estimate, and must now be included, at the rate of three pounds to every hundred pounds of rations.

General Scott replied, " as the Cherokee people are exclusively interested in the cost as well as the comfort of the removal," he did not feel himself at liberty to withhold his sanction from these estimates.   In the report of the Indian Commissioner, also, it is stated that " the cost of removal, according to the Indian estimate, is high ;" but the commissioner adds, " as their own fund pays it, and it was insisted on by their own confidential agents, it was thought it could not be rejected."

Noble liberality ! This nation of eighteen thousand industrious, self-supporting people, compelled at the point of the bayonet to leave their country and seek new homes in a wilderness, are to be permitted, as a favor, to spend on their journey to this wilderness as much of their own money as they think necessary, and have all the soap they want.

The record which the United States Government has left in official papers of its self-congratulations in the matter of this Cherokee removal has an element in it of the ludicrous, spite of the tragedy and shame.

Says the Secretary of War : " The generous and enlightened policy evinced in the measures adopted by Congress toward that people during the last session was ably and judiciously carried into effect by the general appointed to conduct their removal. The reluctance of the Indians to relinquish the land of their birth in the East, and remove to their new homes in the West, was entirely overcome by the judicious conduct of that officer, and they departed with alacrity under the guidance of their own chiefs. The arrangements for this purpose made by General Scott, in compliance with his previous instructions, although somewhat costly to the Indians themselves, met the entire approbation of the Department, as it was deemed of the last importance that the Cherokees should remove to the West voluntarily, and that upon their arrival at the place of their ultimate destination they should recur to the manner in which they had been treated with kind and grateful feelings. Humanity no less than good policy dictated this course toward these children of the forest; and in carrying out in this instance with an unwavering hand the measures resolved upon by the Government, in the hope of preserving the Indians and of maintaining the peace and tranquillity of the whites, it will always be gratifying to reflect that this has been effected not only without violence, but with every proper regard for the feelings and interests of that people."

The Commissioner of Indian Affairs says, in his report: "The case of the Cherokees is a striking example of the liberality of the Government in all its branches. * * * A retrospect of the last eight months in reference to this numerous and more than ordinarily enlightened tribe cannot fail to be refreshing to well-constituted minds."

A further appropriation had been asked by the Cherokee chiefs to meet the expense of their removal (they not thinking $5,000,000 a very munificent payment for a country as large as all Massachusetts, Rhode Island, and Connecticut together), and Congress had passed a law giving them $1147 67 more, and the commissioner says of this: "When it is considered that by the treaty of December, 1835, the sum of $5,000,000 was stipulated to be paid them as the full value of their lands, after that amount was declared by the Senate of the United States to be an ample consideration for them, the spirit of this whole proceeding cannot be too much admired. By some the measure may be regarded as just; by others generous: it perhaps partook of both attributes. If it went farther than naked justice could have demanded, it did not stop short of what liberality approved. * * * If our acts have been generous, they have not been less wise and politic. A large mass of men have been conciliated; the hazard of an effusion of human blood has been put by; good feeling has been preserved, and we have quietly and gently transported eighteen thousand friends to the west bank of the Mississippi."

To dwell on the picture of this removal is needless. The fact by itself is more eloquent than pages of detail and description could make it. No imagination so dull, no heart so hard as not to see and to feel, at the bare mention of such an emigration, what horrors and what anguish it must have involved. "Eighteen thousand friends!" Only a great magnanimity of nature, strengthened by true Christian principle, could have prevented them from being changed into eighteen thousand bitter enemies.

For some years after this removal fierce dissensions rent the Cherokee nation. The party who held that the treaty of 1835 had been unfair, and that the nation still had an unextinguished right to its old country at the East, felt, as was natural, a bitter hatred toward the party which, they claimed, had wrongfully signed away the nation's lands. Several of the signers of the treaty, influential men of the nation, were murdered. Party-spirit ran to such a height that the United States Government was compelled to interfere; and in 1846, after long negotiations and dissensions, a new treaty was made, by the terms and concessions of which the anti-treaty party were appeased, a general amnesty provided for, and comparative harmony restored to the nation.

The progress of this people in the ten years following this removal is almost past belief. In 1851 they had twenty-two primary schools, and had just built two large houses for a male and female seminary, in which the higher branches of education were to be taught. They had a temperance society with three thousand members, and an auxiliary society in each of the eight districts into which the country was divided. They had a Bible Society and twelve churches; a weekly newspaper, partly in English, partly in Cherokee; eight district courts, two circuit courts, and a supreme court. Legislative business was transacted as before by the national council and committee, elected for four years. Nearly one thousand boys and girls were in the public schools.

In 1860 the agitation on the subject of slavery began to be felt, a strong antislavery party being organized in the nation. There were stormy scenes also in that part of the country nearest the Kansas line. For several years white settlers had persisted in taking up farms there, and the Cherokees had in vain implored the Government to drive them away. The officer at last sent to enforce the Cherokees' rights and dislodge the squatters was obliged to burn their cabins over their heads before they would stir, so persuaded were they of the superior right of the white man over the Indian. "The only reason the settlers gave for not heeding the notices was that they had been often notified before to quit the reservation; and, no steps having been taken to enforce obedience, they supposed they would be allowed to remain with like security in this instance."

"It is surprising," says the Commissioner of Indian Affairs, "to see the growing disposition on the part of our citizens to wholly disregard our treaty obligations with Indian tribes within our borders; and it is to be hoped that in future their rights will be held more sacred, or that the Government will in every instance promptly see that they are observed and respected."

In the first year of the Civil War a large number of the

Cherokees took up arms on the rebel side. That this was not from any love or liking for the Southern cause, it would seem, must be evident to any one who believed that they were possessed of memories. The opportunity of fighting against Georgians could not but have been welcome to the soul of a Cherokee, even if he bought it at the price of fighting on the side of the government which had been so perfidious to his nation. Their defection was no doubt largely due to terror. The forts in their vicinity were surrendered to the rebels; all United States troops were withdrawn from that part of the country. They had no prospect of protection from the Government, and, as if to leave them without one incentive to loyalty, the Government suspended the payment of their annuities.

The Confederate Government stepped in, artfully promising to pay what the Northern Government refused. It would have taken a rare loyalty, indeed, to have stood unmoved in such circumstances as these; yet thousands of the Indians in Indian Territory did remain loyal, and fled for their lives to avoid being pressed into the rebel service; almost half of the Creek nation, many Seminoles, Chickasaws, Quapaws, Cherokees, and half a dozen others—over six thousand in all—fled to Kansas, where their sufferings in the winter of 1862 were heart-rending.

That the Cherokees did not lightly abandon their allegiance is on record in the official history of the Department of the Interior. The Report of the Indian Bureau for 1863 says: "The Cherokees, prior to the Rebellion, were the most numerous, intelligent, wealthy, and influential tribe of this superintendency (the southern). For many months they steadily resisted the efforts made by the rebels to induce them to abandon their allegiance to the Federal Government; but being wholly unprotected, and without the means of resistance, they were finally compelled to enter into treaty stipulations with the rebel authorities. This connection was, however, of short duration, for upon the first appearance of United States forces in their country an entire regiment of Indian troops, raised ostensibly for service in the rebel army, deserted and came over to us, and have ever since been under our command, and upon all occasions have proved themselves faithful and efficient soldiers." In the course of the next year, however, many more joined the rebels: it was estimated that between six and seven thousand of the wealthier portion of the nation co-operated in one way or another with the rebels. The result was that at the end of the war the Cherokee country was ruined.

"In the Cherokee country," says the Report of the Indian Bureau for 1865, "where the contending armies have moved to and fro; where their foraging parties have gone at will, sparing neither friend nor foe; where the disloyal Cherokees in the service ·of the rebel government were determined that no trace of the homesteads of their loyal brethren should remain for their return; and where the swindling cattle-thieves have made their ill-gotten gains for two years past, the scene is one of utter desolation."

The party feeling between the loyal and disloyal Cherokees ran as high as it did between the loyal and disloyal whites, and it looked for a time as if it would be as impossible to make the two opposing parties in the Cherokee nation agree to live peaceably side by side with each other, as it would to make discharged soldiers from Georgia and from Maine settle down in one village together. But after long and troublesome negotiations a treaty was concluded in 1866, by which all the necessary points seemed to be established of a general amnesty and peace.

That the Indians were at a great disadvantage in the making of these new treaties it is unnecessary to state. The peculiarity of the Government's view of their situation and rights is most naïvely stated in one of the reports for 1862. Alluding to the necessity of making at no very distant time new treaties with all these Southern tribes, one of the Indian superintendents says: "While the rebelling of a large portion of most of these tribes abrogates treaty obligations, and places them at our mercy, the very important fact should not be forgotten that the Government first wholly failed to keep its treaty stipulations with those people, and in protecting them, by withdrawing all the troops from the forts in Indian Territory, and leaving them at the mercy of the rebels. It is a well-known fact that self-preservation in many instances compelled them to make the best terms they could with the rebels."

Nevertheless they are "at our mercy," because their making the "best terms they could with the rebels abrogates treaty obligations." The trite old proverb about the poorness of rules that do not work both ways seems to be applicable here.

With a recuperative power far in advance of that shown by any of the small white communities at the South, the Cherokees at once addressed themselves to rebuilding their homes and reconstructing their national life. In one year they established fifteen new schools, set all their old industries going, and in 1869 held a large agricultural fair, which gave a creditable exhibition of stock and farm produce. Thus a second time they recovered themselves, after what would seem to be wellnigh their destruction as a people. But the Indian's fate of perpetual insecurity, alarm, and unrest does not abandon them. In 1870 they are said to be "extremely uneasy about the security of their possession of the lands they occupy." When asked why their high-schools are not re-established, reforms introduced into the administration of justice, desirable improvements undertaken, the reply inevitably comes, "We expect to have our lands taken away: what is the use of all that when our doom as a nation is sealed?"

"Distrust is firmly seated in their minds. National apathy depresses them, and until they realize a feeling of assurance that their title to their lands will be respected, and that treaties are an inviolable law for all parties, the Cherokees will not make the efforts for national progress of which they are capable."

When their delegates went to Washington, in 1866, to make the new treaty, they were alarmed by the position taken by the Government that the nation, as a nation, had forfeited its rights. They were given to understand that "public opinion held them responsible for complicity in the Rebellion; and, although they could point to the fact that the only countenance the rebels received came from less than one-third of the population, and cite the services of two Cherokee regiments in the Union cause, it was urged home to them that, before being rehabilitated in their former rights by a new treaty, they were not in a position to refuse any conditions imposed. Such language from persons they believed to possess the power of injuring their people intimidated the Cherokee delegates. They sold a large tract in South-eastern Kansas at a dollar an acre to an association of speculators, and it went into the possession of a railroad company. They also acceded, against the wishes of the Cherokee people, to a provision in the treaty granting right of way through the country for two railroads. This excited great uneasiness among the Indians."

And well it might. The events of the next few years amply justified this uneasiness. The rapacity of railroad corporations is as insatiable as their methods are unscrupulous. The phrase "extinguishing Indian titles" has become, as it were, a mere technical term in the transfer of lands. The expression is so common that it has probably been one of the agencies in fixing in the minds of the people the prevalent impression that extinction is the ultimate and inevitable fate of the Indian; and this being the case, methods and times are not, after all, of so much consequence; they are merely foreordained conditions of the great foreordained progression of events. This is the only explanation of the unconscious inhumanity of many good men's modes of thinking and speaking in regard to the Indians being driven from home after home, and robbed of tract after tract of their lands.

In the Report of the Indian Bureau for 1875 is an account of a remnant of the Cherokee tribe in North Carolina: "They number not far from seventeen hundred, and there are probably in other parts of North Carolina, and scattered through Georgia and Tennessee, between three and four hundred more. These Cherokees have had an eventful history. When the main portion of the tribe was compelled to remove west of the Mississippi they fled to the mountains, and have steadily refused to leave their homes. The proceeds of their lands, which were sold in accordance with a treaty with the main body of the Cherokees, have been mainly expended in the purchase of lands, and providing funds for the Western Cherokees. At various times previous to the year 1861 the agent for the Eastern Cherokees, at their request, purchased lands with their funds, upon which they might make their homes. These purchases, though probably made with good intent, carelessly left the title in their agent personally, and not in trust. By this neglect, when subsequently the agent became insolvent, all their lands were seized and sold for his debts. By special legislation of Congress their case has been brought before the courts of North Carolina, and their rights to a certain extent asserted, and they are enabled to maintain possession of their lands; and, by the use of their own funds in extinguishing liens, are now in possession of above seventy thousand acres of fair arable, timber, and grazing lands. They have shown themselves capable of self-support, and, I believe, have demonstrated the unwisdom of removing Indians from a country which offers to them a home, and where a white man could make a living. This is shown by the fact that they are now, though receiving scarcely any Government aid, in a more hopeful condition, both as to morals, and industry, and personal property, than the Cherokees who removed West."

The Report of the Indian Bureau for 1876 fully bears out this statement. The North Carolina Cherokees have, indeed, reason to be in a more hopeful condition, for they have their lands secured to them by patent, confirmed by a decision of State courts; but this is what the Department of the Interior has brought itself to say as to the Western Cherokees' lands, and those of all other civilized tribes in the Indian Territory: " By treaty the Government has ceded to the so-called civilized tribes—the Cherokees, Creeks, Choctaws, Chickasaws, and Seminoles — a section of country altogether disproportionate in amount to their needs. * * * The amount susceptible of cultivation must be many-fold greater than can ever be cultivated by the labor of the Indians. But the Indians claim, it is understood, that they hold their lands by sanctions so solemn that it would be a gross breach of faith on the part of the Government to take away any portion thereof without their consent; and that consent they apparently propose to withhold."[15]

Let us set side by side with this last paragraph a quotation from the treaty by virtue of which "the Indians claim, it is understood, that they hold" these lands, which they now " apparently propose to withhold." We will not copy it from the original treaty; we will copy it, and a few other sentences with it, from an earlier report of this same Department of the Interior. Only so far back as 1870 we find the Department in a juster frame of mind toward the Cherokees. "A large part of the Indian tribes hold lands to which they are only fixed by laws that define the reservations to which they shall be confined. It cannot be denied that these are in a great measure dependent on the humanity of the American people. * * * But the Cherokees, and the other civilized Indian nations no less, hold lands in perpetuity by titles defined by the supreme law of the land. The United States agreed 'to possess the Cherokees, and to guarantee it to them forever,' and that guarantee 'was solemnly pledged of seven million acres of land.' The

[15] Regarding Indian removal, see R. S. Cotterill, *The Southern Indians: The Story of the Civilized Tribes Before Removal* (Norman, Oklahoma, 1954), Grant Foreman, *Indian Removal, The Emigration of the Five Civilized Tribes of Indians* (Norman, Oklahoma, 1932), and his *The Last Trek of the Indians* (Chicago, 1946).

consideration for this territory was the same number of acres elsewhere located. The inducement to the bargain set forth in the treaty was 'the anxious desire of the Government of the United States to secure to the Cherokee nation of Indians a permanent home, and which shall, under the most solemn guarantee of the United States, be and remain theirs forever—a home that shall never in all future time be embarrassed by having extended around it the lines or placed over it the jurisdiction of a Territory or State, or be pressed upon by the extension in any way of the limits of any existing State.' To assure them of their title, a patent for the Territory was issued."

This was the view of the Department of the Interior in 1870. In 1876 the Department says that affairs in the Indian Territory are "complicated and embarrassing, and the question is directly raised whether an extensive section of country is to be allowed to remain for an indefinite period practically an uncultivated waste, or whether the Government shall determine to reduce the size of the reservation."

The phrase "whether the Government shall determine to reduce the size of the reservation" sounds much better than "whether the Government shall rob the Indians of a few millions of acres of land;" but the latter phrase is truth, and the other is the spirit of lying.

The commissioner says that the question is a difficult one, and should be "considered with calmness, and a full purpose to do no injustice to the Indians." He gives his own personal opinion on it "with hesitancy," but gives it nevertheless, that "public policy will soon require the disposal of a large portion of these lands to the Government for the occupancy either of other tribes of Indians or of white people. There is a very general and growing opinion that observance of the strict letter of treaties with Indians is in many cases at variance with their own best interests and with sound public policy." He adds, however, that it must not be understood from this recommendation that it is "the policy or purpose of this office to in any way encourage the spirit of rapacity which demands the throwing open of the Indian Territory to white settlement." He says, "the true way to secure its perpetual occupancy by Indians is to fill it up with other Indians, to give them lands in severalty, and to provide a government strong and intelligent enough to protect them effectually from any and all encroachments on the part of the whites."

Comment on these preposterously contradictory sentences would be idle. The best comment on them, and the most fitting close to this sketch of the Cherokee nation, is in a few more quotations from the official reports of the Indian Bureau.

Of this people, from whom the Department of the Interior proposes, for "public policy," to take away "a large portion" of their country, it has published within the last three years these records:

"It has been but a few years since the Cherokees assembled in council under trees or in a rude log-house, with hewed logs for seats. Now the legislature assembles in a spacious brick council-house, provided with suitable committee-rooms, senate chamber, representative hall, library, and executive offices, which cost $22,000.

"Their citizens occupy neat hewed double log-cabins, frame, brick, or stone houses, according to the means or taste of the individual, with ground adorned by ornamental trees, shrubbery, flowers, and nearly every improvement, including orchards of the choicest fruits. Some of these orchards have existed for nearly twenty years, and are now in a good, fruitful condition. Their women are usually good house-keepers, and give great attention to spinning and weaving yarns, jeans, and linsey, and make most of the pants and hunter-jackets of the men and boys. The farmers raise most of their own wool and cotton, and it is not an uncommon sight, in a well-to-do Cherokee farmer's house, to see a sewing-machine and a piano.

"They have ample provision for the education of all their children to a degree of advancement equal to that furnished by an ordinary college in the States. They have seventy-five common day-schools, kept open ten months in the year, in the different settlements. For the higher education of their young men and women they have two commodious and well-furnished seminaries, one for each sex; and, in addition to those already mentioned, they have a manual labor school and an orphan asylum. The cost of maintaining these schools the past year (1877) was, as reported by the superintendent of public instruction, $73,441 65, of which $41,475 was paid as salary to teachers.

"They have twenty-four stores, twenty-two mills, and sixty-five smith-shops, owned and conducted by their own citizens.

"Their constitution and laws are published in book form; and from their printing-house goes forth among the people in their own language, and also in English, the *Cherokee Advocate*, a weekly paper, which is edited with taste and ability.

"They have (and this is true also of the Choctaws, Creeks, Chickasaws, and Seminoles) a constitutional government, with legislative, judicial, and executive departments, and conducted upon the same plan as our State governments, the entire expenses of which are paid out of their own funds, which are derived from interest on various stocks and bonds—the invested proceeds of the sale of their lands, and held in trust by the Government of the United States—which interest is paid the treasurers of the different nations semi-annually, and by them disbursed on national warrants issued by the principal chief and secretary, and registered by the auditors.

"They are an intelligent, temperate, and industrious people, who live by the honest fruits of their labor, and seem ambitious to advance both as to the development of their lands and the conveniences of their homes. In their council may be found men of learning and ability; and it is doubtful if their rapid progress from a state of wild barbarism to that of civilization and enlightenment has any parallel in the history of the world. What required five hundred years for the Britons to accomplish in this direction they have accomplished in one hundred years."

Will the United States Government determine to " reduce the size of the reservation ?"

CHAPTER IX.

I.—*The Conestoga Massacre.*

WHEN the English first entered Pennsylvania messengers from the Conestoga Indians met them, bidding them welcome, and bringing gifts of corn and venison and skins. The whole tribe entered into a treaty of friendship with William Penn, which was to last "as long as the sun should shine or the waters run into the rivers."

The records of Pennsylvania history in the beginning of the eighteenth century contain frequent mention of the tribe. In 1705 the governor sent the secretary of his council, with a delegation of ten men, to hold an interview with them at Conestoga, for purposes of mutual understanding and confidence. And in that same year Thomas Chalkley, a famous Quaker preacher, while sojourning among the Maryland Quakers, was suddenly seized with so great a "concern" to visit these Indians that he laid the matter before the elders at the Nottingham meeting; and, the idea being "promoted" by the elders, he set off with an interpreter and a party of fourteen to make the journey. He says: "We travelled through the woods about fifty miles, carrying our provisions with us; and on the journey sat down by a river and spread our food on the grass, and refreshed ourselves and horses, and then went on cheerfully and with good-will and much love to the poor Indians. And when we came they received us kindly, treating us civilly in their way. We treated about having a meeting with them in a religious way; upon which they called a council, in which they were very grave, and spoke, one after another, without any heat or jarring. Some of the most esteemed of their women speak in their councils."

When asked why they suffered the women to speak, they replied that "some women were wiser than some men." It was said that they had not for many years done anything without the advice of a certain aged and grave woman, who was always present at their councils. The interpreter said that she was an empress, and that they gave much heed to what she said. This wise queen of Conestoga looked with great favor on the Quakers, the interpreter said, because they "did not come to buy or sell, or get gain;" but came "in love and respect" to them, "and desired their well-doing, both here and hereafter." Two nations at this time were represented in this Conestoga band—the Senecas and the Shawanese.

The next year the governor himself, anxious to preserve their inalienable good-will, and to prevent their being seduced by emissaries from the French, went himself to visit them. On this occasion one of the chiefs made a speech, still preserved in the old records, which contains this passage: "Father, we love quiet; we suffer the mouse to play; when the woods are rustled by the wind, we fear not; when the leaves are disturbed in ambush, we are uneasy; when a cloud obscures your brilliant sun, our eyes feel dim; but when the rays appear, they give great heat to the body and joy to the heart. Treachery darkens the chain of friendship; but truth makes it brighter than ever. This is the peace we desire."

A few years later a Swedish missionary visited them, and preached them a sermon on original sin and the necessity of a mediator. When he had finished, an Indian chief rose and replied to him; both discourses being given through an interpreter. The Swede is said to have been so impressed with the Indian's reasoning that, after returning to Sweden, he wrote out his own sermon and the Indian's reply in the best Latin at his command, and dedicated the documents to the University of Upsal, respectfully requesting them to furnish him with some arguments strong enough to confute the strong reasonings of this savage.

"Our forefathers," said the chief, "were under a strong persuasion (as we are) that those who act well in this life will be rewarded in the next according to the degrees of their virtues; and, on the other hand, that those who behave wickedly here will undergo such punishments hereafter as were proportionate to the crimes they were guilty of. This has been constantly and invariably received and acknowledged for a truth through every successive generation of our ancestors. It could not, then, have taken its rise from fable; for human fiction, however artfully and plausibly contrived, can never gain credit long among people where free inquiry is allowed, which was never denied by our ancestors. * * * Now we desire to propose some questions. Does he believe that our forefathers, men eminent for their piety, constant and warm in their pursuit of virtue, hoping thereby to merit eternal happiness, were all damned? Does he think that we who are zealous imitators in good works, and influenced by the same motives as we are, earnestly endeavoring with the greatest circumspection to tread the path of integrity, are in a state of damnation? If that be his sentiment, it is surely as impious as it is bold and daring. * * * Let us suppose that some heinous crimes were committed by some of our ancestors, like to that we are told of another race of people. In such a case God would certainly punish the criminal, but would never involve us that are innocent in the guilt. Those who think otherwise must make the Almighty a very whimsical, evil-natured being. * * * Once more: are the Christians more virtuous, or, rather, are they not more vicious than we are? If so, how came it to pass that they are the objects of God's beneficence, while we are neglected? Does he daily confer his favors without reason and with so much partiality? In a word, we find the Christians much more depraved in their morals than we are; and we judge from their doctrine by the badness of their lives."

It is plain that this Indian chief's speech was very much Latinized in the good Swede's hands; but if the words even approached being a true presentation of what he said, it is wonderful indeed.

In 1721 His Excellency Sir William Keith, Bart., Governor of the Province of Pennsylvania, went with an escort of eighty horsemen to Conestoga, and spent several days in making a treaty with the representatives of the Five Nations, "the Indians of Conestoga and their friends." He was entertained at "Captain Civility's cabin." When he left them, he desired them to give his "very kind love and the love of all our people to your kings and to all their people." He invited them to visit him in Philadelphia, saying, "We can provide better for you and make you more welcome. People always receive their friends best at their own homes." He then took out a coronation medal of the King, and presented it to the Indian in these words: "That our children when we are dead may not forget these things, but keep this treaty between us in perpetual remembrance, I here deliver to you a picture in gold, bearing the image of my great master, the King of all the English. And when you return home, I charge you to deliver this piece into the hands of the first man or greatest chief of all the Five Nations, whom you call Kannygoodk, to be laid up and kept as a token to our children's children that an entire and lasting friendship is now established forever between the English in this country and the great Five Nations."

At this time the village of Conestoga was described as lying "about seventy miles west of Philadelphia. The land thereabout being exceeding rich, it is now surrounded with divers fine plantations and farms, where they raise quantities of wheat, barley, flax, and hemp, without the help of any dung."

The next year, also, was marked by a council of great significance at Conestoga. In the spring of this year an Indian called Saanteenee had been killed by two white men, brothers, named Cartledge. At this time it was not only politic but necessary for the English to keep on good terms with as many Indians as possible. Therefore, the old record says, "Policy and justice required a rigid inquiry" into this affair, and the infliction of "exemplary punishment."

Accordingly, the Cartledges were arrested and confined in Philadelphia, and the high-sheriff of Chester County went, with two influential men of the province, to Conestoga, to confer with the Indians as to what should be done with them. The Indians were unwilling to decide the matter without advice from the Five Nations, to whom they owed allegiance. A swift runner (Satcheecho) was, therefore, sent northward with the news of the occurrence; and the governor, with two of his council, went to Albany to hear what the Five Nations had to say about it. What an inconceivable spectacle to us to-day: the governments of Pennsylvania and New York so fully recognizing an Indian to be a "person," and his murder a thing to be anxiously and swiftly atoned for if possible!

Only a little more than a hundred and fifty years lie between this murder of Saanteenee in Conestoga and the murder of Big Snake at Fort Reno, Indian Territory, in 1880. Verily, Policy has kept a large assortment of spectacles for Justice to look through in a surprising short space of time.

On the decision of the king and chiefs of the Five Nations hung the fate of the murderers. Doubtless the brothers Cartledge made up their minds to die. The known principles of the Indians in the matter of avenging injuries certainly left them little room for hope. But no! The Five Nations took a different view. They "desired that the Cartledges should not suffer death, and the affair was at length amicably settled," says the old record. "One life," said the Indian king, "on this occasion, is enough to be lost. There should not two die."

This was in 1722. In 1763 there were only twenty of these Conestoga Indians left—seven men, five women, and eight children. They were still living in their village on the Shawanee Creek, their lands being assured to them by manorial gift; but they were miserably poor—earned by making brooms, baskets, and wooden bowls a part of their living, and begged the rest. They were wholly peaceable and unoffending, friendly to their white neighbors, and pitifully clinging and affectionate, naming their children after whites who were kind to them, and striving in every way to show their gratitude and good-will.

Upon this little community a band of white men, said by some of the old records to be "Presbyterians," from Paxton, made an attack at daybreak on the 14th of December. They found only six of the Indians at home—three men, two women, and a boy. The rest were away, either at work for the white farmers or selling their little wares. "These poor defenceless creatures were immediately fired upon, stabbed, and hatcheted to death; the good Shebaes, among the rest, cut to pieces in his bed. All of them were scalped and otherwise horribly mangled, then their huts were set on fire, and most of them burnt down."

"Shebaes was a very old man, having assisted at the second treaty held with Mr. Penn, in 1701, and ever since continued a faithful friend to the English. He is said to have been an exceeding good man, considering his education; being naturally of a most kind, benevolent temper."

From a manuscript journal kept at this time, and belonging to the great-granddaughter of Robert Barber, the first settler in Lancaster County, are gathered the few details known of this massacre. "Some of the murderers went directly from the scene of their crime to Mr. Barber's house. They were strangers to him; but, with the hospitality of those days, he made a fire for them and set refreshments before them.

" While they warmed themselves they inquired why the Indians were suffered to live peaceably here. Mr. Barber said they were entirely inoffensive, living on their own lands and injuring no one. They asked what would be the consequence if they were all destroyed. Mr. Barber said he thought they would be as liable to punishment as if they had destroyed so many white men. They said *they* were of a different opinion, and in a few minutes went out. In the mean time two sons of Mr. Barber's, about ten or twelve years old, went out to look at the strangers' horses, which were hitched at a little distance from the house.

"After the men went the boys came in, and said that they had tomahawks tied to their saddles which were all bloody, and that they had Christy's gun. Christy was a little Indian boy about their own age. They were much attached to him, as he was their playmate, and made bows and arrows for them."

While the family were talking over this, and wondering what it could mean, a messenger came running breathless to inform them of what had happened. Mr. Barber went at once to the spot, and there he found the murdered Indians lying in the smouldering ruins of their homes, " like half-consumed logs." He, " with some trouble, procured their bodies, to administer to them the rights of sepulture."

"It was said that at the beginning of the slaughter an Indian mother placed her little child under a barrel, charging it to make no noise, and that a shot was fired through the barrel which broke the child's arm, and still it kept silent."

The magistrates of Lancaster, shocked, as well they might be, at this frightful barbarity, sent messengers out immediately, and took the remaining Indians, wherever they were found, brought them into the town for protection, and lodged them in the newly-erected workhouse or jail, which was the strongest building in the place. The Governor of Pennsylvania issued a proclamation, ordering all judges, sheriffs, and "all His Majesty's liege subjects in the province," to make every effort to apprehend the authors and perpetrators of this crime, also their abettors and accomplices. But the "Paxton Boys" held magistrates and governor alike in derision. Two weeks later they assembled again, fifty strong, rode to Lancaster, dismounted, broke open the doors of the jail, and killed every Indian there.

"When the poor wretches saw they had no protection nigh, nor could possibly escape, and being without the least weapon of defence, they divided their little families, the children clinging to their parents. They fell on their faces, protested their innocence, declared their love to the English, and that in their whole lives they had never done them injury. And in this posture they all received the hatchet. Men, women, and children were every one inhumanly murdered in cold blood. * * * The barbarous men who committed the atrocious act, in defiance of government, of all laws, human and divine, and to the eternal disgrace of their country and color, then mounted their horses, huzzaed in triumph, as if they had gained a victory, and rode off unmolested. * * * The bodies of the murdered were then brought out and exposed in the street till a hole could be made in the earth to receive and cover them. But the wickedness cannot be covered, and the guilt will lie on the whole land till justice is done on the murderers. The blood of the innocent will cry to Heaven for vengeance."

These last extracts are from a pamphlet printed in Philadelphia at the time of the massacre; printed anonymously, because "so much had fear seized the minds of the people" that neither the writer nor the printer dared to give "name or place of abode."

There are also private letters still preserved which give accounts of the affair. A part of one from William Henry, of Lancaster, to a friend in Philadelphia, is given in "Rupp's His-

tory of Lancaster County." He says, "A regiment of High-
landers were at that time quartered at the barracks in the
town, and yet these murderers were permitted to break open
the doors of the city jail and commit the horrid deed. The
first notice I had of the affair was that, while at my father's
store near the court-house, I saw a number of people running
down-street toward the jail, which enticed me and other lads
to follow them. At about six or eight yards from the jail we
met from twenty-five to thirty men, well mounted on horses,
and with rifles, tomahawks, and scalping-knives, equipped for
murder. I ran into the prison-yard, and there, oh, what a horrid sight presented itself to my view! Near the back door of
the prison lay an old Indian and his squaw, particularly well
known and esteemed by the people of the town on account of
his placid and friendly conduct. His name was Will Soc.
Around him and his squaw lay two children, about the age of
three years, whose heads were split with the tomahawk and
their scalps taken off. Toward the middle of the jail-yard,
along the west side of the wall, lay a stout Indian, whom I particularly noticed to have been shot in his breast. His legs
were chopped with the tomahawk, his hands cut off, and finally
a rifle-ball discharged in his mouth, so that his head was blown
to atoms, and the brains were splashed against and yet hanging
to the wall for three or four feet around. This man's hands
and feet had been chopped off with a tomahawk. In this
manner lay the whole of them—men, women, and children—
spread about the prison-yard, shot, scalped, hacked, and cut to
pieces."

After this the Governor of Pennsylvania issued a second
proclamation, still more stringent than the first, and offering a
reward of $600 for the apprehension of any three of the
ringleaders.

But the "Paxton Boys" were now like wild beasts that had
tasted blood. They threatened to attack the Quakers and all

persons who sympathized with or protected Indians. They openly mocked and derided the governor and his proclamations, and set off at once for Philadelphia, announcing their intention of killing all the Moravian Indians who had been placed under the protection of the military there.

Their march through the country was like that of a band of maniacs. In a private letter written by David Rittenhouse at this time, he says, "About fifty of these scoundrels marched by my workshop. I have seen hundreds of Indians travelling the country, and can with truth affirm that the behavior of these fellows was ten times more savage and brutal than theirs. Frightening women by running the muzzles of guns through windows, hallooing and swearing; attacking men without the least provocation, dragging them by the hair to the ground, and pretending to scalp them; shooting dogs and fowls: these are some of their exploits."

It is almost past belief that at this time many people justified these acts. An Episcopalian clergyman in Lancaster wrote vindicating them, "bringing Scripture to prove that it was right to destroy the heathen;" and the "Presbyterians think they have a better justification—nothing less than the Word of God," says one of the writers on the massacre.

"With the Scriptures in their hands and mouths, they can set at naught that express command, 'Thou shalt do no murder,' and justify their wickedness by the command given to Joshua to destroy the heathen. Horrid perversion of Scripture and religion, to father the worst of crimes on the God of Love and Peace!" It is a trite saying that history repeats itself; but it is impossible to read now these accounts of the massacres of defenceless and peaceable Indians in the middle of the eighteenth century, without the reflection that the record of the nineteenth is blackened by the same stains. What Pennsylvania pioneers did in 1763 to helpless and peaceable Indians of Conestoga, Colorado pioneers did in 1864 to helpless and peaceable Cheyennes at Sand Creek, and have threatened to do again to helpless and peaceable Utes in 1880. The word "extermination" is as ready on the frontiersman's tongue to-day as it was a hundred years ago; and the threat is more portentous now, seeing that we are, by a whole century of prosperity, stronger and more numerous, and the Indians are, by a whole century of suffering and oppression, fewer and weaker. But our crime is baser and our infamy deeper in the same proportion.

Close upon this Conestoga massacre followed a "removal" of friendly Indians — the earliest on record, and one whose cruelty and cost to the suffering Indians well entitle it to a place in a narrative of massacres.

Everywhere in the provinces fanatics began to renew the old cry that the Indians were the Canaanites whom God had commanded Joshua to destroy; and that these wars were a token of God's displeasure with the Europeans for permitting the "heathen" to live. Soon it became dangerous for a Moravian Indian to be seen anywhere. In vain did he carry one of the Pennsylvania governor's passports in his pocket. He was liable to be shot at sight, with no time to pull his passport out. Even in the villages there was no safety. The devoted congregations watched and listened night and day, not knowing at what hour they might hear the fatal warwhoop of hostile members of their own race, coming to slay them; or the sudden shots of white settlers, coming to avenge on them outrages committed by savages hundreds of miles away.

With every report that arrived of Indian massacres at the North, the fury of the white people all over the country rose to greater height, including even Christian Indians in its unreasoning hatred. But, in the pious language of a narrative written by one of the Moravian missionaries, "God inclined the hearts of the chief magistrates to protect them. November 6th an express arrived from Philadelphia, bringing an order that all the baptized Indians from Nain and Wechquetank should be brought to Philadelphia, and be protected in that city, having first delivered up their arms."

Two days later both these congregations set out on their sad journey, weeping as they left their homes. They joined forces at Bethlehem, on the banks of the Lecha, and "entered upon their pilgrimage in the name of the Lord, the congregation of Bethlehem standing spectators, and, as they passed, commending them to the grace and protection of God, with supplication and tears."

Four of the Moravian missionaries were with them, and some of the brethren from Bethlehem accompanied them all the way, "the sheriff, Mr. Jennings, caring for them as a father."

The aged, the sick, and the little children were carried in wagons. All the others, women and men, went on foot. The November rains had made the roads very heavy. As the weary and heart-broken people toiled slowly along through the mud, they were saluted with curses and abuse on all sides. As they passed through the streets of Germantown a mob gathered and followed them, taunting them with violent threats of burning, hanging, and other tortures. It was said that a party had been organized to make a serious attack on them, but was deterred by the darkness and the storm. Four days were consumed in this tedious march, and on the 11th of November they reached Philadelphia. Here, spite of the governor's positive order, the officers in command at the barracks refused to allow them to enter. From ten in the forenoon till three in the afternoon there the helpless creatures stood before the shut gate — messengers going back and forth between the defiant garrison and the bewildered and impotent governor; the mob, thickening and growing more and more riotous hour by hour, pressing the Indians on every side, jeering them, reviling them, charging them with all manner of outrages, and threatening to kill them on the spot. The missionaries, brave-ly standing beside their flock, in vain tried to stem or turn the torrent of insult and abuse. All that they accomplished was to draw down the same insult and abuse on their own heads.

Nothing but the Indians' marvellous patience and silence saved them from being murdered by this exasperated mob. To the worst insults they made no reply, no attempt at retaliation or defence. They afterward said that they had comforted themselves "by considering what insult and mockery our Saviour had suffered on their account."

At last, after five hours of this, the governor, unable to compel the garrison to open the barracks, sent an order that the Indians should be taken to Province Island, an island in the Delaware River joined to the main-land by a dam. Six miles more, every mile in risk of their lives, the poor creatures walked. As they passed again through the city, thousands followed them, the old record says, and "with such tumultuous clamor that they might truly be considered as sheep among wolves."

Long after dark they reached the island, and were lodged in some unused buildings, large and comfortless. There they kept their vesper service, and took heart from the fact that the verse for the day was that verse of the beautiful thirty-second psalm which has comforted so many perplexed souls: "I will teach thee in the way thou shalt go."

Here they settled themselves as best they could. The missionaries had their usual meetings with them, and humane people from Philadelphia, "especially some of the people called Quakers," sent them provisions and fuel, and tried in various ways to "render the inconvenience of their situation less grievous."

Before they had been here a month some of the villages they had left were burnt, and the riotous Paxton mob, which had murdered all the peaceful Conestoga Indians, announced its intention of marching on Province Island and killing every Indian there. The Governor of Pennsylvania launched proclamation after proclamation, forbidding any one, under severest penalties, to molest the Indians under its protection, and offering a reward of two hundred pounds for the apprehension of the ringleaders of the insurgents. But public sentiment was inflamed to such a degree that the Government was practically powerless. The known ringleaders and their sympathizers paraded contemptuously in front of the governor's house, mocking him derisively, and not even two hundred pounds would tempt any man to attack them. In many parts of Lancaster County parties were organized with the avowed intention of marching on Philadelphia and slaughtering all the Indians under the protection of the Government. Late on the 29th of December rumors reached Philadelphia that a large party of these rioters were on the road; and the governor, at daybreak the next day, sent large boats to Province Island, with orders to the missionaries to put their people on board as quickly as possible, row to Leek Island, and await further orders. In confusion and terror the congregations obeyed, and fled to Leek Island. Later in the day came a second letter from the governor, telling them that the alarm had proved a false one. They might return to Province Island, where he would send them a guard; and that they would better keep the boats, to be ready in case of a similar emergency.

"They immediately returned with joy to their former habitation," says the old record, "comforted by the text for the day—'The Lord is my strength and my shield; my heart trusted in him' (Ps. xxviii., 7)—and closed this remarkable year with prayer and thanksgiving for all the proofs of the help of God in so many heavy trials."

Four days later the missionaries received a second order for instant departure. The reports of the murderous intentions of the rioters being confirmed, and the governor seeing only too clearly his own powerlessness to contend with them, he had resolved to send the Indians northward, and put them under the protection of the English army, and especially of Sir William Johnson, agent for the Crown among the Northern Indians. No time was to be lost in carrying out this plan, for at any moment the mob might attack Province Island. Accordingly, at midnight of January 4th, the fugitives set out once more, passed through Philadelphia, undiscovered, to the meeting-house of the Moravian Brethren, where a breakfast had been provided for them. Here they were met by the commissary, Mr. Fox, who had been detailed by the governor to take charge of their journey. Mr. Fox, heart-stricken at their suffering appearance, immediately sent out and bought blankets to be distributed among them, as some protection against the cold. Wagons were brought for the aged, sick, blind, little children, and the heavy baggage; and again the pitiful procession took up its march. Again an angry mob gathered fast on its steps, cursing and reviling in a terrible manner, only restrained by fear from laying violent hands on them. Except for the protection of a military escort they would scarcely have escaped murderous assault.

At Amboy two sloops lay ready to transport them to New York; but just as they reached this place, and were preparing to go on shore, a messenger arrived from the Governor of New York with angry orders that not an Indian should set foot in that territory. Even the ferry-men were forbidden, under heavy penalties, to ferry one across the river.

The commissioner in charge of them, in great perplexity, sent to the Governor of Pennsylvania for further orders, placing the Indians, meantime, in the Amboy barracks. Here they held their daily meetings, singing and praying with great unction, until finally many of their enemies were won to a hearty respect and sympathy for them; even soldiers being heard to say, "Would to God all the white people were as good Christians as these Indians."

The Pennsylvania governor had nothing left him to do but to order the Indians back again, and, accordingly, says the record, "The Indian congregation set out with cheerfulness on their return, in full confidence that the Lord in his good providence, for wise purposes best known to himself, had ordained their travelling thus to and fro. This belief supported them under all the difficulties they met with in their journeys made in the severest part of winter."

They made the return journey under a large military escort, one party in advance and one bringing up the rear. This escort was composed of soldiers, who, having just come from Niagara, where they had been engaged in many fights with the North-western savages, were at first disposed to treat these defenceless Indians with brutal cruelty; but they were soon disarmed by the Indians' gentle patience, and became cordial and friendly.

The return journey was a hard one. The aged and infirm people had become much weakened by their repeated hardships, and the little children suffered pitiably. In crossing some of the frozen rivers the feeble ones were obliged to crawl on their hands and feet on the ice.

On the 24th of January they reached Philadelphia, and were at once taken to the barracks, where almost immediately mobs began again to molest and threaten them. The governor, thoroughly in earnest now, and determined to sustain his own honor and that of the province, had eight heavy pieces of cannon mounted and a rampart thrown up in front of the barracks. The citizens were called to arms, and so great was the excitement that it is said even Quakers took guns and hurried to the barracks to defend the Indians; and the governor himself went at midnight to visit them, and reassure them by promises of protection.

On February 4th news was received that the rioters in large force were approaching the city. Hearing of the preparations made to receive them, they did not venture to enter. On the night of the 5th, however, they drew near again. The whole city was roused, church-bells rung, bonfires lighted, cannon fired, the inhabitants waked from their sleep and ordered to the town-house, where arms were given to all. Four more cannon were mounted at the barracks, and all that day was spent in hourly expectation of the rebels. But their brave boasts were not followed up by action. Seeing that the city was in arms against them, they halted. The governor then sent a delegation of citizens to ask them what they wanted.

They asserted, insolently, that there were among the Indians some who had committed murders, and that they must be given up. Some of the ringleaders were then taken into the barracks and asked to point out the murderers. Covered with confusion, they were obliged to admit they could not accuse one Indian there. They then charged the Quakers with having taken away six and concealed them. This also was disproved, and finally the excitement subsided.

All through the spring and summer the Indians remained prisoners in the barracks. Their situation became almost insupportable from confinement, unwholesome diet, and the mental depression inevitable in their state. To add to their misery small-pox broke out among them, and fifty-six died in the course of the summer from this loathsome disease.

"We cannot describe," said the missionaries, "the joy and fervent desire which most of them showed in the prospect of seeing their Saviour face to face. We saw with amazement the power of the blood of Jesus in the hearts of poor sinners." This was, no doubt, true; but there might well have entered into the poor, dying creatures' thoughts an ecstasy at the mere prospect of freedom, after a year of such imprisonment and suffering.

At last, on December 4th, the news of peace reached Philadelphia. On the 6th a proclamation was published in all the newspapers that war was ended and hostilities must cease. The joy with which the prisoned Indians received this news can hardly be conceived. It "exceeded all descriptions," says the record, and "was manifested in thanksgivings and praises to the Lord."

It was still unsafe, however, for them to return to their old homes, which were thickly surrounded by white settlers, who were no less hostile now at heart than they had been before the proclamation of peace. It was decided, therefore, that they should make a new settlement in the Indian country on the Susquehanna River. After a touching farewell to their old friends of the Bethlehem congregation, and a grateful leave-taking of the governor, who had protected and supported them for sixteen months, they set out on the 3d of April for their new home in the wilderness. For the third time their aged, sick, and little children were placed in overloaded wagons, for a long and difficult journey—a far harder one than any they had yet taken. The inhospitalities of the lonely wilderness were worse than the curses and revilings of riotous mobs. They were overtaken by severe snow-storms. They camped in icy swamps, shivering all night around smouldering fires of wet wood. To avoid still hostile whites they had to take great circuits through unbroken forests, where each foot of their path had to be cut tree by tree. The men waded streams and made rafts for the women and children. Sometimes, when the streams were deep, they had to go into camp, and wait till canoes could be built. They carried heavy loads of goods for which there was no room in the wagons. Going over high, steep hills, they often had to divide their loads into small parcels, thus doubling and trebling the road. Their provisions gave out. They ate the bitter wild potatoes. When the children cried with hunger, they peeled chestnut-trees, and gave them the sweet-juiced inner bark to suck. Often they had no water except that from shallow, muddy puddles. Once they were environed by blazing woods, whose fires burnt fiercely for hours around their encampment. Several of the party died, and were buried by the way.

"But all these trials were forgotten in their daily meetings, in which the presence of the Lord was most sensibly and comfortably felt. These were always held in the evening, around a large fire, in the open air."

They celebrated a "joyful commemoration" of Easter, and spent the Passion-week "in blessed contemplation" of the sufferings of Jesus, whose "presence supported them under all afflictions, insomuch that they never lost their cheerfulness and resignation" during the five long weeks of this terrible journey.

On the 9th of May they arrived at Machwihilusing, and "forgot all their pain and trouble for joy that they had reached the place of their future abode. * * * With offers of praise and thanksgiving, they devoted themselves anew to Him who had given them rest for the soles of their feet."

"With renewed courage" they selected their home on the banks of the Susquehanna, and proceeded to build houses. They gave to the settlement the name of Friedenshutten—a name full of significance, as coming from the hearts of these persecuted wanderers: Friedenshutten—"Tents of Peace."

If all this persecution had fallen upon these Indians because they were Christians, the record, piteous as it is, would be only one out of thousands of records of the sufferings of Christian martyrs, and would stir our sympathies less than many another. But this was not the case. It was simply because they were Indians that the people demanded their lives, and would have taken them, again and again, except that all the power of the Government was enlisted for their protection. The fact of their being Christians did not enter in, one way or the other, any more than did the fact that they were peaceable. They were Indians, and the frontiersmen of Pennsylvania intended either to drive all Indians out of their State or kill them, just as the frontiersmen of Nebraska and of Colorado now intend to do if they can. We shall see whether the United States Government is as strong to-day as the Government of the Province of Pennsylvania was in 1763; or whether it will try first (and fail), as John Penn did, to push the helpless, hunted creatures off somewhere into a temporary makeshift of shelter, for a temporary deferring of the trouble of protecting them.

Sixteen years after the Conestoga massacre came that of Gnadenhütten, the blackest crime on the long list; a massacre whose equal for treachery and cruelty cannot be pointed out in the record of massacres of whites by Indians.

II.—*The Gnadenhütten Massacre.*

In the year 1779 the congregations of Moravian Indians living at Gnadenhütten, Salem, and Schonbrun, on the Muskingum River, were compelled by hostile Indians to forsake their villages and go northward to the Sandusky River. This movement was instigated by the English, who had become suspicious that the influence of the Moravian missionaries was thrown on the side of the colonies, and that their villages were safe centres of information and supplies. These Indians having taken no part whatever in the war, there was no pretext for open interference with them; but the English agents found it no difficult matter to stir up the hostile tribes to carry out their designs. And when the harassed congregations finally consented to move, the savages who escorted them were commanded by English officers.

"The savages drove them forward like cattle," says an old narrative; "the white brethren and sisters in the midst, surrounded by the believing Indians." "One morning, when the latter could not set out as expeditiously as the savages thought proper, they attacked the white brethren, and forced them to set out alone, whipping their horses forward till they grew wild, and not even allowing mothers time to suckle their children. The road was exceeding bad, leading through a continuance of swamps. Sister Zeisberger fell twice from her horse, and once, hanging in the stirrup, was dragged for some time; but assistance was soon at hand, and the Lord preserved her from harm. Some of the believing Indians followed them as fast as possible, but with all their exertions did not overtake them till night."

For one month these unfortunate people journeyed through the wilds in this way. When they reached the Sandusky Creek the savages left them to take care of themselves as best they might. They were over a hundred miles from their homes, "in a wilderness where there was neither game nor provisions." Here they built huts of logs and bark. They had neither beds nor blankets. In fact, the only things which the savages had left them were their utensils for making maple sugar. It was the middle of October when they reached Sandusky. Already it was cold, and the winter was drawing near. In November Governor De Peyster, the English commander at Fort Detroit, summoned the missionaries to appear before him and refute the accusations brought against their congregations of having aided and abetted the colonies.

"The missionaries answered that they doubted not in the least but that very evil reports must have reached his ears, as the treatment they had met with had sufficiently proved that they were considered as guilty persons, but that these reports were false. * * * That Congress, indeed, knew that they were employed as missionaries to the Indians, and did not disturb them in their labors; but had never in anything given them directions how to proceed."

The governor, convinced of the innocence and single-heartedness of these noble men, publicly declared that " he felt great satisfaction in their endeavors to civilize and Christianize the Indians, and would permit them to return to their congregations." He then gave them passports for their journey back to Sandusky, and appended a permission that they should perform the functions of their office among the Christian Indians without molestation.

This left them at rest so far as apprehensions of attack from hostile Indians were concerned; but there still remained the terrible apprehension of death by starvation and cold. Deep snows lay on the ground. Their hastily-built huts were so small that it was impossible to make large fires in them. Their floors being only the bare earth, whenever a thaw came the water forced itself up and then froze again. Cattle died for lack of food, and their carcasses were greedily devoured; nursing children died for want of nourishment from their starving mothers' breasts; the daily allowance of corn to each adult was one pint, and even this pittance it was found would not last till spring.

Nevertheless, "they celebrated the Christmas holidays with cheerfulness and blessing, and concluded this remarkable year with thanks and praise to Him who is ever the Saviour of his people. But, having neither bread nor wine, they could not keep the communion."

Meantime the corn still stood ungathered in their old fields on the Muskingum River. Weather-beaten, frozen, as it was, it would be still a priceless store to these starving people. The project of going back there after it began to be discussed. It was one hundred and twenty-five miles' journey; but food in abundance lay at the journey's end. Finally it was decided that the attempt should be made. Their first plan was to hide their families in the woods at some distance from the settlements lest there might be some danger from hostile whites. On their way, however, they were met by some of their brethren from Schonbrun, who advised them to go back openly into their deserted towns, assuring them that the Americans were friendly to them now. They accordingly did

so, and remained for several weeks at Salem and Gnadenhütten, working day and night gathering and husking the weather-beaten corn, and burying it in holes in the ground in the
woods for future supply.   On the very day that they were to
have set off with their packs of corn, to return to their starving friends and relatives at Sandusky, a party of between one
and two hundred whites made their appearance at Gnadenhütten.   Seeing the Indians scattered all through the cornfields, they rode up to them, expressing pleasure at seeing
them, and saying that they would take them into Pennsylvania, to a place where they would be out of all reach of persecution from the hostile savages or the English.   They represented themselves as "friends and brothers, who had purpose-
ly come out to relieve them from the distress brought on them
on account of their being friends to the American people.
* * * The Christian Indians, not in the least doubting their
sincerity, walked up to them and thanked them for being so
kind ; while the whites again gave assurances that they would
meet with good treatment from them.   They then advised
them to discontinue their work and cross over to the town, in
order to make necessary arrangements for the journey, as they
intended to take them out of the reach of their enemies, and
where they would be supplied abundantly with all they stood
in need of."

They proposed to take them to Pittsburg, where they
would be out of the way of any assault made by the English
or the savages.   This the Indians heard, one of their missionaries writes, "with resignation, concluding that God would
perhaps choose this method to put an end to their sufferings.
Prepossessed with this idea, they cheerfully delivered their
guns, hatchets, and other weapons to the murderers, who promised to take good care of them, and in Pittsburg to return
every article to its rightful owner.   Our Indians even showed
them all those things which they had secreted in the woods,

assisted in packing them up, and emptied all their beehives for these pretended friends."

In the mean time one of the assistants, John Martin by name, went to Salem, ten miles distant, and carried the good news that a party of whites had come from the settlements to carry them to a place of safety and give them protection. " The Salem Indians," says the same narrative, " did not hesitate to accept of this proposal, believing unanimously that God had sent the Americans to release them from their disagreeable situation at Sandusky, and imagining that when arrived at Pittsburg they might soon find a safe place to build a settlement, and easily procure advice and assistance from Bethlehem."

Some of the whites expressed a desire to see the village of Salem, were conducted thither, and received with much friendship by the Indians. On the way they entered into spiritual conversation with their unsuspecting companions, feigning great piety and discoursing on many religious and scriptural subjects. They offered also to assist the Salem Indians in moving their effects.

In the mean time the defenceless Indians at Gnadenhütten were suddenly attacked, driven together, bound with ropes, and confined. As soon as the Salem Indians arrived, they met with the same fate.

The murderers then held a council to decide what should be done with them. By a majority of votes it was decided to kill them all the next day. To the credit of humanity be it recorded, that there were in this band a few who remonstrated, declared that these Indians were innocent and harmless, and should be set at liberty, or, at least, given up to the Government as prisoners. Their remonstrances were unavailing, and, finding that they could not prevail on these monsters to spare the Indians' lives, " they wrung their hands, calling God to witness that they were innocent of the blood of these Christian Indians. They then withdrew to some distance from the scene of slaughter."

The majority were unmoved, and only disagreed as to the method of putting their victims to death. Some were for burning them alive; others for tomahawking and scalping them. The latter method was determined on, and a message was sent to the Indians that, "as they were Christian Indians, they might prepare themselves in a Christian manner, for they must all die to-morrow."

The rest of the narrative is best told in the words of the Moravian missionaries: "It may be easily conceived how great their terror was at hearing a sentence so unexpected. However, they soon recollected themselves, and patiently suffered the murderers to lead them into two houses, in one of which the brethren were confined and in the other the sisters and children. * * * Finding that all entreaties to save their lives were to no purpose, and that some, more blood-thirsty than others, were anxious to begin upon them, they united in begging a short delay, that they might prepare themselves for death, which request was granted them. Then asking pardon for whatever offence they had given, or grief they had occasioned to each other, they knelt down, offering fervent prayers to God their Saviour and kissing one another. Under a flood of tears, fully resigned to his will, they sung praises unto him, in the joyful hope that they would soon be relieved from all pains and join their Redeemer in everlasting bliss. * * * The murderers, impatient to make a beginning, came again to them while they were singing, and, inquiring whether they were now ready for dying, they were answered in the affirmative, adding that they had commended their immortal souls to God, who had given them the assurance in their hearts that he would receive their souls. One of the party, now taking up a cooper's mallet which lay in the house, saying, 'How exactly this will answer for the purpose,' began with Abraham, and

continued knocking down one after another until he counted
fourteen that he had killed with his own hands. He now
handed the instrument to one of his fellow-murderers, saying:
'My arm fails me. Go on in the same way. I think I have
done pretty well.' In another house, where mostly women
and children were confined, Judith, a remarkably pious aged
widow, was the first victim. After they had finished the horrid deed they retreated to a small distance from the slaughter-
houses; but, after awhile, returning again to view the dead
bodies, and finding one of them (Abel), although scalped and
mangled, attempting to raise himself from the floor, they so
renewed their blows upon him that he never rose again. * * *
Thus ninety-six persons magnified the name of the Lord by
patiently meeting a cruel death. Sixty-two were grown persons and thirty-four children. Many of them were born of
Christian parents in the society, and were among those who in
the year 1763 were taken under the protection of the Pennsylvania Government at the time of the riots of the Paxton
Boys. * * * Two boys, about fourteen years of age, almost
miraculously escaped from this massacre. One of them was
scalped and thrown down for dead. Recovering himself, he
looked around; but, with great presence of mind, lay down
again quickly, feigning death. In a few moments he saw the
murderers return, and again bury their hatchets in the head of
Abel, who was attempting to rise, though scalped and terribly
mangled. As soon as it was dark, Thomas crept over the dead
bodies and escaped to the woods, where he hid himself till night.
The other lad, who was confined in the house with the women,
contrived unnoticed to slip through a trap-door into the cellar,
where he lay concealed through the day, the blood all the
while running down through the floor in streams. At dark he
escaped through a small window and crept to the woods, where
he encountered Thomas, and the two made their way together, after incredible hardships, to Sandusky. To describe the

grief and terror of the Indian congregation on hearing that so
large a number of its members was so cruelly massacred is impossible.   Parents wept and mourned for the loss of their children, husbands for their wives, and wives for their husbands,
children for their parents, sisters for brothers, and brothers for
sisters.   But they murmured not, nor did they call for vengeance on the murderers, but prayed for them.   And their
greatest consolation was a full assurance that all their beloved
relatives were now at home in the presence of the Lord, and in
full possession of everlasting happiness."

An account of this massacre was given in the *Pennsylvania
Gazette* of April 17th, 1782.   It runs as follows:

"The people being greatly alarmed, and having received intelligence that the Indian towns on the Muskingum had not
moved, as reported, a number of men, properly provided, collected and rendezvoused on the Ohio, opposite the Mingo Bottom, with a desire to surprise the above towns.

"One hundred men swam the river, and proceeded to the
towns on the Muskingum, where the Indians had collected a
large quantity of provisions to supply their war-parties.   They
arrived at the town in the night, undiscovered, attacked the Indians in their cabins, and so completely surprised them that
they killed and scalped upward of ninety—but a few making
their escape—about forty of whom were warriors, the rest old
women and children.   About eighty horses fell into their hands,
which they loaded with the plunder, the greatest part furs and
skins, and returned to the Ohio without the loss of a man."

III.—*Massacres of Apaches.*

In less than one hundred years from this Gnadenhütten massacre an officer of the United States Army, stationed at Camp
Grant, in Arizona Territory, writes to his commanding officer the
following letter:

"Camp Grant, Arizona Territory, May 17th, 1871.

"DEAR COLONEL,—Thanks for your kind letter of last week. If I could see you and have a long talk, and answer all your questions, I could come nearer giving you a clear idea of the history of the Indians at this post than by any written account. Having had them constantly under my observation for nearly three months, and the care of them constantly on my mind, certain things have become so much a matter of certainty to me that I am liable to forget the amount of evidence necessary to convince even the most unprejudiced mind that has not been brought in contact with them. I will, however, try and give you a connected account, and if it proves not sufficiently full in detail, you may be sure all its positive statements will be sustained by the testimony of all competent judges who have been at this post and cognizant of the facts.

"Sometime in February a party of five old women came in under a flag of truce, with a letter from Colonel Greene, saying they were in search of a boy, the son of one of the number taken prisoner near Salt River some months before. This boy had been well cared for, and had become attached to his new mode of life, and did not wish to return. The party were kindly treated, rationed while here, and after two days went away, asking permission to return. They came in about eight days, I think, with a still larger number, with some articles for sale, to purchase manta, as they were nearly naked. Before going away they said a young chief would like to come in with a party and have a talk. This I encouraged, and in a few days he came with about twenty-five of his band. He stated in brief that he was chief of a band of about one hundred and fifty of what were originally the Aravapa Apaches; that he wanted peace; that he and his people had no home, and could make none, as they were at all times apprehensive of the approach of the cavalry. I told him he should go to the White Mountains. He said, 'That is not our country, neither are they our people. We are at peace with them, but never have mixed with them. Our fathers and their fathers before them have lived in these mountains, and have raised corn in this valley. We are taught to make mescal, our principal article of food, and in summer and winter here we have a never-failing supply. At the White Mountains there is none, and without it now we get sick. Some of our people have been in at Goodwin, and for a short time at the White Mountains; but they are not contented, and they all say, " Let us go to the Aravapa and make a final peace, and never break it." '

" I told him I had no authority to make any treaty with him, or to promise him that he would be allowed a permanent home here, but that he could bring in his band, and I would feed them, and report his wishes to the Department commander. In the mean time runners had been in from two other small bands, asking the same privileges and giving the same reasons. I made the same reply to all, and by about the 11th of March I had over three hundred here. I wrote a detailed account of the whole matter, and sent it by express to Department Head-quarters, asking for instructions, having only the general policy of the Government in such cases for my guidance. After waiting more than six weeks my letter was returned to me without comment, except calling my attention to the fact that it was not briefed properly. At first I put them in camp, about half a mile from the post, and counted them, and issued their rations every second day. The number steadily increased until it reached the number of five hundred and ten.

" Knowing, as I did, that the responsibility of the whole movement rested with me, and that, in case of any loss to the Government coming of it, I should be the sufferer, I kept them continually under my observation till I came not only to know the faces of the men, but of the women and children. They were nearly naked, and needed everything in the way of clothing. I stopped the Indians from bringing hay, that I might buy of these. I arranged a system of tickets with which to pay them and encourage them; and to be sure that they were properly treated, I personally attended to the weighing. I also made inquiries as to the kind of goods sold them, and prices. This proved a perfect success; not only the women and children engaged in the work, but the men. The amount furnished by them in about two months was nearly 300,000 pounds.

"During this time many small parties had been out with passes for a certain number of days to burn mescal. These parties were always mostly women, and I made myself sure by noting the size of the party, and from the amount of mescal brought in, that no treachery was intended. From the first I was determined to know not only all they did, but their hopes and intentions. For this purpose I spent hours each day with them in explaining to them the relations they should sustain to the Government, and their prospects for the future in case of either obedience or disobedience. I got from them in return much of their habits of thought and rules of action. I made it a point to tell them all they wished to know, and in the plainest and most positive manner. They were readily obedient, and remarkably quick of comprehension. They were happy and contented, and took every opportunity to show it. They had sent out runners to two other bands which were connected with them by intermarriages, and had received promises from them that they would come in and join them. I am confident, from all I have been able to learn, that but for this unlooked-for butchery, by this time we would have had one thousand persons, and at least two hundred and fifty able-bodied men. As their number increased and the weather grew warmer, they asked and obtained permission to move farther up the Aravapa to higher ground and plenty of water, and opposite to the ground they were proposing to plant. They were rationed every third day. Captain Stanwood arrived about the first of April, and took command of the post. He had received, while *en route*, verbal instructions from General Stoneman to recognize and feed any Indians he might find at the post as prisoners of war. After he had carefully inspected all things pertaining to their conduct and treatment, he concluded to make no changes, but had become so well satisfied of the integrity of their intentions that he left on the 24th with his whole troop for a long scout in the lower part of the Territory. The ranchmen in this vicinity were friendly and kind to them, and felt perfectly secure, and had agreed with me to employ them at a fair rate of pay to harvest their barley. The Indians seemed to have lost their characteristic anxiety to purchase ammunition, and had, in many instances, sold their best bows and arrows. I made frequent visits to their camp, and if any were absent from count, made it my business to know why.

"Such was the condition of things up to the morning of the 30th of April. They had so won on me that, from my first idea of treating them justly and honestly, as an officer of the army, I had come to feel a strong personal interest in helping to show them the way to a higher civilization. I had come to feel respect for men who, ignorant and naked, were still ashamed to lie or steal; and for women who would work cheerfully like slaves to clothe themselves and children, but, untaught, held their virtue above price. Aware of the lies industriously circulated by the puerile press of the country, I was content to know I had positive proof they were so.

"I had ceased to have any fears of their leaving here, and only dreaded for them that they might be at any time ordered to do so. They frequently expressed anxiety to hear from the general, that they might have confidence to build for themselves better houses; but would always say, 'You know what we want, and if you can't see him you can write, and do for us what you can.' It is possible that, during this time, individuals from here had visited other bands; but that any number had ever been out to assist in any marauding expedition I know is false. On the morning of April 30th I was at breakfast at 7.30 o'clock, when a despatch was brought to me by a sergeant of Company P, 21st Infantry, from Captain Penn, commanding Camp Lowell, informing me that a large party had left Tucson on the 28th with the avowed purpose of killing all the Indians at this post. I immediately sent the two interpreters, mounted, to the Indian camp, with orders to tell the chiefs the exact state of things, and for them to bring their entire party inside the post. As I had no cavalry, and but about fifty infantry (all recruits), and no other officer, I could not leave the post to go to their defence. My messengers returned in about an hour with intelligence that they could find no living Indians.

"Their camp was burning, and the ground strewed with their dead and mutilated women and children. I immediately mounted a party of about twenty soldiers and citizens, and sent them with the post surgeon with a wagon to bring in the wounded, if any could be found. The party returned late in the afternoon, having found no wounded, and without having been able to communicate with any of the survivors. Early the next morning I took a similar party with spades and shovels, and went out and buried the dead immediately in and about the camp. I had, the day before, offered the interpreters, or any one who would do so, $100 to go to the mountains and communicate with them, and convince them that no officer or soldier of the United States Government had been concerned in the vile transaction; and, failing in this, I thought the act of caring for their dead would be an evidence to them of our sympathy, at least, and the conjecture proved correct; for while we were at the work, many of them came to the spot and indulged in expressions of grief too wild and terrible to be described.

"That evening they began to come in from all directions, singly and in small parties, so changed as hardly to be recognizable in the forty-eight hours during which they had neither eaten

nor slept. Many of the men, whose families had all been killed, when I spoke to them and expressed sympathy for them,
were obliged to turn away, unable to speak, and too proud to
show their grief. The women whose children had been killed
or stolen were convulsed with grief, and looked to me appeal-
ingly, as if I were their last hope on earth. Children, who two
days before had been full of frolic, kept at a distance, expressing wondering horror.

"I did what I could : I fed them, talked to them, and listened patiently to their accounts. I sent horses to the mountains
to bring in two badly wounded women, one shot through the
left leg, one with an arm shattered. These were attended to,
and are doing well, and will recover.

"Their camp was surrounded and attacked at daybreak.
So sudden and unexpected was it, that I found a number of
women shot while asleep beside their bundles of hay, which
they had collected to bring in on that morning. The wounded who were unable to get away had their brains beaten out
with clubs or stones, while some were shot full of arrows after
having been mortally wounded by gun-shots. The bodies were
all stripped. Of the number buried, one was an old man, and
one was a well-grown boy ; all the rest women and children.
Of the whole number killed and missing—about one hundred
and twenty-five—only eight were men. It has been said that
the men were not there: they were all there. On the 28th
we counted one hundred and twenty-eight men, a small number being absent for mescal, all of whom have since been in.
I have spent a good deal of time with them since the affair,
and have been astonished at their continued unshaken faith in
me, and their perfectly clear understanding of their misfortune. They say, ' We know there are a great many white men
and Mexicans who do not wish us to live at peace. We know
that the Papagos would never have come out against us at
this time unless they had been persuaded to do so.' What

they do not understand is, while they are at peace and are conscious of no wrong intent, that they should be murdered.

"One of the chiefs said : 'I no longer want to live; my women and children have been killed before my face, and I have been unable to defend them. Most Indians in my place would take a knife and cut their throats; but I will live to show these people that all they have done, and all they can do, shall not make me break faith with you so long as you will stand by us and defend us, in a language we know nothing of, to a great governor we never have and never shall see.'

"About their captives they say : 'Get them back for us. Our little boys will grow up slaves, and our girls, as soon as they are large enough, will be diseased prostitutes, to get money for whoever owns them. Our women work hard, and are good women, and they and our children have no diseases. Our dead you cannot bring to life; but those that are living we gave to you, and we look to you, who can write and talk and have soldiers, to get them back.'

" I assure you it is no easy task to convince them of my zeal when they see so little being done. I have pledged my word to them that I never would rest, day or night, until they should have justice, and just now I would as soon leave the army as to be ordered away from them, or be obliged to order them away from here. But you well know the difficulties in the way. You know that parties who would engage in murder like this could and would make statements and multiply affidavits without end in their justification. I know you will use your influence on the right side. I believe, with them, this may be made either a means of making good citizens of them and their children, or of driving them out to a hopeless war of extermination. They ask to be allowed to live here in their old homes, where nature supplies nearly all their wants. They ask for a fair and impartial trial of their faith, and they ask that all their captive children may be returned to them. Is their demand unreasonable ?"

This letter was written to Colonel T. G. C. Lee., U.S.A., by Lieut. Royal E. Whitman, 3d U.S. Cavalry. It is published in the Report of the Board of Indian Commissioners for 1871. There is appended to it the following affidavit of the post surgeon at Camp Grant:

"On this 16th day of September, 1871, personally appeared Conant B. Brierley, who, being duly sworn according to law, deposeth and saith : 'I am acting-assistant surgeon, U.S.A., at Camp Grant, Arizona, where I arrived April 25th, 1871, and reported to the commanding officer for duty as medical officer. Some four hundred Apache Indians were at that time held as prisoners of war by the military stationed at Camp Grant, and during the period intervening between April 25th and 30th I saw the Indians every day. They seemed very well contented, and were busily employed in bringing in hay, which they sold for manta and such little articles as they desired outside the Government ration. April 29th Chiquita and some of the other chiefs were at the post, and asked for seeds and for some hoes, stating that they had ground cleared and ready for planting. They were told that the garden-seeds had been sent for, and would be up from Tucson in a few days. They then left, and I saw nothing more of them until after the killing.

"'Sunday morning I heard a rumor that the Indians had been attacked, and learned from Lieutenant Whitman that he had sent the two interpreters to the Indian camp to warn the Indians, and bring them down where they could be protected, if possible. The interpreters returned and stated that the attack had already been made and the Indians dispersed, and that the attacking party were returning.

"'Lieutenant Whitman then ordered me to go to the Indian camp to render medical assistance, and bring down any wounded I might find. I took twelve men and a wagon, and pro-

ceeded without delay to the scene of the murder.   On my arrival I found that I should have but little use for the wagon
or medicine.   The work had been too thoroughly done.   The
camp had been fired, and the dead bodies of twenty-one wom-
en and children were lying scattered over the ground; those
who had been wounded in the first instance had their brains
beaten out with stones.   Two of the squaws had been first rav-
ished, and then shot dead.   One infant of some two months
was shot twice, and one leg nearly hacked off. * * * I know
from my own personal observations that, during the time the
Indians were in, after my arrival, they were rationed every
three days, and Indians absent had to be accounted for; their
faces soon became familiar to me, and I could at once tell when
any strange Indian came in.

   "'And I furthermore state that I have been among nearly
all the tribes on the Pacific coast, and that I have never seen
any Indians who showed the intelligence, honesty, and desire
to learn manifested by these Indians.   I came among them
greatly prejudiced against them; but, after being with them, I
was compelled to admit that they were honest in their intentions, and really desired peace.

"'C. B. BRIERLEY,
"'Acting Assistant Surgeon, U.S.A.'"

   This is not the only instance of cruel outrage committed by
white men on the Apaches.   In the Report of the Board of
Indian Commissioners for 1871 is the following letter from
one of the Arizona pioneers, Mr. J. H. Lyman, of Northamp-
ton, Mass.   Mr. Lyman spent the years of 1840–'41 among the
Apaches, and thus briefly relates an occurrence which took
place at a time when they were friendly and cordial to all
Americans going among them:

   "The Indians were then, as now, hostile to the Mexicans of
Sonora, and they were constantly making raids into the State

and driving off the cattle. The Mexicans feared them, and were unable to meet them man to man. At that time American trappers found the beaver very abundant about the headwaters of the Gila River, among those rich mountain valleys where the Apaches had, and still have, their secure retreats. At the time I speak of there were two companies of trappers in that region. One of the companies, about seventeen men, was under a captain named Johnson. The other company consisted of thirty men, I think. I was trapping on another head of the Gila, several miles north. The valleys were full of Apaches, but all peaceful toward the white men, both Indians and whites visiting each other's camps constantly and fearlessly, with no thought of treachery or evil. Besides the Mexicans, the only enemies of the Apaches were the Piutes and Navajoes, in the north-west. But here in their fastnesses they felt safe from all foes.

"One day Johnson concluded to go down into Sonora on a spree, as was occasionally the way with mountain-men. He there saw the Governor of Sonora, who, knowing that he had the confidence of the ˌIndians, offered him an ounce of gold for every Apache scalp he would bring him. The bargain was struck. Johnson procured a small mountain howitzer, and then, with supplies for his party, returned to his camp. Previous to entering it he loaded his howitzer with a quantity of bullets. On approaching the valley he was met by the Indians, who joyfully welcomed him back, and proceeded at once to prepare the usual feast. While they were boiling and roasting their venison and bear meat, and were gathered in a small group around the fire laughing, and chatting in anticipation of the pleasure they expected in entertaining their guests, Johnson told those of his party who had remained behind of the offer of the governor, and with such details of temptation as easily overcame any scruples such men might have.

"As they were all armed with rifles, which were always in

hand day and night, together with pistols in belt, they needed no preparation. The howitzer, which the Indians might have supposed to be a small keg of whiskey, was placed on the ground and pointed at the group of warriors, squaws, and little children round the fire, watching the roasting meal.

" While they were thus engaged, with hearts full of kindly feelings toward their white friends, Johnson gave the signal. The howitzer was discharged, sending its load of bullets scattering and tearing through the mass of miserable human beings, and nearly all who were not stricken down were shot by the rifles. A very few succeeded in escaping into the ravine, and fled over the dividing ridge into the northern valleys, where they met others of their tribe, to whom they told the horrible story.

" The Apaches at once showed that they could imitate their more civilized brothers. Immediately a band of them went in search of the other company of trappers, who, of course, were utterly unconscious of Johnson's infernal work. They were attacked, unprepared, and nearly all killed ; and then the story that the Apaches were treacherous and cruel went forth into all the land, but nothing of the wrongs they had received."

Is it to be wondered at that the Apaches became one of the most hostile and dangerous tribes on the Pacific coast?

These are but four massacres out of scores, whose history, if written, would prove as clearly as do these, that, in the long contest between white men and Indians, the Indian has not always been the aggressor, and that treachery and cruelty are by no means exclusively Indian traits.

CHAPTER X.

CONCLUSION.

THERE are within the limits of the United States between two hundred and fifty and three hundred thousand Indians, exclusive of those in Alaska. The names of the different tribes and bands, as entered in the statistical tables of the Indian Office Reports, number nearly three hundred. One of the most careful estimates which has been made of their numbers and localities gives them as follows: "In Minnesota and States east of the Mississippi, about 32,500; in Nebraska, Kansas, and the Indian Territory, 70,650; in the Territories of Dakota, Montana, Wyoming, and Idaho, 65,000; in Nevada and the Territories of Colorado, New Mexico, Utah, and Arizona, 84,000; and on the Pacific slope, 48,000."

Of these, 130,000 are self-supporting on their own reservations, "receiving nothing from the Government except interest on their own moneys, or annuities granted them in consideration of the cession of their lands to the United States."*

This fact alone would seem sufficient to dispose forever of the accusation, so persistently brought against the Indian, that he will not work.

Of the remainder, 84,000 are partially supported by the Government—the interest money due them and their annuities, as provided by treaty, being inadequate to their subsistence on the reservations where they are confined. In many cases, however, these Indians furnish a large part of their sup-

---

* Annual Report of Indian Commissioner for 1872.

port—the White River Utes, for instance, who are reported by the Indian Bureau as getting sixty-six per cent. of their living by "root-digging, hunting, and fishing;" the Squaxin band, in Washington Territory, as earning seventy-five per cent., and the Chippewas of Lake Superior as earning fifty per cent. in the same way. These facts also would seem to dispose of the accusation that the Indian will not work.

There are about 55,000 who never visit an agency, over whom the Government does not pretend to have either control or care. These 55,000 "subsist by hunting, fishing, on roots, nuts, berries, etc., and by begging and stealing;" and this also seems to dispose of the accusation that the Indian will not "work for a living." There remains a small portion, about 31,000, that are entirely subsisted by the Government.

There is not among these three hundred bands of Indians one which has not suffered cruelly at the hands either of the Government or of white settlers. The poorer, the more insignificant, the more helpless the band, the more certain the cruelty and outrage to which they have been subjected. This is especially true of the bands on the Pacific slope. These Indians found themselves of a sudden surrounded by and caught up in the great influx of gold-seeking settlers, as helpless creatures on a shore are caught up in a tidal wave. There was not time for the Government to make treaties; not even time for communities to make laws. The tale of the wrongs, the oppressions, the murders of the Pacific-slope Indians in the last thirty years would be a volume by itself, and is too monstrous to be believed.

It makes little difference, however, where one opens the record of the history of the Indians; every page and every year has its dark stain. The story of one tribe is the story of all, varied only by differences of time and place; but neither time nor place makes any difference in the main facts. Colorado is as greedy and unjust in 1880 as was Georgia in 1830, and Ohio in 1795; and the United States Government breaks promises now as deftly as then, and with an added ingenuity from long practice.

One of its strongest supports in so doing is the wide-spread sentiment among the people of dislike to the Indian, of impatience with his presence as a "barrier to civilization," and distrust of it as a possible danger. The old tales of the frontier life, with its horrors of Indian warfare, have gradually, by two or three generations' telling, produced in the average mind something like an hereditary instinct of unquestioning and unreasoning aversion which it is almost impossible to dislodge or soften.

There are hundreds of pages of unimpeachable testimony on the side of the Indian; but it goes for nothing, is set down as sentimentalism or partisanship, tossed aside and forgotten.

President after president has appointed commission after commission to inquire into and report upon Indian affairs, and to make suggestions as to the best methods of managing them. The reports are filled with eloquent statements of wrongs done to the Indians, of perfidies on the part of the Government; they counsel, as earnestly as words can, a trial of the simple and unperplexing expedients of telling truth, keeping promises, making fair bargains, dealing justly in all ways and all things. These reports are bound up with the Government's Annual Reports, and that is the end of them. It would probably be no exaggeration to say that not one American citizen out of ten thousand ever sees them or knows that they exist, and yet any one of them, circulated throughout the country, read by the right-thinking, right-feeling men and women of this land, would be of itself a "campaign document" that would initiate a revolution which would not subside until the Indians' wrongs were, so far as is now left possible, righted.

In 1869 President Grant appointed a commission of nine men, representing the influence and philanthropy of six leading

States, to visit the different Indian reservations, and to "examine all matters appertaining to Indian affairs."

In the report of this commission are such paragraphs as the following: "To assert that 'the Indian will not work' is as true as it would be to say that the white man will not work.

"Why should the Indian be expected to plant corn, fence lands, build houses, or do anything but get food from day to day, when experience has taught him that the product of his labor will be seized by the white man to-morrow? The most industrious white man would become a drone under similar circumstances. Nevertheless, many of the Indians" (the commissioners might more forcibly have said 130,000 of the Indians) "are already at work, and furnish ample refutation of the assertion that 'the Indian will not work.' There is no escape from the inexorable logic of facts.

"The history of the Government connections with the Indians is a shameful record of broken treaties and unfulfilled promises. The history of the border white man's connection with the Indians is a sickening record of murder, outrage, robbery, and wrongs committed by the former, as the rule, and occasional savage outbreaks and unspeakably barbarous deeds of retaliation by the latter, as the exception.

"Taught by the Government that they had rights entitled to respect, when those rights have been assailed by the rapacity of the white man, the arm which should have been raised to protect them has ever been ready to sustain the aggressor.

"The testimony of some of the highest military officers of the United States is on record to the effect that, in our Indian wars, almost without exception, the first aggressions have been made by the white man; and the assertion is supported by every civilian of reputation who has studied the subject. In addition to the class of robbers and outlaws who find impunity in their nefarious pursuits on the frontiers, there is a large class of professedly reputable men who use every means in their power to bring on Indian wars for the sake of the profit to be realized from the presence of troops and the expenditure of Government funds in their midst. They proclaim death to the Indians at all times in words and publications, making no distinction between the innocent and the guilty. They irate the lowest class of men to the perpetration of the darkest deeds against their victims, and as judges and jurymen shield them from the justice due to their crimes. Every crime committed by a white man against an Indian is concealed or palliated. Every offence committed by an Indian against a white man is borne on the wings of the post or the telegraph to the remotest corner of the land, clothed with all the horrors which the reality or imagination can throw around it. Against such influences as these the people of the United States need to be warned."

To assume that it would be easy, or by any one sudden stroke of legislative policy possible, to undo the mischief and hurt of the long past, set the Indian policy of the country right for the future, and make the Indians at once safe and happy, is the blunder of a hasty and uninformed judgment. The notion which seems to be growing more prevalent, that simply to make all Indians at once citizens of the United States would be a sovereign and instantaneous panacea for all their ills and all the Government's perplexities, is a very inconsiderate one. To administer complete citizenship of a sudden, all round, to all Indians, barbarous and civilized alike, would be as grotesque a blunder as to dose them all round with any one medicine, irrespective of the symptoms and needs of their diseases. It would kill more than it would cure. Nevertheless, it is true, as was well stated by one of the superintendents of Indian Affairs in 1857, that, "so long as they are not citizens of the United States, their rights of property must remain insecure against invasion. The doors of the federal tribunals being barred against them while wards and dependents, they can

only partially exercise the rights of free government, or give
to those who make, execute, and construe the few laws they
are allowed to enact, dignity sufficient to make them respectable.   While they continue individually to gather the crumbs
that fall from the table of the United States, idleness, improvidence, and indebtedness will be the rule, and industry, thrift,
and freedom from debt the exception.   The utter absence of
individual title to particular lands deprives every one among
them of the chief incentive to labor and exertion—the very
mainspring on which the prosperity of a people depends."

All judicious plans and measures for their safety and salva-
tion must embody provisions for their becoming citizens as
fast as they are fit, and must protect them till then in every
right and particular in which our laws protect other " persons "
who are not citizens.

There is a disposition in a certain class of minds to be
impatient with any protestation against wrong which is unac-
companied or unprepared with a quick and exact scheme of
remedy.   This is illogical.   When pioneers in a new country
find a tract of poisonous and swampy wilderness to be reclaim-
ed, they do not withhold their hands from fire and axe till
they see clearly which way roads should run, where good water will spring, and what crops will best grow on the redeemed
land.   They first clear the swamp.   So with this poisonous
and baffling part of the domain of our national affairs—let us
first " clear the swamp."

However great perplexity and difficulty there may be in the
details of any and every plan possible for doing at this late
day anything like justice to the Indian, however hard it may
be for good statesmen and good men to agree upon the things
that ought to be done, there certainly is, or ought to be, no
perplexity whatever, no difficulty whatever, in agreeing upon
certain things that ought not to be done, and which must cease
to be done before the first steps can be taken toward right-

ing the wrongs, curing the ills, and wiping out the disgrace to us of the present condition of our Indians.

Cheating, robbing, breaking promises—these three are clearly things which must cease to be done.   One more thing, also, and that is the refusal of the protection of the law to the Indian's rights of property, " of life, liberty, and the pursuit of happiness."

When these four things have ceased to be done, time, statesmanship, philanthropy, and Christianity can slowly and surely do the rest.   Till these four things have ceased to be done, statesmanship and philanthropy alike must work in vain, and even Christianity can reap but small harvest.

Revised November, 1964

hARPER ✦ TORCHBOOKS

HUMANITIES AND SOCIAL SCIENCES

American Studies

JOHN R. ALDEN: The American Revolution, 1775-1783.† Illus. TB/3011

BERNARD BAILYN: The New England Merchants in the Seventeenth Century TB/1149

RAY STANNARD BAKER: Following the Color Line: American Negro Citizenship in the Progressive Era.‡ Illus. Edited by Dewey W. Grantham, Jr. TB/3053

RAY A. BILLINGTON: The Far Western Frontier, 1830-1860.† Illus. TB/3012

JOSEPH L. BLAU, Ed.: Cornerstones of Religious Freedom in America. Selected Basic Documents, Court Decisions and Public Statements. Revised and Enlarged Edition TB/118

RANDOLPH S. BOURNE: War and the Intellectuals: Collected Essays, 1915-1919.‡ Edited by Carl Resek TB/3043

A. RUSSELL BUCHANAN: The United States and World War II. † Illus. Vol. I TB/3044
Vol. II TB/3045

ABRAHAM CAHAN: The Rise of David Levinsky: a novel. Introduction by John Higham TB/1028

JOSEPH CHARLES: The Origins of the American Party System TB/1049

THOMAS C. COCHRAN: The Inner Revolution: Essays on the Social Sciences in History TB/1140

T. C. COCHRAN & WILLIAM MILLER: The Age of Enterprise: A Social History of Industrial America TB/1054

EDWARD S. CORWIN: American Constitutional History: Essays edited by Alpheus T. Mason and Gerald Garvey TB/1136

FOSTER RHEA DULLES: America's Rise to World Power, 1898-1954.† Illus. TB/3021

W. A. DUNNING: Reconstruction, Political and Economic, 1865-1877 TB/1073

A. HUNTER DUPREE: Science in the Federal Government: A History of Policies and Activities to 1940 TB/573

CLEMENT EATON: The Freedom-of-Thought Struggle in the Old South. Revised Edition. Illus. TB/1150

CLEMENT EATON: The Growth of Southern Civilization, 1790-1860.† Illus. TB/3040

HAROLD U. FAULKNER: Politics, Reform and Expansion, 1890-1900.† Illus. TB/3020

LOUIS FILLER: The Crusade against Slavery, 1830-1860.† Illus. TB/3029

EDITORS OF FORTUNE: America in the Sixties: the Economy and the Society. 72 two-color charts TB/1015

DIXON RYAN FOX: The Decline of Aristocracy in the Politics of New York.‡ Edited by Robert V. Remini TB/3064

LAWRENCE HENRY GIPSON: The Coming of the Revolution, 1763-1775.† Illus. TB/3007

FRANCIS J. GRUND: Aristocracy in America: Jacksonian Democracy TB/1001

ALEXANDER HAMILTON: The Reports of Alexander Hamilton.‡ Edited by Jacob E. Cooke TB/3060

OSCAR HANDLIN, Editor: This Was America: As Recorded by European Travelers to the Western Shore in the Eighteenth, Nineteenth, and Twentieth Centuries. Illus. TB/1119

MARCUS LEE HANSEN: The Atlantic Migration: 1607-1860. Edited by Arthur M. Schlesinger, Sr.; Introduction by Oscar Handlin TB/1052

MARCUS LEE HANSEN: The Immigrant in American History. Edited with a Foreword by Arthur M. Schlesinger, Sr. TB/1120

JOHN D. HICKS: Republican Ascendancy, 1921-1933.† Illus. TB/3041

JOHN HIGHAM, Ed.: The Reconstruction of American History TB/1068

---

† The New American Nation Series, edited by Henry Steele Commager and Richard B. Morris.
‡ American Perspectives series, edited by Bernard Wishy and William E. Leuchtenburg.
* The Rise of Modern Europe series, edited by William L. Langer.
‖ Researches in the Social, Cultural, and Behavioral Sciences, edited by Benjamin Nelson.
§ The Library of Religion and Culture, edited by Benjamin Nelson.
Σ Harper Modern Science Series, edited by James R. Newman.
º Not for sale in Canada.

1

DANIEL H. HUNDLEY: Social Relations in our Southern States.‡ Edited by William R. Taylor   TB/3058

HELEN HUNT JACKSON: A Century of Dishonor: The Early Crusade for Indian Reform.‡ Edited by Andrew F. Rolle   TB/3063

ROBERT H. JACKSON: The Supreme Court in the American System of Government   TB/1106

THOMAS JEFFERSON: Notes on the State of Virginia.‡ Edited by Thomas Perkins Abernethy   TB/3052

JOHN F. KENNEDY: A Nation of Immigrants. Revised and Enlarged Edition. Illus.   TB/1118

WILLIAM L. LANGER & S. EVERETT GLEASON: The Challenge to Isolation: The World Crisis of 1937-1940 and American Foreign Policy   Vol. I   TB/3054
Vol. II   TB/3055

WILLIAM E. LEUCHTENBURG: Franklin D. Roosevelt and the New Deal, 1932-1940.† Illus.   TB/3025

LEONARD W. LEVY: Freedom of Speech and Press in Early American History: Legacy of Suppression   TB/1109

ARTHUR S. LINK: Woodrow Wilson and the Progressive Era, 1910-1917.† Illus.   TB/3023

ROBERT GREEN McCLOSKEY: American Conservatism in the Age of Enterprise, 1865-1910   TB/1137

BERNARD MAYO: Myths and Men: Patrick Henry, George Washington, Thomas Jefferson   TB/1108

JOHN C. MILLER: Alexander Hamilton and the Growth of the New Nation   TB/3057

JOHN C. MILLER: The Federalist Era, 1789-1801.† Illus.   TB/3027

PERRY MILLER: Errand into the Wilderness   TB/1139

PERRY MILLER & T. H. JOHNSON, Editors: The Puritans: A Sourcebook of Their Writings
Vol. I   TB/1093
Vol. II   TB/1094

GEORGE E. MOWRY: The Era of Theodore Roosevelt and the Birth of Modern America, 1900-1912.† Illus.   TB/3022

WALLACE NOTESTEIN: The English People on the Eve of Colonization, 1603-1630.† Illus.   TB/3006

RUSSEL BLAINE NYE: The Cultural Life of the New Nation, 1776-1801.† Illus.   TB/3026

RALPH BARTON PERRY: Puritanism and Democracy   TB/1138

RALPH BARTON PERRY: The Thought and Character of William James: Briefer Version   TB/1156

GEORGE E. PROBST, Ed.: The Happy Republic: A Reader in Tocqueville's America   TB/1060

WALTER RAUSCHENBUSCH: Christianity and the Social Crisis.‡ Edited by Robert D. Cross   TB/3059

HEINRICH STRAUMANN: American Literature in the Twentieth Century. Revised Edition   TB/1168

FRANK THISTLETHWAITE: America and the Atlantic Community: Anglo-American Aspects, 1790-1850   TB/1107

TWELVE SOUTHERNERS: I'll Take My Stand: The South and the Agrarian Tradition. Introduction by Louis D. Rubin, Jr.; Biographical Essays by Virginia Rock   TB/1072

A. F. TYLER: Freedom's Ferment: Phases of American Social History from the Revolution to the Outbreak of the Civil War. Illus.   TB/1074

GLYNDON G. VAN DEUSEN: The Jacksonian Era, 1828-1848.† Illus.   TB/3028

WALTER E. WEYL: The New Democracy: An Essay on Certain Political and Economic Tendencies in the United States.‡ Edited by Charles Forcey   TB/3042

LOUIS B. WRIGHT: The Cultural Life of the American Colonies, 1607-1763.† Illus.   TB/3005

LOUIS B. WRIGHT: Culture on the Moving Frontier   TB/1053

Anthropology & Sociology

BERNARD BERELSON, Ed.: The Behavioral Sciences Today   TB/1127

JOSEPH B. CASAGRANDE, Ed.: In the Company of Man: 20 Portraits of Anthropological Informants. Illus.   TB/3047

W. E. LE GROS CLARK: The Antecedents of Man: An Introduction to the Evolution of the Primates.° Illus.   TB/559

THOMAS C. COCHRAN: The Inner Revolution: Essays on the Social Sciences in History   TB/1140

ALLISON DAVIS & JOHN DOLLARD: Children of Bondage: The Personality Development of Negro Youth in the Urban South ‖   TB/3049

ST. CLAIR DRAKE & HORACE R. CAYTON: Black Metropolis: A Study of Negro Life in a Northern City   Vol. I   TB/1086; Vol. II   TB/1087

CORA DU BOIS: The People of Alor. New Preface by the author. Illus.   Vol. I   TB/1042; Vol. II   TB/1043

EMILE DURKHEIM et al.: Essays on Sociology and Philosophy: With Analyses of Durkheim's Life and Work. ‖ Edited by Kurt H. Wolff   TB/1151

LEON FESTINGER, HENRY W. RIECKEN & STANLEY SCHACHTER: When Prophecy Fails: A Social and Psychological Account of a Modern Group that Predicted the Destruction of the World ‖   TB/1132

RAYMOND FIRTH, Ed.: Man and Culture: An Evaluation of the Work of Bronislaw Malinowski ‖ °   TB/1133

L. S. B. LEAKEY: Adam's Ancestors: The Evolution of Man and his Culture. Illus.   TB/1019

KURT LEWIN: Field Theory in Social Science: Selected Theoretical Papers. ‖ Edited with a Foreword by Dorwin Cartwright   TB/1135

ROBERT H. LOWIE: Primitive Society. Introduction by Fred Eggan   TB/1056

R. M. MacIVER: Social Causation   TB/1153

BENJAMIN NELSON: Religious Traditions and the Spirit of Capitalism: From the Church Fathers to Jeremy Bentham   TB/1130

TALCOTT PARSONS & EDWARD A. SHILS, Editors: Toward a General Theory of Action: Theoretical Foundations for the Social Sciences   TB/1083

JOHN H. ROHRER & MUNRO S. EDMONSON, Eds.: The Eighth Generation Grows Up: Cultures and Personalities of New Orleans Negroes ‖   TB/3050

ARNOLD ROSE: The Negro in America: The Condensed Version of Gunnar Myrdal's An American Dilemma   TB/3048

HENRI DE SAINT-SIMON: Social Organization, The Science of Man, and Other Writings. ‖ Edited and translated by Felix Markham   TB/1152

KURT SAMUELSSON: Religion and Economic Action: A Critique of Max Weber's The Protestant Ethic and the Spirit of Capitalism.‖ ° Trans. by E. G. French; Ed. with Intro. by D. C. Coleman   TB/1131

History: Renaissance & Reformation

R. R. BOLGAR: The Classical Heritage and Its Benefici-aries: *From the Carolingian Age to the End of the Renaissance*   TB/1125

JACOB BURCKHARDT: The Civilization of the Ren-aissance in Italy. Introduction by Benjamin Nelson and Charles Trinkaus. Illus.   Volume I TB/40
Volume II TB/41

ERNST CASSIRER: The Individual and the Cosmos in Renaissance Philosophy. *Translated with an Intro-duction by Mario Domandi*   TB/1097

EDWARD P. CHEYNEY: The Dawn of a New Era, 1250-1453.* *Illus.*   TB/3002

DESIDERIUS ERASMUS: Christian Humanism and the Reformation: *Selected Writings. Edited and translated by John C. Olin*   TB/1166

WALLACE K. FERGUSON et al.: Facets of the Ren-aissance   TB/1098

WALLACE K. FERGUSON et al.: The Renaissance: *Six Essays. Illus.*   TB/1084

MYRON P. GILMORE: The World of Humanism, 1453-1517.* *Illus.*   TB/3003

FRANCESCO GUICCIARDINI: Maxims and Reflec-tions of a Renaissance Statesman: *Ricordi. Trans. by Mario Domandi. Intro. by Nicolai Rubinstein*   TB/1160

JOHAN HUIZINGA: Erasmus and the Age of Refor-mation. *Illus.*   TB/19

ULRICH VON HUTTEN et al.: On the Eve of the Reformation: *"Letters of Obscure Men." Introduction by Hajo Holborn*   TB/1124

PAUL O. KRISTELLER: Renaissance Thought: *The Classic, Scholastic, and Humanist Strains* TB/1048

PAUL O. KRISTELLER: Renaissance Thought II: *Papers on Humanism and the Arts*   TB/1163

NICCOLO MACHIAVELLI: History of Florence and of the Affairs of Italy: *from the earliest times to the death of Lorenzo the Magnificent. Introduction by Felix Gilbert*   TB/1027

ALFRED VON MARTIN: Sociology of the Renaissance. *Introduction by Wallace K. Ferguson*   TB/1099

GARRETT MATTINGLY et al.: Renaissance Profiles. *Edited by J. H. Plumb*   TB/1162

MILLARD MEISS: Painting in Florence and Siena after the Black Death. *The Arts, Religion and Society in the Mid-Fourteenth Century. 169 illus.*   TB/1148

J. E. NEALE: The Age of Catherine de Medici⁰   TB/1085

ERWIN PANOFSKY: Studies in Iconology: *Humanistic Themes in the Art of the Renaissance. 180 illustra-tions*   TB/1077

J. H. PARRY: The Establishment of the European He-gemony: 1415-1715   TB/1045

HENRI PIRENNE: Early Democracies in the Low Countries: *Urban Society and Political Conflict in the Middle Ages and the Renaissance. Introduction by John Mundy*   TB/1110

J. H. PLUMB: The Italian Renaissance: *A Concise Survey of Its History and Culture*   TB/1161

FERDINAND SCHEVILL: The Medici. Illus.   TB/1010

FERDINAND SCHEVILL: Medieval and Renaissance Florence. *Illus. Volume I: Medieval Florence* TB/1090
Volume II: *The Coming of Human-ism and the Age of the Medici*   TB/1091

G. M. TREVELYAN: England in the Age of Wycliffe, 1368-1520⁰   TB/1112

VESPASIANO: Renaissance Princes, Popes, and Prel-ates: *The Vespasiano Memoirs: Lives of Illustrious Men of the XVth Century. Introduction by Myron P. Gilmore*   TB/1111

History: Modern European

FREDERICK B. ARTZ: Reaction and Revolution, 1815-1832.* *Illus.*   TB/3034

MAX BELOFF: The Age of Absolutism, 1660-1815   TB/1062

ROBERT C. BINKLEY: Realism and Nationalism, 1852-1871.* *Illus.*   TB/3038

CRANE BRINTON: A Decade of Revolution, 1789-1799.* *Illus.*   TB/3018

J. BRONOWSKI & BRUCE MAZLISH: The Western Intellectual Tradition: *From Leonardo to Hegel*   TB/3001

GEOFFREY BRUUN: Europe and the French Imperium, 1799-1814.* *Illus.*   TB/3033

ALAN BULLOCK: Hitler, A Study in Tyranny.⁰ *Illus.*   TB/1123

E. H. CARR: The Twenty Years' Crisis, 1919-1939: *An Introduction to the Study of International Relations*⁰   TB/1122

GORDON A. CRAIG: From Bismarck to Adenauer: *Aspects of German Statecraft. Revised Edition*   TB/1171

WALTER L. DORN: Competition for Empire, 1740-1763.* *Illus.*   TB/3032

CARL J. FRIEDRICH: The Age of the Baroque, 1610-1660.* *Illus.*   TB/3004

LEO GERSHOY: From Despotism to Revolution, 1763-1789.* *Illus.*   TB/3017

ALBERT GOODWIN: The French Revolution TB/1064

CARLTON J. H. HAYES: A Generation of Materialism, 1871-1900.* *Illus.*   TB/3039

J. H. HEXTER: Reappraisals in History: *New Views on History and Society in Early Modern Europe*   TB/1100

A. R. HUMPHREYS: The Augustan World: *Society, Thought, and Letters in Eighteenth Century England*   TB/1105

HANS KOHN, Ed.: The Mind of Modern Russia: *His-torical and Political Thought of Russia's Great Age*   TB/1065

SIR LEWIS NAMIER: Vanished Supremacies: *Essays on European History, 1812-1918*⁰   TB/1088

JOHN U. NEF: Western Civilization Since the Renais-sance: *Peace, War, Industry, and the Arts* TB/1113

FREDERICK L. NUSSBAUM: The Triumph of Science and Reason, 1660-1685.* *Illus.*   TB/3009

RAYMOND W. POSTGATE, Ed.: Revolution from 1789 to 1906: *Selected Documents*   TB/1063

PENFIELD ROBERTS: The Quest for Security, 1715-1740.* *Illus.*   TB/3016

PRISCILLA ROBERTSON: Revolutions of 1848: *A So-cial History*   TB/1025

ALBERT SOREL: Europe Under the Old Regime. *Trans-lated by Francis H. Herrick*   TB/1121

N. N. SUKHANOV: The Russian Revolution, 1917: *Eyewitness Account*. Edited by Joel Carmichael
Vol. I TB/1066; Vol. II TB/1067

JOHN B. WOLF: The Emergence of the Great Powers, 1685-1715.* *Illus.* TB/3010

JOHN B. WOLF: France: 1814-1919: *The Rise of a Liberal-Democratic Society* TB/3019

Intellectual History

HERSCHEL BAKER: The Image of Man: *A Study of the Idea of Human Dignity in Classical Antiquity, the Middle Ages, and the Renaissance* TB/1047

J. BRONOWSKI & BRUCE MAZLISH: The Western Intellectual Tradition: *From Leonardo to Hegel*
TB/3001

ERNST CASSIRER: The Individual and the Cosmos in Renaissance Philosophy. *Translated with an Introduction by Mario Domandi* TB/1097

NORMAN COHN: The Pursuit of the Millennium: *Revolutionary Messianism in medieval and Reformation Europe and its bearing on modern Leftist and Rightist totalitarian movements* TB/1037

ARTHUR O. LOVEJOY: The Great Chain of Being: *A Study of the History of an Idea* TB/1009

ROBERT PAYNE: Hubris: *A Study of Pride. Foreword by Sir Herbert Read* TB/1031

BRUNO SNELL: The Discovery of the Mind: *The Greek Origins of European Thought* TB/1018

ERNST LEE TUVESON: Millennium and Utopia: *A Study in the Background of the Idea of Progress.|| New Preface by the Author* TB/1134

Literature, Poetry, The Novel & Criticism

JAMES BAIRD: Ishmael: *The Art of Melville in the Contexts of International Primitivism* TB/1023

JACQUES BARZUN: The House of Intellect TB/1051

W. J. BATE: From Classic to Romantic: *Premises of Taste in Eighteenth Century England* TB/1036

RACHEL BESPALOFF: On the Iliad TB/2006

R. P. BLACKMUR et al.: Lectures in Criticism. *Introduction by Huntington Cairns* TB/2003

ABRAHAM CAHAN: The Rise of David Levinsky: *a novel. Introduction by John Higham* TB/1028

ERNST R. CURTIUS: European Literature and the Latin Middle Ages TB/2015

GEORGE ELIOT: Daniel Deronda: *a novel. Introduction by F. R. Leavis* TB/1039

ETIENNE GILSON: Dante and Philosophy TB/1089

ALFRED HARBAGE: As They Liked It: *A Study of Shakespeare's Moral Artistry* TB/1035

STANLEY R. HOPPER, Ed.: Spiritual Problems in Contemporary Literature§ TB/21

A. R. HUMPHREYS: The Augustan World: *Society, Thought, and Letters in Eighteenth Century England*°
TB/1105

ALDOUS HUXLEY: Antic Hay & The Gioconda Smile.° *Introduction by Martin Green* TB/3503

HENRY JAMES: Roderick Hudson: *a novel. Introduction by Leon Edel* TB/1016

HENRY JAMES: The Tragic Muse: *a novel. Introduction by Leon Edel* TB/1017

ARNOLD KETTLE: An Introduction to the English Novel. Volume I: *Defoe to George Eliot* TB/1011
Volume II: *Henry James to the Present* TB/1012

ROGER SHERMAN LOOMIS: The Development of Arthurian Romance TB/1167

JOHN STUART MILL: On Bentham and Coleridge. *Introduction by F. R. Leavis* TB/1070

PERRY MILLER & T. H. JOHNSON, Editors: The Puritans: *A Sourcebook of Their Writings* Vol. I TB/1093
Vol. II TB/1094

KENNETH B. MURDOCK: Literature and Theology in Colonial New England TB/99

SAMUEL PEPYS: The Diary of Samuel Pepys.° *Edited by O. F. Morshead. Illus. by Ernest Shepard* TB/1007

ST.-JOHN PERSE: Seamarks TB/2002

O. E. RÖLVAAG: Giants in the Earth TB/3504

GEORGE SANTAYANA: Interpretations of Poetry and Religion§ TB/9

C. P. SNOW: Time of Hope: *a novel* TB/1040

HEINRICH STRAUMANN: American Literature in the Twentieth Century. *Revised Edition* TB/1168

DOROTHY VAN GHENT: The English Novel: *Form and Function* TB/1050

E. B. WHITE: One Man's Meat. *Introduction by Walter Blair* TB/3505

MORTON DAUWEN ZABEL, Editor: Literary Opinion in America. Vol. I TB/3013; Vol. II TB/3014

Myth, Symbol & Folklore

JOSEPH CAMPBELL, Editor: Pagan and Christian Mysteries. *Illus.* TB/2013

MIRCEA ELIADE: Cosmos and History: *The Myth of the Eternal Return*§ TB/2050

C. G. JUNG & C. KERÉNYI: Essays on a Science of Mythology: *The Myths of the Divine Child and the Divine Maiden* TB/2014

ERWIN PANOFSKY: Studies in Iconology: *Humanistic Themes in the Art of the Renaissance. 180 illustrations* TB/1077

JEAN SEZNEC: The Survival of the Pagan Gods: *The Mythological Tradition and its Place in Renaissance Humanism and Art. 108 illustrations* TB/2004

HELLMUT WILHELM: Change: *Eight Lectures on the I Ching* TB/2019

HEINRICH ZIMMER: Myths and Symbols in Indian Art and Civilization. *70 illustrations* TB/2005

Philosophy

HENRI BERGSON: Time and Free Will: *An Essay on the Immediate Data of Consciousness*° TB/1021

H. J. BLACKHAM: Six Existentialist Thinkers: *Kierkegaard, Nietzsche, Jaspers, Marcel, Heidegger, Sartre*°
TB/1002

ERNST CASSIRER: The Individual and the Cosmos in Renaissance Philosophy. *Translated with an Introduction by Mario Domandi* TB/1097

ERNST CASSIRER: Rousseau, Kant and Goethe. *Introduction by Peter Gay* TB/1092

FREDERICK COPLESTON: Medieval Philosophy°
TB/376

NATURAL SCIENCES
AND MATHEMATICS

GEORGE SARTON: Ancient Science and Modern Civilization TB/501

HANS THIRRING: Energy for Man: *From Windmills to Nuclear Power* TB/556

WILLIAM LAW WHYTE: Essay on Atomism: *From Democritus to 1960* TB/565

A. WOLF: A History of Science, Technology and Philosophy in the 16th and 17th Centuries.º *Illus.*
Vol. I TB/508; Vol. II TB/509

A. WOLF: A History of Science, Technology, and Philosophy in the Eighteenth Century.º *Illus.*
Vol. I TB/539; Vol. II TB/540

Mathematics

H. DAVENPORT: The Higher Arithmetic: *An Introduction to the Theory of Numbers* TB/526

H. G. FORDER: Geometry: *An Introduction* TB/548

GOTTLOB FREGE: The Foundations of Arithmetic: *A Logico-Mathematical Enquiry* TB/534

S. KÖRNER: The Philosophy of Mathematics: *An Introduction* TB/547

D. E. LITTLEWOOD: Skeleton Key of Mathematics: *A Simple Account of Complex Algebraic Problems* TB/525

GEORGE E. OWEN: Fundamentals of Scientific Mathematics TB/569

WILLARD VAN ORMAN QUINE: Mathematical Logic TB/558

O. G. SUTTON: Mathematics in Action.º *Foreword by James R. Newman. Illus.* TB/518

FREDERICK WAISMANN: Introduction to Mathematical Thinking. *Foreword by Karl Menger* TB/511

Philosophy of Science

R. B. BRAITHWAITE: Scientific Explanation TB/515

J. BRONOWSKI: Science and Human Values. *Illus.* TB/505

ALBERT EINSTEIN ET AL.: Albert Einstein: Philosopher-Scientist. *Edited by Paul A. Schilpp*
Volume I TB/502
Volume II TB/503

WERNER HEISENBERG: Physics and Philosophy: *The Revolution in Modern Science* TB/549

JOHN MAYNARD KEYNES: A Treatise on Probability.º *Introduction by N. R. Hanson* TB/557

STEPHEN TOULMIN: Foresight and Understanding: *An Enquiry into the Aims of Science. Foreword by Jacques Barzun* TB/564

STEPHEN TOULMIN: The Philosophy of Science: *An Introduction* TB/513

G. J. WHITROW: The Natural Philosophy of Timeº TB/563

Physics and Cosmology

DAVID BOHM: Causality and Chance in Modern Physics. *Foreword by Louis de Broglie* TB/536

P. W. BRIDGMAN: The Nature of Thermodynamics TB/537

P. W. BRIDGMAN: A Sophisticate's Primer of Relativity TB/575

A. C. CROMBIE, Ed.: Turning Point in Physics TB/535

C. V. DURELL: Readable Relativity. *Foreword by Freeman J. Dyson* TB/530

ARTHUR EDDINGTON: Space, Time and Gravitation: *An outline of the General Relativity Theory* TB/510

GEORGE GAMOW: Biography of PhysicsΣ TB/567

MAX JAMMER: Concepts of Force: *A Study in the Foundation of Dynamics* TB/550

MAX JAMMER: Concepts of Mass *in Classical and Modern Physics* TB/571

MAX JAMMER: Concepts of Space: *The History of Theories of Space in Physics. Foreword by Albert Einstein* TB/533

EDMUND WHITTAKER: History of the Theories of Aether and Electricity
Volume I: *The Classical Theories* TB/531
Volume II: *The Modern Theories* TB/532

G. J. WHITROW: The Structure and Evolution of the Universe: *An Introduction to Cosmology. Illus.* TB/504

Code to Torchbook Libraries:

TB/1+	: The Cloister Library
TB/301+	: The Cathedral Library
TB/501+	: The Science Library
TB/1001+	: The Academy Library
TB/2001+	: The Bollingen Library
TB/3001+	: The University Library

Jackson, Helen Maria (Fiske) Hunt, 1831-1885.
A century of dishonor; the early crusade for
Indian reform. Edited by Andrew F. Rolle.
New York, Harper & Row [c1965]
342p. 21cm. (Harper torchbook, TB-3063

"Originally published as A Century of Dishonor
Dishonor: A Sketch of the United State Government's Dealings with Some of the Indian Tribes...
in 1881. The Torchbook edition omits the
Appendix."

1.Indians of North Ameri   ca-Government relations.
2.Indians of North Ameri   ca-California. I.Title.